From Iowa to the mountains of Glacier National Park . . .

Doris Ashley left Iowa and came to Montana as the frontier era came to a close and the hard transition to the modern West began. In 1925, already a widow at the age of 24, she took a job as "cheap help" in Glacier National Park and thus began a lifelong affair with Montana's landscape, wildlife, and people. Doris soon met the love of her life, native son Dan Huffine, another park worker with an abiding love for the region. Together, they shared many adventures over the next 60 years, helping to shape the character of northwest Montana and to participate in the growth of Glacier Park on both sides of the Continental Divide. Between them, the Huffines shared stints as backcountry park ranger, driver of the classic Glacier Park tour buses, and cook for the crew that did the perilous work surveying the famous Going-to-the-Sun Road. The couple operated tourist camps along the Glacier Park boundary, and became co-proprietors of the Huffine Montana Museum. Many people considered the couple endearingly eccentric, and for good reason, as they kept skunks, badgers, coyotes, bears, a mountain goat, and a beaver as pets. Doris scolded hunting law violators in her *Hungry Horse News* column, yet participated in questionable hunts herself. The Huffines were also world-class raconteurs, and enjoyed telling their tales later in life to author John Fraley, who shared their love of the outdoors and of Glacier Park. Using many hours of tape recordings, numerous journals, and a great deal of research, Fraley has pieced together the story of Doris's early life in Iowa, her fateful meeting with Dan, and their love story which is also very much a work story—a tale of building a life together while at the same time helping to build the "Crown of the Continent" region of our country.

Advance praise for

A Woman's Way West

"For years beyond count, the Huffine Museum was an inviting and mysterious place for me. Now John Fraley's book gives the rest of the story and it is a tale of fascinating proportions, swirling about the lives of the unusual pioneer couple who lived there. Thank you John."

— GEORGE OSTROM
*(Montana's most colorful newsman and author of
Glacier's Secrets: Beyond the Roads and Above the Clouds)*

"John Fraley has captured the determined spirit of Doris Huffine, and in so doing has paid tribute to both this strong pioneering woman and the many other women who helped cultivate Montana as it grew up."

—JO ANN SPEELMAN
*(Founding member of Glacier National Park Associates
and former board member of Glacier Natural History Association)*

A Woman's Way West
In and Around Glacier National Park from 1925 to 1990

by

John Fraley

Foreword by Bert Gildart,
author of *Montana's Early Day Rangers* and *Glacier Country*

Big Mountain Publishing
Whitefish, Montana

Library of Congress Cataloging-in-Publication Data

Fraley, John, 1954-

A Woman's Way West: In and Around Glacier National Park, 1925-1990
Includes source list and index
ISBN 0-9622429-6-9
1. Glacier National Park Region (Montana)—History 2. Doris and Dan
Huffine—Historical ties to Glacier Park Country, Going-To-The-Sun-Road
(Montana). 3. Middle Fork Flathead River Drainage (Montana)—Tourist
camps, oldtimer history, wildlife as pets. 4. Flathead National Forest (Montana)—Hunting, poaching, and wildlife. 5. Huffine Montana Museum—
Montana memorabilia. I. Title

Library of Congress Catalog Card Number: 98-71492

A Woman's Way West
In and Around Glacier National Park from 1925 to 1990

ISBN 0-9622429-6-9

Table of Contents

All photos are from the Dan and Doris Huffine collections unless otherwise noted.

GLACIER NATIONAL PARK
AND THE FLATHEAD VALLEY
WITH DORIS AND DAN HUFFINE LOCATIONS 1925-1990

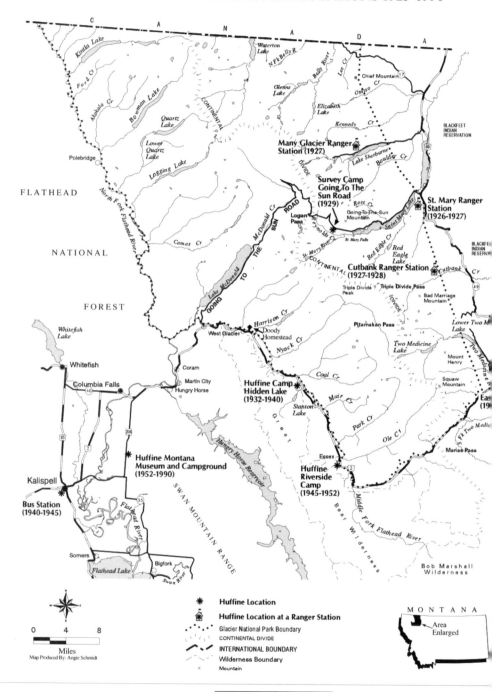

Huffine Location

Huffine Location at a Ranger Station

Glacier National Park Boundary

CONTINENTAL DIVIDE

INTERNATIONAL BOUNDARY

Wilderness Boundary

Mountain

MONTANA

Area Enlarged

0   4   8

Miles

Map Produced By: Angie Schmidt

Acknowledgements

I couldn't have written this book without the help of many people.

Maxine (Ashley) Conrad, Doris's youngest sister, provided Doris's and Dan's journals and many of their personal papers, writings, and photos. Maxine's recollections also were a major source of information. It is a sad note that she died in 1995 before this book could be published, but until her death she was a constant source of encouragement.

Many other relatives and friends supplied information and help including Doris's sister, Shirley (Ashley) Reinking, and her brother Frank Ashley. Norma Reinking, Shirley's daughter-in-law, helped me greatly by interviewing some of Doris's Iowa relatives and friends, especially Sadie (Brune) Murphy, and Bernice (Weaver) Manker. Irma (Huffine) Fritts, Dan's sister, provided information and insights about Dan and Doris in interviews and letters. Reminiscinces of Doris's long-time friends Lilian Carlson, Esther Overland, and Sandra Rosetti added greatly to the project. Glenna Ferrone of the Woodbury County Genealogical Society located vital records of Doris and others.

I began thinking about this book and writing parts of it more than a decade ago. Writer and former Glacier Park Ranger Bert Gildart encouraged me from the start and his comments greatly improved the manuscript as the project went along. He also contributed a foreword to the book. Thanks, Bert. Kay Ellerhoff, Ben Long, Rick Hull, Peggy Pace, and Marilyn Grant provided useful suggestions on earlier versions of the manuscript. I thank *Montana the Magazine of Western History* for permission to use material from my article "Winter at Cut Bank Ranger Station," and *Montana Outdoors* for permission to use material from my article "Doris." Deirdre Shaw of Glacier National Park allowed me to use documents in the Park's historical archives. I thank Brian Kennedy of the *Hungry Horse News* for allowing me to quote from Doris's "Essex News" columns.

Ron Wright of Big Mountain Publishing believed in the book and graciously brought it to publication. Writer Frank Miele ably edited the book for Big Mountain Publishing.

Most of all, I thank Doris, who waited patiently for years until I finally realized that she knew everything and I knew nothing. I treasured my time with Doris, laboring around her place and listening to her stories. She generously allowed me to record her reminiscences over the years even though she remained suspicious about what I would do with the information.

My family gave me the moral support I needed to complete the book. My children, Kevin, Heather, and Troy were not born in time to meet Doris or Dan, but they learned a lot about them and about Glacier Park as I wrote the book. Finally, I thank my wife, Dana — Dan and Doris's great niece — for her encouragement and tolerance, and for her willingness to live with someone Doris once described as a "banty rooster."

John Fraley
Kalispell, Montana
January 1998

Doris, in her later years, remained a force in northwestern Montana, both as an active member of the East Side Grange, and here as the proprietor of the Huffine Montana Museum. (Photo courtesy of The Daily Inter Lake)

Foreword:

"John Fraley, Doris Huffine, and the Cut Bank Valley"

by Bert Gildart
(author of "Montana's Early Day Rangers" and "Glacier Country")

To the best of my recollection I met John Fraley sometime in the early 1980s when I was stationed at Cut Bank Ranger Station. Subsequent to our meeting, it was inevitable that a camaraderie would develop, for we both shared an interest in the early-day rangers who had patrolled Cut Bank and beyond.

Fraley was most interested in the earliest days of the station's occupancy, and I was too. In the course of researching Glacier for various books and articles of my own, I had discovered that one of the very first rangers to occupy the station was Dan Huffine, and that he did so with his wife, Doris, during the winter of 1927 and 1928. When I learned from John that his great aunt was, in fact, Huffine's wife, and that she was still alive, our meetings increased in frequency. "We'll have to have lunch and talk about Doris," I said. "Sure," Fraley said, "but we'll have to talk about Glacier and Cut Bank Valley, too." Of course, I also hoped to meet Doris, which John said he'd try and arrange.

What I could tell Fraley was that the Cut Bank Valley was — and still is — one of the park's most primitive areas. In fact, as far as I was concerned, Cut Bank provided variety that exceeded other Glacier Park areas and made it a perfect backdrop for a story. Indian tribes once fought there, and one historic battle occurred not more than a few hundred yards from the ranger station. The valley had giant grizzlies, too, and on more than one occasion, I had ridden trails on which grizzlies had followed me. I wondered whether

Dan or Doris ever had experienced such traumatic moments. Reading this manuscript, I know now that they did, though in different settings.

As well, I knew just how rugged the winters there could be, for once I'd trudged on skis up the valley, only to be turned back when harsh winds blasted down from Pitamakin Pass. I wanted to know if Dan's experiences had equaled mine. Later, I learned they far exceeded anything I'd ever done.

But what I could tell John was vastly overshadowed by what he could tell me about Doris and her husband Dan. Here was a fascinating woman, a Midwestern woman who was attracted to the West and was content to live in a small ranger station on the edge of an Indian reservation where rugged mountains met a vast sprawling prairie. What, I wondered was the ranger station like in the '20s? Did they ever get out together? How did she fare when they once, as I learned, snowshoed to St. Mary for Christmas? And when at the cabin, how did they heat water? What did they do for refrigeration? And how did they lay away enough food and other supplies to last them during times when snowdrifts virtually covered the station?

Obviously, the Huffines managed to withstand the rigors together. But probably the demands on her were greater, for often she was alone for days, while her husband made his obligatory winter patrols. Sometimes, these patrols were short ones concluding eight miles along the boundary at Lake Creek Patrol Cabin. But sometimes, his patrols required that he proceed to Two Medicine — or even on to East Glacier — distances that required several days afoot. During such times, Doris was left alone to tend the home fires. How did she fare? What was it like for her? And what was it like for Dan during his patrols? As I learned more, my desire to meet this remarkable woman only intensified.

Unfortunately, I met Doris only once, and when I did, she was almost 89 and quite tired, and so my questions remained of necessity but brief. Still, I consider myself privileged, for I had seen a spark of vitality, a smile and a frown of mixed memories. "Those were some of the best — and worst — years of our lives," said Doris. And, of course, I wanted to know more.

Doris passed away several months after I met her, but Fraley and I continued to visit. When he informed me he was writing a book about Doris, I was elated, for who better to tell the story of her life than a family member who is also a first-class writer? And how better to obtain answers to my many and varied questions.

I envy my friend John Fraley, who had the opportunity to hear Doris relive her memories not only about Cut Bank, but about Glacier. I am grateful, too, that he had the good sense to record what Doris revealed and that he had the determination to see this book through to publication. I'm thankful he was able to document not only her times at Cut Bank, but her times, too, here in the Flathead, for indeed Doris Huffine was a pioneer woman who lived in a pioneer period. What's more, she lived at a time when Glacier was still young. For John's excellent work, I am sincerely grateful.

Introduction
My Affair With Doris

I should confess right at the start that this can't be a completely objective book. After all, we had an affair, Doris and I. It was intense, but of course it wasn't physical. It began when I was 25 and she was nearly 80. It was an affair of the mind.

I first met her in 1979, as I passed through the Flathead Valley on a trip from Bozeman to Glacier National Park with my girlfriend, Dana. Dana told me we had to stop and visit her Great Aunt Doris and Great Uncle Dan, who had both worked in the park and owned the Huffine Montana Museum, raspberry ranch, and chicken farm between Kalispell and Glacier. Doris was kind of stubborn, Dana had said.

It turned out that calling Doris kind of stubborn was like calling the spectacular, glacier-carved mountains of Glacier Park kind of pretty.

Doris stood only about five feet tall, but her posture was straight and she moved with an easy grace. She sported curly red hair, dyed monthly by her friends. As she stared at me through her cat-style glasses, I caught her intense green eyes, still as bright as a teenager's. She spoke in a clear, commanding yet polite tone that melted away her age and made her seem young and vital. Though a striking woman, it was the force of her personality that intimidated me and caught my interest right away. As a young fish-and-wildlife biologist, I had a lot of opinions on how grizzly bears should be managed, how the elk were doing, and so on. Doris held equally strong opinions, and we clashed. On top of that, Doris wasn't too happy to see her unmarried niece traveling with some kid who worked for the government.

"Sure doesn't appeal to me," Doris wrote in her diary that August day, referring to me. "Little guy [she crossed out an expletive] and so blowy — like a banty rooster."

I had made a poor first impression.

A year later my work with Montana's state wildlife agency brought me to Kalispell, and my assigned area encompassed much of Doris's old stomping grounds in Glacier Park and the Middle Fork Flathead River Drainage. In her diary, Doris noted our return to the Flathead (Dana was now my wife) but didn't have anything good to say about it.

I got to know Doris and Dan slowly. I began to find out how key they were in the history of Glacier Park and the surrounding area. Dan had driven the classic red tour buses in Glacier, and after years of interpreting the park for tourists he had become a master storyteller. Both he and Doris relished their job of sharing the history of the area through their museum artifacts. Doris was guarded, but she slowly began to see my genuine interest in the history of her beloved piece of Montana and her opinions about it. Doris could recall details of long-ago events as if they had just happened; her keen observations of nature came from a lifetime in the outdoors.

We entertained each other with stories. I told Doris and Dan about the high mountain lakes and streams, the cutthroat trout, and the bull trout. I brought to her fish packed in snow that I had caught in a wilderness lake so they could enjoy eating them; she told me what the lake had been like 50 years ago. I described the skeleton of an old cabin on a Glacier Park ridge; Doris told me when it was built and talked of the characters who had lived there. Through each other we shared the past and present.

Drawn to Doris, I worked around the couple's 10-acre place, rototilling and doing little repairs. I picked up feed for her treasured banty hens, leghorns, and Rhode Island Reds. I even lopped off their heads when needed, a job Doris hated.

From time to time, she sent me out behind the house to fetch something from her root cellar. That cellar spoke volumes about her frugal ways. I loved ribbing her about it. Jars of moldy fish and meat, canned whole in the 1930s, stood on the shelves. She boasted that one box of dried huckleberries was 40 years old and still fine. ("They are good forever if the bugs don't get into them too bad," she had said.) Sickening-looking jars of putrefied, unidentifiable things were sealed with rusty lids. She claimed that everything in the cellar was palatable in a pinch; lucky for her she never got in a pinch.

Within a few years Doris began to trust me. "We rather like John now," she wrote in her diary. "He helps us."

Doris was as self-sufficient as a wolverine. That was fortunate, because Dan had been disabled for a number of years and could offer little help with chores. Legs that had once carried him on 20-mile snowshoe trips as one of Glacier Park's early rangers failed him. He died in 1984, just shy of his 80th birthday.

After Dan died, I helped Doris more, and the gap between us narrowed. But she still supervised everything I did around her place, even to the extent of holding onto and trying to direct my arm as I cleaned her stovepipe.

Doris ran her place with the iron hand of a construction foreman. Some areas were simply off limits. She didn't allow me to enter her cherished, income-producing raspberry patch, but it was my job to keep the weeds down by rototilling around it.

Once, she went into town with a friend and forgot that it was rototilling day.

I remember arriving at Doris's and backing the rototiller down the ramp from her shed. I tilled around and around the patch, looking at cane after cane loaded with huge red raspberries highlighted by the midday sun. Finally, my will power dissolved and I thought, what the heck, Doris isn't even around today. Soon I was stuffing berries into my mouth as fast as I could. I figured I had a feeding frenzy coming after all the work I'd done on the patch.

Just as I was thinking that it would be embarrassing if anyone saw me gobbling the berries like a guilty thief, I heard a car door slam.

"Uh-oh," I thought, that must be Doris and Lilian. I'd better get out of the berries." But I didn't react quickly enough. Only a few feet away through the brush I heard Doris scream, "WHO'S IN MY RASPBERRIES!"

She had jumped out of the moving car and covered the 50 yards between the museum parking lot and the raspberry patch in what must have been world record time for women over 80.

"Oh, hi Doris," I said nonchalantly. "This is rototilling day, remember? I was just checking the edge of the plant row."

Silence.

"Well, Doris, I'll just restart the old rototiller and finish up now, OK?"

Doris still didn't reply. She just looked at me through her cat-glasses with her mouth held crooked. I'm sure she had seen me wolfing down her beloved berries, but she let it go and never scolded me about it. I may be the only person caught eating Doris's berries without permission who lived to tell about it.

Even in her mid-80s, Doris still moved quickly. Once when we went huckleberrying, I bent to pick a few berries, looked up, and Doris was gone. She had disappeared around the bend of a logging road faster than I thought possible. When I finally caught up with her, at one of her old special patches, she didn't look winded. That day she told me that as a young girl she outran all the other children, boys and girls, at the county fair races. "I could take them all in the broad jump, too," she boasted. I believed her. In fact I wondered what she could have done in her prime with a scientific training program and a pair of Nikes.

We continued to clash occasionally. On one repair job I was adding shingles to the roof of one of her old sheds. She told me where to put the ladder, which nail to use, how to hold the hammer — tried to direct every movement I made. Finally I snapped at her and she became hurt. Later that day she tried to pay me, thinking I was angry because she didn't. After I convinced her that the last thing I wanted was to be paid to be around her place, we made up. That one incident seemed to create a closer understanding between us. She finally believed that I was genuinely interested in her; I finally saw that Doris had to be in charge.

After chores that day, Doris shared with Dana and me sips of syrupy

Doris managed her museum and grounds, including this large flower plot, with help from her friends and relatives.

"wine" made from huckleberries picked in the Great Bear Wilderness 50 years before. The concoction had a bite, and very much of it would probably have made anyone sick. But it preserved the taste of the berries and of the time; Doris was a true Montana Character, I thought, and her and Dan's story needed to be preserved, too. I had already made my mind up then that I would one day write this book. It was the one last chore I would gladly do for Doris.

Doris and I grew closer in those final years. She remained tough to work for but she rewarded us with her wit and her stories. After years of listening to her talk about earlier days in Glacier Park I recognized that she was a pioneer. She had defied grizzlies when she cooked for the Going-to-the-Sun road crew, hiked the park's trails in clothes reserved for men, owned wilderness lodges, kept bears, coyotes, beaver, and mountain goats for pets, managed a museum, written an outdoor news column, and taught in one-room schools. She was an uncommon, common woman who reflected the rugged spirit and grit of the men and women who paved Montana's transition to the modern West.

I believe that Doris was a "Show-You" feminist, although she would have balked at being called any kind of feminist. In her wake she left a trail of men who became believers in the intellect, physical prowess and toughness of women. She convinced these men by showing them, not by talking. I know she convinced me.

I felt everyone could learn from her life, and that was what I wanted to get across in a book about her. Doris was mostly cool to the idea. She did allow me to write one magazine article about her, but then wouldn't speak to me after it appeared. It seems that our generational differences led to a misunderstanding about what "Mountain Dew" meant.

Doris had become hooked on caffeine-charged Mountain Dew pop. She drank so much that she actually had various people buy it for her, so her grocer wouldn't know how much she was drinking. I'm ashamed to admit that I bought for her too.

Once I went out to her feed shed to get something, and when I opened the door dozens of two-liter empty pop bottles that Doris had stacked cascaded down the steps. I finally asked her about her habit and she admitted she couldn't stop, that she was "crazy about the stuff." When I wrote that magazine profile about her, I mentioned her Mountain Dew habit, but didn't specify I meant "pop." Some of her friends thought she was drinking bottles of moonshine.

Doris's sister, Maxine, confided in me that, secretly, Doris liked the article, except for the Mountain Dew part. Doris forgave me eventually and we grew closer still. I treasured my time with her, laboring around her place and visiting with her in the evenings. She allowed me to tape hours and hours of her stories. I had finally accepted the wisdom of her age and experience, and her diary reflected it. "John is real nice," she wrote. "We got used to each other."

Doris met her final battle with the defiance of a badger caught in a leghold trap. She received transfusions and chemotherapy for multiple myeloma for three years, still living alone and managing her place until the last few months of her life. She finally succumbed to the cancer a month before her 89th birthday.

Maxine had also become a friend and she knew I'd been working on Doris's story. Maxine gave me what I considered Doris's most valuable belongings: diaries, correspondence, and photos of Dan and Doris that covered 1924-1989. The diaries and papers shed light on many things I had long wondered about. I learned that Doris faced untold tragedy earlier in life, that she and Dan were both protectors and poachers of wildlife. I learned that she seemed to have a passion for off-color jokes.

As I dug deeper I learned that Doris was one of the first to record events in official ranger station journals in Glacier Park. She served as Dan's assistant at the remote Cut Bank Ranger Station; her flowing handwriting fills the pages of the station journal for 1928. I also learned that Doris held a great interest in the Blackfeet tribes and their connection with the park, and that she spent a lot of time with tribal members when she lived in East Glacier during the glory days of Great Northern Railroad's "See America First" campaign.

I spent years after Doris's death interviewing relatives and friends, and searching historical records for information about Dan and Doris, and Glacier Park. I felt to some degree possessed by her story, driven as if I were on both ends of a whip. I stood in places where she spent time and tried to feel her presence. One evening I sat alone in the old grange hall she loved so. The last rays of the sun cast an eerie, golden light on the rich wood floor. Around the room hung mementos of her time in the Grange; but I felt little inspiration. The same was true for her gravesite and places around Glacier Park. I was chasing Doris's ghost, but I wasn't finding it.

Finally, on a warm spring day more than seven years after her death I returned to her home and museum grounds. A Realtor's sign faced the highway. Doris's carefully maintained flower gardens no longer decorated the front yard. Doris's house and museum building stood as empty shells. Not a trace of Doris's presence remained.

I walked around the back and found myself at the root cellar.

The root cellar door was mostly intact. I lifted it sideways and stepped down. I expected the labyrinth to be long empty or caved in, but I was surprised at what I found.

About three feet of water filled the entry space but I could stand on boards which kept me mostly dry. Jumbles of electrical wires that would have caused an electrician to cringe hung from the low ceiling. I turned on my flashlight and, looking through a mass of cobwebs, saw about 200 jars of fruit and vegetables in various stages of decomposition still standing on the shelves. Red raspberries had faded to the color of pale flesh. Some of the canned huckleberries had dissolved into a fibrous, pale mass in the bottom of the jars. A tall bottle marked "Wine" held a black liquid covered with floating scum.

I had to admit that the jars of "food" didn't look any worse, and may have even looked better, than they did years before. I couldn't find a single date on any of the rusty lids or dust-covered jars. I guess Doris figured that, since this stuff was supposed to be good forever, why date it?

It struck me right away why the cellar was virtually untouched. Over the years, renters had simply been afraid to go down there, fearing rotting food or electrical shock. The root cellar persisted as a lasting example of her lifetime of nickel-nursing and frugality. I had found Doris's time capsule.

I replaced the door on the root cellar and walked past the back shed that once housed the rototiller. I reached what used to be the main raspberry patch. Renters had neglected the 7,500 square-foot patch and allowed it to nearly vanish into weeds.

I stood at the spot where Doris caught me red handed and red-toothed that summer day years before. I paced the sprint she had made to catch me and found it to be almost exactly 50 yards. I marveled at how quickly she covered the distance.

She was known for her speed. When in her 20s, she had kept up with a Montana University track star, a fellow park worker, on a roundabout, 18-mile jog to the top of Squaw Peak and back to Glacier Park Lodge in half a day. I thought about Doris in her prime; I imagined what it must have been like to hike with her over the new trails of Glacier. I was gaining on Doris's ghost.

I remembered a passage from her journal. One sunny day in May she noted a hike to Triple Divide, nestled amongst Glacier's peaks at the head of the magnificent Cut Bank Valley. She hiked alone that day, covering 15 miles; snow still covered the higher part of the trail. I could almost see her. She moved quickly, skipping over the snow banks like a hoary marmot. It was 1928, and Doris and Glacier Park were both very young...

Doris on a hiking trip along a Glacier Park creek, about 1926. She's wearing her ever-present high-top leather boots.

1
Triple Divide

"It was on the trip up Mt. Henry that I first learned of your speed,
Oh Doris, Oh Doris, you're a terror in speed."

On May 23, 1928, 27-year-old Doris Huffine woke up before dawn. Packing a small lunch and pocketing her tiny, porcupine quill-decorated journal, she left the isolated Cut Bank Ranger Station where she had spent the winter assisting in and recording patrols with her new husband, Dan, and began hiking up the trail along Cut Bank Creek. As she had many times in the past few years Doris steeled herself for an arduous hike. The creek, named Punak'iksi Ituktai by the Blackfeet Indians for the cliff-like banks along its lower reaches, meanders gently for the first few miles above the ranger station, then gains gradient quickly where it flows from the spine of the Rocky Mountains. She planned to scale the Continental Divide at Triple Divide Pass, 7,400 feet above sea level, and return to the station in time to cook dinner, covering a total distance of 16 miles with about 5,000 feet of elevation gain and loss. The Blackfeet considered the alpine, wind-battered Triple Divide Pass a spiritual place along the Backbone of the World, where water from melting snow eventually flows to three oceans, and Doris enjoyed the hike as much for its meditative rewards as for its physical challenges.

At 5-feet 4-inches tall and about 100 pounds, Doris' small wiry frame understated her athletic prowess and inner strength. A few years before, she had escaped the tragedy of her loved ones' deaths in Iowa by fleeing to Glacier National Park in northwestern Montana. The park's grandeur captured her. Blackfeet Tribal members she'd met during the previous sum-

The tiny Cut Bank Ranger Station in spring, 1928, where Doris began her hike to Triple Divide. That's Ranger Dan Huffine, Doris's new husband, standing on the porch. The sign reads, "File Complaints Here."

mers while working at Glacier Park Lodge, ceremonies she'd witnessed, and the tribal history she had studied stirred her imagination. Doris wanted to learn more about the Blackfeet and their ties to the magnificent country bordering their reservation on the east side of Glacier.

"Here is the last home of a vanishing race — the Blackfeet Indians," wrote famed novelist and frequent park visitor Mary Roberts Rinehart in "The Call of the Mountains," a park travel magazine used as an autograph book by Doris and other park workers. "Here is the last stand of the Rocky Mountain sheep and the Rocky Mountain goat... here are meadows of June roses, forget-me-not, larkspur, and Indian paint-brush growing beside glaciers, snow fields and trails of a beauty to make you gasp."

All this and more was what led Doris on her arduous journey that day. In the first hour of her hike, she passed Cut Bank Chalets, a cluster of three log backcountry hostels built by Louis Hill and the Great Northern Railway about 15 years earlier during the heyday of the early promotion of the park. Wildflowers adorned the meadows along the trail. Glacier lilies thrust stamens toward the sun, yellow petals trailing behind like arms of a star. The first paintbrush, deep red and orange, stood among the trailside grasses. Doris crossed the foot bridge over Cut Bank Creek and noted that the stream, swollen with water from melting snow fields, measured seven feet above the normal water mark. A beaver swam in a side channel pond, formed by a low dam that it had built from sticks and mud.

"Saw three dandy beaver," Doris recorded in one of the journals that she would keep for most of her life. She loved to observe all of nature's majestic displays, whether in the stunning vistas of the Northern Rockies or the fragile stubbornness of an alpine flower. That was one of the things that had led her West from Iowa, the cornucopia of wilderness experiences that were fresh every day. She had a particular admiration for beavers, for their industriousness and social skills, and later would raise one from a small kit to a 50-pound behemoth that lived in her bathtub.

Doris had hiked or traveled on skis to this reach of the Cut Bank Creek often during the past few months to watch the beavers work on their dams. The area had long been an important camping site for the Blackfeet. Here they gathered "weasel eyes," or huckleberries, cut lodge poles from the narrow-bore trees that today still bear the name lodgepole, and waited for warriors to return from their raids on the west-side tribes. The ponds were "dotted with beaver houses" even in the Blackfeet times, according to their history, and it is easy to believe that the Indian visitors and Doris shared a vision of the totemic animal as a powerful ally.

Doris continued on the trail along the edge of the beaver ponds and around the base of 8,690-foot Amphitheater Mountain, called by the Blackfeet Three Horns Mountain after a famous chief who stole a wife from the west-side tribes. The glacier-carved mountain forms a giant horseshoe with Mount James, or Lone Chief Mountain, to the south. Together, the two mountains form the north wall of the Cut Bank Creek drainage.

"Sure some snow and mosquitos," Doris wrote in her journal that day. "Water all over everywhere." She reached the tributary stream discharging from the great cirque of Amphitheater Mountain and removed her calf-high leather hiking boots to wade the icy, rushing waters. Like the experienced

Ridges of Glacier Park looking towards the "Backbone of the World" in spring.

Otto Bessey and Doris on top of Squaw Peak, Glacier Park, in 1926. According to Doris, she and Otto made the roundabout 18-mile jog from East Glacier and back in 4 hours and 10 minutes.

mountain traveler she had become, Doris ignored the dull, throbbing pain in her feet and ankles created by the snowmelt water, and the sharp pain on the soles of her feet caused by the angular rocks. These were the rewards of her long walk, more likely to be cherished than the subject of a complaint.

At the forks of Cut Bank Creek, Doris continued up the west branch known as Atlantic Creek. Had she turned south, up the North Fork of Cut Bank Creek as she had on other hikes, she would have passed Morning Star Lake, named by the Blackfeet for the son of the sun and the moon. Continuing on, she would have followed the trail over Pitamakan Pass, named after a famous Blackfeet woman with whom Doris shared many characteristics. According to legend, Pitamakan, or Running Eagle, was a Pikuni warrior, a member of one of the three tribes in the Blackfeet Confederacy, and the only woman in the Blackfeet tribes ever given a man's name. Pitamakan too lost her mother at age 15, shouldered the burden of raising four younger brothers and sisters, and became hardened by the experience. Pitamakan led warriors up Cut Bank Creek and over the pass to raid the tribes on the west side of the mountains. On one raid, she turned down a marriage proposal by the Blood chief, Falling Bear, because he failed to meet her challenge. Pitamakan had crept into the enemy camp several times, stealing a total of 15 horses while Falling Bear stole only 9 horses. "I gave you your chance," Pitamakan said when Falling Bear proposed. "The answer would have been yes had you taken more horses than I did..."

Like Pitamakan, Doris was forceful and endowed with great athletic prowess. If born toward the end of the century instead of at its beginning, she very easily could have made a name for herself in any of several sports. She had the competitor's heart. Two years before this, she had jogged with Montana University track runner Otto Bessey from Glacier Park Lodge to the top of Squaw Mountain and back, covering the 18 rugged miles in four hours and 10 minutes. "I measured the distance in lengths and puffs," she wrote in her photo album next to pictures of the two on the peak. No wonder, since Bessey was an athletic champion who led Flathead County High School teams to championships in football as their star quarterback, and in basketball as their star forward. He set long-standing high school records in the javelin. Later, at Montana University, he set records in the javelin again, and he was the Pacific Coast Conference javelin champion. Although he was not much taller than Doris, he was known for his speed and referred to as the "Little Giant" of the Montana University track squad. He and Doris made a good match.

On another hike, to the top of Mount Henry, her hiking ability inspired another lodge worker, Bud Johnson, to write a poem about her which began, "It was on the trip up Mt. Henry that I first learned of your speed, Oh

Trick Falls (now called Running Eagle Falls) on the upper Two Medicine River, at high water level. Features like these spectacular falls enticed Doris to stay in Glacier Park country.

The Glacier Park Hotel, where Doris worked and developed the closest friendships of her life. Near this photo she wrote, "the good old place where we had fun."

Doris, Oh Doris, you're a terror in speed." Her reputation as a young woman gave credence to her claim that as a young girl she could outrun all the other children at the annual county fair races.

Also like Pitamakan, Doris's physical grace, her intelligence — she held a college degree and had taught school — and her feminine qualities — striking face and deep, dreamy green eyes — had attracted many suitors. Dude ranch cowboys and lodge co-workers wrote longing tributes to her beauty on the pages of her 1925 and 1926 autograph books. "To the little dreamy eyed Doris!" wrote cowboy artist and East Glacier resident C.A. Beil, "We hate to see you leave Glacier Park. The horses will miss you, the goats will miss you, the mountain sheep will miss you, the bears will miss you, the moon lillys will miss you, the cowboys gonna miss you, and poor me is gonna miss you too." In concluding that Doris would always be welcome, Beil may have been hinting at a romance, but it was not long afterward that Doris met Dan, falling for his humor, physical prowess, and independence as a backcountry ranger. In her lifelong commitment to a man she considered her equal, she achieved something that apparently escaped Pitamakan.

Passing through the narrow gorge formed by Medicine Grizzly Peak, which divides the drainage, Doris saw a band of four bighorn sheep, the animals which had one time attracted hunting parties from the west-side tribes — Kootenais, Kalispels, Spokanes, and Stonies — and later, white hunters from the east. Rather than linger to admire the creatures, Doris continued up the slope as though in homage of them. She gained elevation more quickly now past scattered yellow buttercups and glacier lilies, poking up from the edges of melting snowfields. A thousand feet below, the turquoise waters of Medicine Grizzly Lake backed against the sheer cirque-wall formed by the base of Triple Divide Peak and Razoredge Mountain at the head of the drainage. Snowmelt from the flanks of the peaks tumbled hundreds of feet over huge rocks and cliff faces into the upper end of the lake, forming one of the most impressive waterfalls in the park.

Medicine Grizzly Lake bears the name of a huge bear that once lived in the Cut Bank drainage and terrorized the Blackfeet. The Blackfeet called grizzlies Pah'-ksi-kwo-yi, "sticky mouths," or real-bears. Only medicine men, or sun priests, could take the skin of one of the great bears. James Willard Schultz, a writer who Doris had met and admired and who had lived among the Blackfeet, wrote, "None of the [Blackfeet] women would venture out after fuel or poles for lodge or travois without an escort. Many of the hunters never molested a grizzly, the bear being regarded as a sort of medicine or sacred animal, many believing that it was really a human being." Blackfeet women believed that grizzlies could carry them away to their dens and enslave them.

Doris held respect for grizzlies, but did not fear them. She accepted their presence in the park and later demonstrated her coolness in encounters with them, and their lesser cousin, the black bear, on both sides of the Divide. Indeed, throughout her life, Doris possessed a special skill and understanding with wildlife, leading her eventually to raise several black bears as pets.

This particular afternoon in May 1928, however, she saw no bears or bear tracks as she hiked up the drainage. By that late in the spring, most grizzlies would have already emerged from their dens, but fewer grizzlies lived in the Cut Bank Valley in the 1920s than in the Blackfeet times because sheep ranchers and others had shot many bears. Hikers still encountered them around the park, but it was something of an event. About a decade earlier, a huge grizzly had chased two women over a bank and into Cut Bank Creek near the chalets.

In the early afternoon that day, Doris left the mosquitos behind and reached Triple Divide Pass, one of the most profound geographic points in North America. On the peak above her, formed by some of the world's oldest sedimentary rocks, snowmelt waters gathered to eventually cascade into three watersheds: east and south to the Missouri and Atlantic Ocean, west to the Columbia River and Pacific Ocean, and north to the St. Mary River and Hudson Bay. It was a place that was rich in metaphoric potential and could easily inspire an aware consciousness such as Doris's to examine the course of her own life, and where it was heading. Even without the magical thought of how the waters from this spot found their natural destiny, Doris was enchanted by the special beauty of the vistas from Triple Divide Pass. To the north, she looked down a trail running along the Red Eagle drainage past Red Eagle Lake, named after a Blackfeet sun priest. Then, a little further beyond were the two St. Mary Lakes, together nearly 20 miles long, called by the Blackfeet the "Lakes Inside," because of the spectacular peaks that tower above their shores. Upon seeing the lakes for the first time, on a hunting expedition with James Willard Schultz, a British banker named Colonel Robert Baring remarked, "I have been in the Alps of Switzerland, the Himalayas in India, but in neither of those ranges have I seen any setting of lake and mountains that can compare with this..."

Along the Divide to the west of where Doris stood, the park's namesakes clung to the peaks like huge, irregular pearls in a great necklace. In the distance, Doris could make out the peaks of Mt. Logan, Mt. Jackson, and Blackfoot Mountain, which dominate the Divide and shield the glaciers below their summits. This series of glaciers, or "ices" as the Blackfeet called them, is the most extensive in the park. Red Eagle, Logan, Blackfoot, Jackson and Harrison glaciers link together to form nearly an eight-mile chain of ice. Looking east from the Divide, Doris could see the route she had just traveled up the glacially carved Cut Bank Valley; the greening plains stretched beyond the mountain foothills.

The Backbone, as the Blackfeet referred to the Continental Divide, is home to the "bigheads" or mountain goats, another symbol of the park and an animal Doris found fascinating, perhaps aware that she shared many traits with the tenacious and canny cliff dwellers. Early explorers called them white buffaloes because of their humped backs and small hind quarters. Schultz was one of the first to write about goats in the park, describing their "...long, wavy fringes of hair down to the knees of the forelegs, reminding one of a girl's pantalettes in the wind." Mary Roberts Rinehart wrote perhaps with more sensitivity, when she noted: "The call of the mountains is a real call. Go out and ride the mountain trails — look across the valleys to wild peaks where mountain goats stand impassive on the edge of space — then the mountains will get you."

After a series of tragedies in Iowa, Doris found spiritual renewal in Glacier's wildflowers, alpine meadows and spectacular vistas.

Doris had expected to see some that day, sitting dog-like on their haunches along a cliff face. Over the years, she would mount many photos of goats in her album, and later in life painted scenes of the agile animals clinging to the precipitous ledges of the park's mountains. With her husband Dan, living on the west side of the Backbone years later, Doris would even keep a goat as a pet, nursing its injuries. On this particular hike to Triple Divide Peak, however, Doris was to be disappointed. The goats were staying out of sight.

Standing in one of the more remote points in the park, dwarfed by the vastness of this spectacular country, Doris shed the indecision that had plagued her. She turned and strode back down the Cut Bank drainage, splashing through the melt-waters running in the narrow trail. She felt like a little girl again, refreshed and excited. She reached the ranger station by late afternoon, thinking about what she'd cook for dinner. Doris had fled to Montana as a way of escaping sadness, viewing Iowa as flat and full of despair. The splendor of Glacier Park, the close friends she'd made, and the independent feel of Montana held her.

She had heard that same "call of the mountains" that Rinehart had written about. Montana's spectacular mountains, melting snowfields and explosions of glacier lilies offered renewal. She had decided to stay.

Doris, age 15 or 16. Doris lost her mother, Austa, during this period and took on adult responsibilities around the Ashley homestead.

2
Snake in the Cornpatch, 1901-24

*"My poor Aunt. I just went up her front like I was climbing up a tree.
And Eva said, 'Gosh! Get down, get down off of me!' And I said, 'No
sir, not while there's a snake down there.'"*

Doris had been born Doris Ashley. Her family roots were sunk deep in
some of the world's richest soil in western Iowa, where two related homesteads sprawled across hundreds of acres of gently rolling corn country.
Doris's parents came there as children with their families in the 1870s, and
Doris probably had every expectation that like most of her relatives she
would not only grow up but grow old there.

Doris's father, Bert Ashley, had come from Illinois in 1877 to Highland
Home near Council Bluffs when he was four and his brother George was 11.
The two boys were destined to have more in common than lives as Iowa
farmers. George grew up to marry Eva Drake, while Bert would wed Eva's
sister, Austa. Eva had come to the homestead when she was four, traveling
from Belle Plain, Iowa, to Battle Creek by train, then making the rest of the
journey to the homestead by sled. That was in 1878. Grandpa Drake, Austa's
father, traded a horse team for his 40 acres and built a tiny one-room house.
They brought along some flour, beans, side meat and cows. The cows were
dry when they arrived and the kids nearly starved for milk until a calf
arrived.

Living in relative isolation as they did, the two families grew intertwined.
After all, only two houses stood along the 22 miles between Battle Creek
and the homesteads. A dirt track connected the two homesteads, nestled
among rows of shelterbelt willow, maple, oak, elm, and ash. Corn, cows and

The homestead belonging to Doris's Aunt Eva and Uncle George. Doris spent much of her time at Aunt Eva's, who was her closest confidant during her childhood.

sheep provided the families with their livelihood. The Ashleys and Drakes hauled grain to Sioux City to sell, and to Correctionville to grind into flour. Doris recounted stories of those days, as if she had been there herself. "The first time Aunt Eva went to a store she and Uncle Kelly walked four miles to Lucky Valley," she remembered Eva telling her. "The store was closed for some horse races and the kids were so scared they just stood around until the races were over and the store opened. Then they were so bashful that everyone else was waited on first so it was nearly dark when they got the groceries and started home. It got dark when they were a mile on their way, and Grandpa met them when they were about half way home."

Doris's mother, Austa, was born on the Drake homestead in 1883. As time went on, the Drake sisters and the Ashley brothers became close friends. Indeed, their relationship developed into an extended family on adjoining land. Austa and Eva were very close, and apparently their desire to stay together had something to do with their decision to marry the neighboring brothers.

Eva chose not to have children, but Austa wasted no time. She gave birth to Doris Dorothy on a cold first day of February in 1901. Austa, just 18, was thrilled to have a girl. From the beginning, Doris was precocious and charmed everyone. She quickly developed the gift for writing that she would later in life put to good use in her journals and a newspaper column. As young as three, she was already scrawling letters to Aunt Eva, who had taken to spending winters in California with George to find a climate more friendly to Eva, who suffered from an unnamed illness. Austa speaks of Doris's letters in several contemporary references.

"Dear Sister," Austa wrote to Eva on January 14, 1905. "Doris is writing a letter to you so I will write a little. Doris says that she told you all of the news in her letter and I expect you can read it. Doris says we are having lots of fun this winter, her birthday comes soon and she is thinking about that." Doris's "letter" actually consisted of scribbles across a small piece of writing paper.

Then a few weeks later, Austa writes to her sister again, telling a humorous anecdote about Doris. The letter was dated February 2, 1905, just one day after Doris's birthday. "Doris is sending you a piece of her birthday cake. This morning just getting up there was an awful racket under the house. I think it was a weasel catching a rabbit from the sound of things. Doris jumped out of her bed over Bert and the baby and down beside me before you could think. I didn't even have time to move the baby, she laid on him in spite of me. She looked like a flying cat coming. She then asked me if I would let the cat get her. All I can say is, she is only four."

Eva had cautioned Austa against having children because of the work required, the lack of doctors in the area, and the strain of birth, but Doris had nonetheless been joined by brothers Eldon in 1902 and Frank in 1904. Eldon had serious respiratory problems early in his life, and Austa began to see Eva's point, worrying that she might lose one or more of her children. The doctor warned that a specialist might be needed for Eldon if his breathing problems and fainting continued.

"Dear sister," Austa, wrote on February 13, 1906. "Eva the sun is shining today, first time we've seen the sun for about a week. It was 30 below by Ashley's thermometer this morning. We are well except Eldon has a cough at night; he coughs an hour or two in the middle of the night. I am going to make him a suit today (or) tomorrow. I am going to make him a coat if nothing happens. I got the children and myself summer dresses from Chicago... I still have some sewing to do. I want to try and get it done while I have a girl.

"Doris is about as leggy as any of the Ashleys," Austa continued, "and she has grown about a foot and a half this winter. She is learning to write so she can write to you. That letter you wrote to her is hardly ever out of her sight.

Doris's grandfather, Jim Drake (right), and George Ashley up on the bundle rack, at the Drake homestead in Iowa. Doris and her Uncle George became good friends.

Doris, about six years old, on the Bert Ashley homestead. Doris surrounded herself with animals throughout her life.

Well, I will have to warm my feet they are about froze."

Doris added a note: "Dear Aunt Eva," she wrote in blocky, backward script, "Sheep are all wright."

Eldon managed to surprise everyone by becoming healthy, but within a year, at age 24, Austa began developing early signs of tuberculosis. No remedies the family tried over the next few years proved effective.

Austa found it especially hard to breath during the hot, muggy, Iowa summers, so in 1910, Bert, Austa and their family, which now included Shirley, born in 1908, moved to the wheat country of McGrath, Alberta, in western Canada, not far from the Montana border. Although the family longed for Iowa, they thought that the dryer mountain air and cooler summers would help Austa's worsening tuberculosis. The family homesteaded some land, and Bert supplemented their income by driving a delivery team that distributed supplies around the town.

Ever busy, nine-year old Doris wrote a steady flow of letters to her beloved aunt. "Dear Aunt Eva," she wrote from McGrath on March 12, 1910. "We got to Lethbridge all write. We are staying in a hotel now. Papa got a house for us and we are going to live in it Monday. Mamma is singing how nice to live in sunny Alberta. She is just singing that to tease us kids. It's snowing today. She wishes she was down there and every body else does. We have 15 jars of fruit left. Mamma says we can come back down there when they are gone."

Even at that early age, Doris was helping with her younger brothers and sisters. "Dear Aunt Eva," Doris wrote on May 26, 1910, "Mamma was downtown today and left me home to take care of Shirley and she did not crie a bite while mama was gone."

Doris wrote often about the outdoors, foreshadowing her interests later in life. "We went to Spring Coulee today," she wrote on June 6, 1910. "We did not see the comet because it don't get dark quick enough. On the road over there we stopped to give the horses a drink and Eldon got out and paddled across the creek and there was a snake swimming in the water. I will send you a blossom off of the columbine we found today."

In her letters, Doris mentioned running and speech contests, and plays she took part in at the McGrath school. More than anything else, these seemed to excite her. She was very competitive. Doris succeeded in school, and often won foot races, and speaking contests. Apparently, she'd inherited her mother's knack for achieving in school, as Austa's one surviving report card (from ninth grade) suggests: "Report of the average standing of Austa Drake for the month ending May 1, 1896: Spelling, 100%; Reading, 95%; Writing, 97%; Arithmetic, 75%; Geography, 97%; Grammar, 95%; History, 98%; Physiology, 98%; Deportment, 100%; Average standing, 97%; Days present, 18. Mrs. M.G. Taylor, Rock Branch Iowa, Woodbury Co., Teacher."

Even though the children longed for Iowa, they enjoyed their stay in Alberta. The family read together and spent evenings around the fireplace. Eventually, it became clear that the stay in Alberta would not produce the magic cure they sought, and the Ashleys returned to Iowa after about three years.

Austa's health had improved some. Bert built a new house near George and Eva's farm, and the family prepared to move in. About the first of March, Eva hitched a team of horses to the family buggy and transported Austa and the children through a snowstorm to their new home. "Doris sat in the front seat next to Eva with her canary bird on her lap under a blanket to keep it warm," remembered Doris's brother Frank. As this incident demon-

Doris, age 12, with her sister, Shirley, age 4. Doris bore child rearing and housekeeping duties early in life because of her mother's poor health. Photo courtesy of Shirley Ashley Reinking.

Doris's sister, Maxine, about age 13, at the family farm in Iowa. Maxine was Doris's favorite sibling and became her lifelong supporter and closest friend.

15

strates, Doris maintained an intense interest and kindness towards animals from early in life.

After their move to the new home, Austa spent much of her time on the breezy, sunny, screened porch on the southwest side, hoping the fresh air would help her lungs. Doris, along with a hired girl, helped with her brothers and sisters. Austa gave birth to Maxine in 1913. Eva was appalled that Austa continued having children given her condition.

The Ashley family centered their life around long, quiet evenings together at home. Bert spent a lot of time reading and memorizing poetry, then reciting it for his family. Doris and her sisters and brothers took part, too. According to Doris's sister, Shirley, Doris was very good to her Papa. But even early in life Doris spoke up and would tell Bert what she thought of things he did. It was no surprise that she stood up to her father on occasion since she was herself a surrogate parent in the family. Because of Austa's illness, Doris had gotten to exercise her penchant for leadership, and she ruled sternly over her younger brothers and sisters. Frank remembered that he and the other children called Doris "Bossy."

"Doris was a very headstrong girl," he remembered. "She ordered the rest of us around all the time but we didn't think about it much because she was the oldest."

Doris spent many of her afternoons at Aunt Eva's house, telling Eva of her troubles and aspirations. "Aunt Eva's was only a half mile from our place," remembered Maxine. "That's where Doris went to do all her hoping, complaining, pouting and talking about good things too."

Aunt Eva's served as a refuge from the heavy responsibilities Doris bore at such an early age. She was very close to Eva and often took walks with her around the homesteads, or helped her around the house. "We couldn't stay nights at Aunt Eva and Uncle George's," remembered Doris, "but we could go over there any time we wanted during the days. We were over there all the time, eating up all the food she had."

Although Doris didn't like to talk about her childhood, one event stood out in her mind and she often laughed as she recalled it later in life. Doris behaved in an uncharacteristic way for the tomboy she'd become.

"I was a big kid, about 12 or 13," Doris began, "probably as big as I am now. One day we went down to the cornpatch way down in the field. We were going to pick sweet corn, and it was kind of weedy down there. All of a sudden I saw a snake. And my poor Aunt! I just went up her like I was going up a tree. It was just the dumbest thing I can remember. I just went right up her front and I sat on top of her.

"And Eva said, 'Gosh! Get down, get down off of me!' And I said, 'No sir, not as long as there's a snake down there.' She couldn't get me down, I just stayed up there like a leech. My land, the way she fought to get me down. I don't know why she didn't kill us."

Fortunately, Eva's love and support carried Doris through the wrenching experience of her mother's illness. As Austa's tuberculosis worsened, Doris spent her time between Eva's farm and Austa's bedside. Austa sewed a white blouse for Doris to wear to her eighth-grade final exams. It proved to be the last project Austa completed and Doris treasured the blouse the rest of her life.

To the chagrin of Eva, Austa became pregnant again in spite of her condition. The fifth Ashley child, Bertie George, was born in 1915, and he turned out to be the sickest of all. Bertie had severe spinal meningitis, and because of Austa's illness, Doris had to bear much of the responsibility of caring for the infant. She supported him as his spine curved and shortened, but Bertie died virtually in Doris's arms in July 1916, at nine months of age. And with so much stress, both physical and psychological, Austa's conditioned worsened, too.

The Ashley family had tried everything known at the time to help Austa. Nothing had worked, and now they had gotten to the point where the only thing left to try was constant medical attention in an institution. Like most "houses of consumption," the sanitarium in Woodbury County, Iowa, served as a warehouse for terminally ill victims of tuberculosis. Doris, who idolized her mother, visited her in the sanitarium frequently, attended to her needs, and wiped the blood following Austa's convulsive coughing spells.

"I remember going out there to tell Mama goodbye," recalled Doris's sister, Maxine, "but she had a coughing spell and blood flew out all over the floor. Doris helped with the clean up equipment, even though they had a trained nurse."

It was just a matter of time before the disease claimed Austa. Doris was just 15, but already a woman from so much hardship. On top of the loss of her mother and infant brother, Doris also suffered the death of her beloved grandfather about the same time.

"Papa was gone a lot because he was the only one who could stand to dress Grandpa's cancer of the throat," remembered Maxine. "Grandpa lived just down over the hill, a quarter mile. Doris was the oldest grandchild, and he thought she was wonderful, and wanted to have her in the room all the time." Doris shut out her emotions and her optimistic outlook on life faded. Each funeral became a trial, and the combined experiences hardened her and paved the way for her to handle other tragedies.

Austa was adored by her family and her death on September 28, 1916, devastated Doris and the Ashleys so much that they avoided talking about it, even among themselves. On Austa's death certificate, Dr. W.L. Stillman listed "tuberculosis of the lungs" as the cause of death. Austa, just 34 when she died, was buried two days later at Oak Hill Cemetery near the Ashley home. Doris attended the third Ashley funeral of the year.

Bert never remarried, and his sister, Lenna, came to live with the family after Austa died. According to Doris's sister, Shirley, Doris resented Aunt Lenna being in the home and being paid by Bert. But Aunt Lenna earned her keep, doing all the household work (with help from Doris) and gardening. The only condition Lenna made for her employment was that she would attend Rock Branch Methodist Church, weather permitting. Doris's brothers usually took Lenna to church, returned home, then went to pick her up after services.

During her high school years, Doris too attended church regularly, thinking it would help her mother in some way. She often brought Maxine, who was only 5 or 6 years old. One Sunday, during a revival, many of the churchgoers were speaking in tongues and moving to the front of the church to answer the call to baptism and grace. The revival leaders and others called Doris again and again, asking her to ensure her trip to heaven, but she refused.

Doris became angry and finally shouted that she didn't wish to be baptized, adding, "My mama wasn't baptized, and if she didn't go to heaven, I don't want to go either. When I die I'm going wherever she is."

The call then went to little Maxine, who began to cry. Doris became angry. "You might as well all go up to the rail, kneel together, and leave us alone!" Doris yelled at the congregation. "Wherever Mama and I are going, Maxine is going too. We're leaving!"

After Austa died Doris spent much of her spare time at Aunt Eva's farm. Eva and Bert never got along well because Eva thought that Austa had worked too hard. Bert probably wasn't too fond of the idea of his daughter spending so much time with her aunt, but they had too much in common to be kept apart. Along with many positive influences, Eva convinced Doris that Austa died from the strain of having her last two children, a thought Doris carried with her all her life, making her reluctant to have children herself.

George, Eva's husband, was a quiet man, but he did like to talk to Doris. Shirley recalled some of their conversations. "She liked to talk to Uncle George and wanted to know his opinion on U.S. politics and world affairs. Uncle George read a lot and studied politics." He may also have been an early feminist. At the very least, he was ahead of his time in listening to what a woman had to say. With Doris, though, perhaps he didn't have any choice. "Doris was outspoken and opinionated," as Shirley noted.

Living on a farm and bearing adult responsibilities shaped Doris's work ethic. She sewed for sisters Maxine and Shirley, making most of their school clothes and party dresses. She also helped with the milking and with chores around the house, and her contact with the animals then probably contributed to her lifelong concern for animals. Successful dairy farming required a big commitment of time from each family member; care for individual cows was vital. Doris remembered that sometimes one of their cows would bloat after eating green silage and the stomach gasses would build with disastrous results if not attended to. Because the Ashleys didn't have much money they provided the remedy themselves, and it "was not pleasant at all," recalled Doris, "oh no."

One day after school, Doris and Maxine had stopped at Aunt Eva's and found her in tears. She'd discovered a bloated cow down by the barn and tried to do something but had been handicapped, possibly as Doris recalled, because she "was always blocky and big." She had a hard time bending over or moving quickly and might not have been effective in using a trochar, an implement used to pierce the cow's stomach to release the gases. To be effective, the user must plunge the sharp trochar into the cow's side between the ribs.

Eva instructed the girls where to drive the trochar. Maxine, only about 10, decided she'd do it. "So I got up on this fence," recalled Maxine, "and I let go with the biggest bang I could. And that sharp trochar went right into the cow's stomach — oh, the smell! I took off for that house at a dead run." Despite Maxine's mortification, the cow lived.

Doris remembered her sister's exploit proudly. "That's Maxine. If you can't do something, get hold of her."

Maxine recalled another experience from the time she and Doris spent on the farm. The girls always brought the sheep back from the pasture on their way home from school; they opened the pasture gate and the sheep walked along behind. One day the sheep didn't come, and Maxine heard scuffling behind her. She turned around and the ram which the Ashleys had just purchased charged with his head down. Maxine jumped up on the gate and the sheep collided with the gate right below her feet and fell over, breaking his own neck.

"Then I had to go tell my dad," recalled Maxine. "When he told me how much that ram cost, I could have died: $400. Papa just told me I was lucky."

Despite her increased chore load and feeling deeply depressed about her mother's death, Doris maintained her excellence in school. And her competitive personality intensified.

"Doris always entered contests, especially races, at community picnics, which were very popular then," remembered Shirley. Doris was proud of her prowess in foot races and, later in life, often boasted about it. "I usually beat everybody in the sprints," Doris remembered. "Boys and girls, I beat them all. I could take 'em in the broad jump too."

Shirley remembered that nearby towns held community nights and anyone could enter a variety of contests. In high school Doris often entered speaking contests and usually finished near the top. She turned that talent to profit in Wednesday night talent contests. Often, she won the $10 prize for reciting a memorized speech. Once she won a set of cookware at a picnic in Moville. Doris also excelled in plays and, sometimes, she and her best friend, Sadie, practiced their parts together.

Doris was outgoing and popular and usually had major parts in church plays. Pastor Cyrus Albertson, of Rock Branch Community Church, liked to include everyone from small children to adults in plays he produced. Sadie usually took smaller parts with less memory work while Doris assumed the larger roles. Once, Doris performed a dramatic speech for the community of Anthon at the Catholic Church. According to Sadie, Bert took the other children and went to town, standing outside a window to listen to his daughter perform because he was too shy to go inside. In fact, he was so shy you

The Bert Ashley farm in Iowa where Doris grew up. That's Doris's dad, Bert, walking toward the camera.

could barely believe he was Doris's father. Yet it was Bert's long recitals around the fireplace to the Ashley children that had instilled in Doris the desire to perform. She enjoyed getting attention for her talents, and thrived on public performance.

In their later teens, Doris and Sadie attended dances together, usually accompanied by Frank, who often drove the 1915 Ford which had no wipers, and only side curtains for windows. "He would sit along the side and patiently wait for us until he was old enough to dance too," remembered Sadie. The dances were held at the Rock Branch Community House, Anthon Catholic Church, or someone's home. Doris and Sadie enjoyed the two-step, waltz, and cheek-to-cheek. The women of the communities would prepare sandwiches, cakes and punch and come along as chaperons.

"Doris was a very good mixer," remembered Sadie. "She was very popular."

Not much later, Doris translated those social skills, along with her success in school and love of learning and her desire to perform, into a career. She graduated from high school in 1919 and immediately began training for work as a teacher. She completed two years in normal training at Morningside College in Sioux City, and then taught at rural schools not far from her family's farm. Of course, she was still an integral part of life on the farm for her younger siblings, and Maxine told a story that illustrates the esteem, and perhaps, awe in which she was held.

"One time," recalled Maxine, "she was driving her little roadster to school and I was going to ride to school with her. We just had to go over the hill to the school I attended, then she had to go four miles to where she taught. But she couldn't get the car started. So she said, 'Go get papa or one of the boys, we only have so much time.' I went running through the pig yard and they'd put up a new barb wire fence which I rammed into. I ripped my arm and cut my eyelid. You can see the scar on my arm, more than 70 years later. I don't remember whether or not we went on to school that day, but knowing Doris she probably patched me up and loaded me in the roadster."

Doris seemed comfortable in her role as single teacher, but her deep sadness over her mother's death created in her an acute need for affection. At the same time, although she was popular and attractive, she apparently feared getting close to anyone. Finally, she began to see more of a young man she'd met in college, a man whose social standing exceeded hers. It was to prove a fateful relationship that would leave Doris even more uncertain of herself and her place in life.

Howard Weaver, Doris's first husband, grew up in a well-to-do family and was considered to be elevated in social standing. Even though they spent their childhoods in the same part of Iowa, Doris didn't officially meet Howard until her years at Morningside College.

3
Until Death, 1924-25

"I was so embarrassed to tell the guys I needed another quarter but Doris insisted."

Doris may have avoided marriage partly because communities expected teachers to be single. Also, travel was difficult on rutted, often muddy, dirt roads, so many people married neighbors. Young men had trouble finding work to support a wife; most young men went into farming with their fathers and were not financially independent. Strict courting rules were in effect; parents insisted on chaperons. And Doris bore an added burden helping with her younger sisters because her mother had died. But when Doris was 22 and had been teaching for a few years, a young man whose parents owned a farm in nearby Moville began courting her.

Doris met Howard Weaver during her years at Morningside College and became reacquainted with him at local barn dances. According to Maxine, who accompanied Doris and Frank to many of the dances, Howard was "higher on the social ladder" than most people who attended.

At the dances, held Wednesday and Saturday nights, young men swarmed around the dreamy-eyed Doris. She wore her hair in a long, luxurious curl over her left shoulder. "I'd watch her with that curling iron, hour after hour," Maxine recalled, describing Doris's careful preparations for the dances. Doris brought Maxine, her lifelong companion and supporter, even though Maxine was barely a teenager. "I was only a brat in jeans," remembered Maxine. "Lots of times I'd go over in the corner and fall asleep on the hay."

Doris gave most of her attention to Howard, a pleasant-looking young man with fine features and light-colored hair. Howard farmed with his father and stood to inherit the family property, and his looks attracted Doris

Doris chose to marry Howard Weaver despite his physical disability (this is Howard's high school graduation photo). Maxine idolized Howard and thought he was a "nice looking guy," influencing Doris in Howard's favor. Photo courtesy of the Weaver family.

as well. On top of that, he became a favorite of Maxine's, a big factor in his favor with Doris. "Howard was a real good looking guy," recalled Maxine. "I thought he was especially nice because he gave me silver dollars."

Sadie Brune remembered that Howard and Doris got along well but didn't seem to have much in common. "I never considered them as a team," Sadie remembered. "The things that Doris enjoyed, Howard didn't." Howard didn't dance, although he did enjoy playing basketball. Sadie believed there must have been some sort of magnetism between the two of them that wasn't apparent to her.

Doris and Howard grew closer and discussed engagement but had not yet begun the rigid courtship process required when, tragically, Howard was stricken with cancer. The family was told that it developed from a sore on his leg resulting from a kick by a horse. Others remembered that Howard was injured in a stock car while taking cows to Chicago on the train, or believed that Howard's problem may have been pre-existing bone marrow cancer. Whatever his exact condition, it proved incurable.

Sadie believed that Doris felt obligated to continue her relationship with Howard because they had begun seeing each other before Howard was stricken with cancer. Then after doctors amputated part of Howard's leg in an operation, Doris felt she had to continue the courtship out of loyalty and no doubt true affection.

Doris's dogged dedication to Howard given his disability was reminiscent of the devotion she had shown to her tuberculosis-stricken mother. The example of Bert's work ethic, and the tragedies Doris weathered early

Doris developed into a stunning woman, with dreamy eyes and elaborately curled hair. Her looks and athletic abilities attracted many young men to her at the local barn dances.

in life had instilled in her an unusual inner strength. As her brother Frank remembered, once the "headstrong" Doris made up her mind about something, she rarely changed it. Said Frank: "Doris was stubborn, and always right."

According to Howard's younger sister, Bernice, Doris made Howard feel happy after all his medical problems. Bernice drove Howard to the Ashley farm to court Doris, then would return to pick him up. Howard couldn't drive safely with his wooden leg. Sometimes, Howard and Doris would go to social events, return to the Ashley home and wait for Bernice to pick up Howard. Bert did not approve of Doris seeing a young man with a disability that might prevent him from supporting her. But Doris wouldn't listen, defied her father, and made up her mind she'd stick with Howard until death.

Finally, Doris and Howard, with the help of Doris's long-time confidant, Eva, eloped when they were both nearly 23. Doris packed up her things and went to Eva's, where Howard met her. Howard wanted to avoid a big ceremony. Pastor Earl Hoon married the couple on January 8, 1924, in Sioux City. Earl's wife, Bessie, served as witness. The honeymoon lasted a few days, and then Doris and Howard came home to a reception put on by the Weaver family. Doris's father, Bert, did not attend..

After they were married, Howard's folks gave them a farm, cows and sheep. The newlyweds moved into a shared home along old Route 20, on the 144-acre Weaver homestead near Moville. Howard planned on farming the place with his father, who lived at the main home on the same property.

Doris worked on the household chores and also helped with the milking and the sheep.

Sadie visited the couple often; she and Doris exchanged recipes and gossip. Sometimes, the three of them attended social events. Sadie believed that Doris was happy with Howard and thought he would recover.

"They hadn't lived there very long before Howard's cancer flared up again," remembered Maxine. "It would not heal, and in those days the only thing the doctors knew to do was to cut off more of his leg."

After the operation, Howard remained in the hospital. Doris asked Maxine to live with her. "Doris had the chickens and animals and everything to take care of and she didn't want to be alone," Maxine recalled. She stayed at the young couple's home to help after Howard returned from the hospital, too. Howard would need a long period of bed rest as the doctors had cut off his leg just below the knee joint.

"He came home and learned how to walk again using crutches," recalled Maxine. "It was a hard thing for him to swallow, and hard for Doris to keep up her spirits. That I know. I remember I played checkers with Howard hour upon hour."

Howard had just learned to walk and made one trip to the barn when the cancer broke out again. He returned to the hospital and doctors removed the leg half-way between the hip and the knee. Amazingly, Howard came home and soon learned to walk again.

"I remember him walking around the kitchen, hanging on to my shoulder," Maxine said. "I must have made a good-sized cane... I was too young to realize it, but Doris must have known he didn't have much of a chance to survive."

Embroiled in the tragedy of Howard's illness, Doris still managed to maintain the household and even sought to make extra money.

"I remember they put the highway through by their house," recalled Maxine. "The night they began laying the pavement Doris decided that she could make a lot of money selling sandwiches to the crew. She baked bread that day and had a lot of bread, and of course she raised her own eggs, and made hot fried egg sandwiches; and (Howard's brother and sister) Dale and Dorothy and I went down and sold them. We'd just get about halfway down there and the crew would meet us. I remember those nights so well, because they had lights on the machines they were using. We were so impressed that they could lay that pavement and light it up at night."

As the sandwich-hawking business boomed, Doris demonstrated her life-long habit of penny-pinching by incrementally raising the prices. "I was so embarrassed to tell the guys I needed another quarter but Doris insisted," remembered Maxine. "The sandwiches started out at 50 cents a piece, then they went up to 75 cents. Anyway, we sold all her egg sandwiches, then she made cheese sandwiches which the men didn't like as well. And you know I don't think Doris ever paid us at all."

Howard's cancer worsened. Finally, doctors disjointed his hip and took the rest of his leg. Sadie remembered visiting Doris at Doris's and Howard's home to lend her moral support. She remembers Doris and Aunt Eva spent lots of time at Howard's bedside as he was in and out of the hospital in Sioux City.

Finally, on January 9, 1925, just a year and a day after he married Doris, Howard died at home. His death certificate lists as cause of death lympho sarcoma based on general symptoms; doctors did not perform an autopsy.

Pastor Albertson served at Howard's funeral, held at the Rock Branch Methodist Church three days after Howard's death. The church was filled, and Doris — who had been a pillar of strength for so many months — finally broke down.

"Howard's death really crushed Doris," remembered Maxine. "She was quite bitter about losing him. They had a big sale, the machinery, the horses, chickens, everything except the little Ford Roadster. And Doris's Airedale dog."

Howard's father finished feeding out the sheep, sold them and gave all the money from the sale to Doris. The family was very grateful to Doris for her bravery during Howard's ordeal, as well as her loyalty. With Sadie's help, Doris collected some of the household things, but Doris couldn't bring herself to sort through Howard's belongings so that task fell to Howard's sister, Bernice, who had adored her big brother.

Bernice gave Howard's clothing to friends. She burned his wooden leg.

"It was a horrible experience, and Doris didn't want people to feel sorry for her," continued Maxine. "She blocked it out of her mind. She wanted no one to give her anything extra, she didn't want sympathy. It changed her attitude about things."

After Howard died, Doris moved back to the Ashley home. She shared the housework and helped with her younger sisters. She sought some way to escape the memories of all the people close to her who had died, and later that winter, she found it.

Doris was visiting a family member in Minneapolis when she learned the secret of escaping her tragedy and all the bad memories of her childhood in Iowa. Her cousin, Helen, had been spending summers working in Glacier Park, out in Montana. Helen described glaciers, sharp mountain peaks, glass-clear water, Swiss-style lodges and cowboys. And she told Doris about the close friendships she'd developed with the other workers in the park. The stories captivated Doris. "I decided," recalled Doris, "to go with her the next spring."

And as Doris and her cousin rode the train north to Glacier Park Lodge in early June, one of Montana's native sons — a man who would soon figure prominently in Doris's life — was on his way to the same place.

Dan, 17, on the porch of the Kelly Canyon Ranch with sister, Irma, age 1.

4

Native Son

"Dan loved the freedom of the mountains and thought that it could only be bigger and better in Glacier."

About the time 4-year-old Doris was scribbling her first letters, Dan Huffine, a rancher's son, was born in Worden, a small eastern Montana town near Billings. Dan grew up on a ranch and experienced a rural life similar to Doris's.

Dan's relatives had emigrated from Germany and settled in Tennessee, where they maintained a large plantation. Huffine Lane in present-day Bozeman bears the name of his great uncle J.D. Huffine, who migrated from Tennessee to Kansas, then Missouri, then finally to Montana in 1873. J.D. homesteaded west of Bozeman. Charles Franklin, J.D.'s brother, followed the same route to Montana but didn't arrive until 1896; Dan's dad, John, then 21, came along. Five years later, on October 23, 1901, John married Mae Brooks of Billings, with the bride's parents serving as witnesses. Mae had been born in Darke County, Iowa, and came to Montana in the 1880s with her family.

John Huffine became an engineman for the Northern Pacific Railway Company; Dan's family album contains work reports his dad filled out for his trips around eastern Montana, and other railroad mementos from his dad's work as an engineer.

John and Mae had five sons: Chester, born in 1902; Harold, born 1903; Franklin Daniel (Dan) born 1905; Thomas, born 1907; and Albert, born 1910. Although Dan was healthy, medical problems plagued all of his brothers. Because Mae couldn't handle the boys herself, John quit his railroad job in

Dan, about age 14, (second from right) with some of his cousins on the Huffine side. Dan's mother died about this time. (Next three photos courtesy of Irma Huffine Fritts)

Dan's mother Mae Brooks Huffine, brother Chester, father J. D. Huffine, and brother Harold; Chester and Harold died in childhood.

Dan, age 16 at the Huffine Ranch in Kelly Canyon near Bozeman in 1921. Dan's riding "Rabe," whom he described as a "fine cow horse." Dan took on more adult responsibilities around the ranch when his mother died and his father became ill.

1910 and homesteaded near Billings. The family lost that farm, but later bought a farm near Kelly Canyon outside Bozeman.

Of the five boys, only Dan survived childhood. Chester died at age 14, Harold died at 12, Thomas died at only 7 months, and Albert died at 6 years old. The two older brothers died of cerebral palsy and muscular dystrophy after years of being "invalids," as cited on their death certificates. The problem apparently ran in the family, as Mae's younger sister, Grace, had several boys who died under the same circumstances. This apparent genetic trait caused Dan to decide against ever having children, according to his half sister Irma.

Dan was closest to the youngest brother, Albert, and though the family thought Albert was going to survive, he contracted pneumonia and died as three of his brothers had done before him.

"Albert's death just broke Dan's heart," remembered Irma. "Dan then became very close to his mother; he was the only one left."

Despite the obvious emotional worries that must have haunted him as a boy growing up in a family beset with mortality, Dan was always a good student. At age 7 when he was in the second grade, Dan was awarded a card of approbation for good conduct and lessons from his teacher Bertha B. Reed of the Worden School. At age 8, his teacher Edith Vernon presented him a prize card for excelling in punctuality and attendance. And in 1917, at age 12, Dan bound together essays he'd written on the American flag and the Pledge of Allegiance. His official composition book, titled simply "Bozeman City Schools," is filled with essays on patriotism and history.

Dan's mother died in March 1919 of complications from diabetes. Dan was then 14 and preparing to graduate from the ninth grade. Perhaps in memory of his mother, Dan carefully kept his Yellowstone County Common School Diploma, which certified his graduation from ninth grade on June 19, 1919.

"Mae's death was a last straw for Dan," remembered Irma. First, he'd lost all his brothers, now his mother. It caused him to lose his faith in God."

Then, less than a year after his mother's death, Dan heard the news that his father had remarried. John Huffine had returned to Tennessee for a visit, and while there he contracted pneumonia. During his convalescence, he married Lena Rhear, the woman who nursed him back to health. John had known Lena when he lived in Tennessee, indeed had grown up within walking distance of her home. He adopted Lena's 3-year old son, Curtis, and the family returned to Montana.

Not long afterward, Dan dropped out of school, and went to work because "they had no money and had Lena on their hands too," according to what he later told Doris. Dan's decision to end his formal education handicapped him for the rest of his life, but for now he was able to find steady work. Indeed, he had several jobs, on the farm, for the telephone company and elsewhere. John Huffine had bought a ranch east of Bozeman, but lost that when he got sick not much later.

Lena's first daughter, Irma, was born March 11, 1921. On the night Lena

Dan's grandmother and grandfather Brooks. Dan had great respect for his Grandma Brooks and often visited her.

Harvesting at the Kelly Canyon ranch, 1924. Dan's father, J.D., is on the harvester with little Irma, while Dan's Grandmother Huffine looks on.

was ready to give birth to Irma, John's first mother-in-law, Grandma Brooks, came over to help. Dan rode 10 miles into town through a blizzard to get the doctor, but by the time they returned, his grandmother was just cutting Irma's cord.

Irma remembers Dan as a great brother, in spite of an age difference of 16 years. She remembered that he always kidded and teased. "He called me Mickey, never Irma, unless he was irritated with me or if he was going to talk to me seriously."

In May 1924, Dan left home to work for the U.S. Forest Service. He began writing detailed descriptions of his activities in a journal, a practice he continued throughout his life. Dan maintained trails, cut telephone poles and packed supplies throughout the Gallatin National Forest west of Bozeman. His area included beautiful, high-country areas like the Yellow Mules, Ramshorn Lake, Bear Basin and Buffalo Horn. Throughout the summer Dan worked hard, but he also managed to find time for dances about once a week.

In October, Dan moved back into Bozeman, where he worked on area ranches, threshing, harvesting and disking. He lived at home, spent time with his family and hunted for deer. Later that winter he visited his Grandmother Brooks's family in Billings, and he spent time entertaining his stepbrother Curtis and little half-sister Irma.

When spring came, Dan worked at area ranches, noting that he disked 45 acres in 22 hours and netted $16.90. He checked at the U.S. Forest Service office but no work was available yet for the summer. Dan longed for the adventure of the backcountry. Early in June, on a lark, Dan and his cousin decided to travel north in an old Ford to Glacier National Park to seek summer work on the trail crews. Dan had no idea that his spontaneous decision would set the course of his life.

Already en route to Glacier, a young widow, accompanied by her cousin, had left the Minneapolis train station a few days earlier, bound for the solace of the high peaks of the park.

"Dan loved the freedom of the mountains and thought that it could only be bigger and better in Glacier," Doris remembered later.

He was right.

George Snyder's steam-powered boat, the "F.I. Whitney" (right) along with the "Emeline." Snyder and others hauled the Whitney overland 3 miles from the Middle Fork Flathead River to launch it in Lake McDonald. That's probably Snyder at the helm. NPS Photo, unknown photographer.

George Snyder's steam boat plied the length of Lake McDonald, here photographed from Apgar Lookout. (Author's Photo)

5
Glacier

The February 11 edition of the Kalispell Inter Lake carried a 10-line story announcing that the Senate passed a bill on February 9, 1910, providing for the "establishment of the Glacier national park in northern Montana."

When naturalist John Muir visited the Glacier Park area in the 1890s he claimed that the "care killing" scenery would "truly make you immortal." Neither Muir nor anyone since has been able to capture adequately in words the essence of this place which has drawn admirers and exploiters since the first Europeans — men like trapper Hugh Monroe and missionary Father Pierre Jean DeSmet — traveled through the area prior to 1850.

Glacier, dubbed "Crown of the Continent" by editor, anthropologist, and explorer George Bird Grinnell, includes some 1,600 square miles straddling two parallel mountain ranges, the Lewis and the Livingstone.The two sides of the Continental Divide in Glacier have been described as "two superb national parks laid side by side." On the precipitous east side, sharp ridges rise nearly straight up from the shores of spectacular lakes like St. Mary and Swiftcurrent. On the west side, the country falls away more gradually, the lakes are long, and the slopes are densely forested. Both sides are home to more than 1,000 plant species and all the wildlife species present in Lewis and Clark's time. Glacier is the only place in the lower 48 states where grizzlies, wolves, and mountain lions still co-exist naturally.

In Glacier, the world's oldest sedimentary rocks lay over younger layers and form jumbled bands of gray, green, red and purple. The landscape bears the mark of recent glaciation, and more than 50 Glaciers remain on the sides of mountains like Heaven's Peak and Mt. Stimpson. Gushing water is

Snyder's frame hotel and associated log buildings, 1907, near the upper end of Lake McDonald. Snyder told Doris that he established a small stop here as early as 1892. NPS photo, W.T. Ridgeley Calendar Co., photographer.

everywhere, from the spectacular Weeping Wall to ribbon-like Bird Woman Falls. Glacier is the only "three-ocean" watershed on the North American Continent. From a single place, Triple Divide Peak, water flows eventually into the Pacific via Pacific Creek and the Flathead River; to the Atlantic via Atlantic Creek and the Missouri River; and to Hudson Bay via Hudson Creek and the St. Mary River.

In the years before 1900, little public discussion had taken place about setting aside the area's natural wonders through national park designation. By 1901, the situation began to change as the country came to the realization that Glacier's greatest value could be fostered through its preservation rather than the development of its natural resources.

In 1901, the year Doris was born, an edition of *Century Magazine* featured an article by George Bird Grinnell entitled, "The Crown of the Continent." In the article Grinnell, widely considered the "Father of Glacier Park," described the scenic beauty and recreational values of the Glacier Park area. He pointed out the fact that the mountains of Glacier gave rise to the headwaters of three great North American river systems and called for protection of the area.

Grinnell had already been instrumental in setting the wonders of the Glacier Park area before the public. As editor of *Forest and Stream* magazine, he had published articles about the St. Mary area by writer and explorer James Willard Schultz, a man whom Doris came to know much later. Grinnell learned a great deal about Glacier from Schultz, who had been in the area since the 1870s and was a good friend of original settler Hugh Monroe. In a series of visits beginning in 1885, Grinnell and Schultz hunted and explored together, often accompanied by Blackfeet tribal members. They named some of the features of the spectacular east side of the park, including some of the glaciers.

"Let us name it Blackfoot Glacier," remarked Grinnell one morning to Schultz on a hunting trip above St. Mary Lake after watching 27 goats cavort on its slopes. "For that takes in the Pikunis, the Bloods and the Blackfeet, all three tribes of the Confederacy." Grinnell and Schultz were trusted by the Blackfeet and knew more about them than any other whites; Schultz had lived among the tribe and had married a tribal member. Both men sympathized with the once great Blackfoot Confederacy, which had dominated the buffalo plains east of the Glacier Park area since the 1700s.

Grinnell became a friend of the Blackfeet; they christened him Pinut-u-ye-is-tsim-o-kan, or "Fisher Cap." At the urging of Schultz and the tribe, Grinnell was appointed in 1895 by President Grover Cleveland as one of three commissioners to meet with the Blackfeet and negotiate the purchase of what is now the eastern portion of Glacier Park. The U.S. government acquired the land for $1.5 million in 1896. Grinnell's efforts netted the Blackfeet $500,000 more than the other commissioners wished to grant for the land.

A few years after the land was acquired, Washington declared it open for mining and hundreds of people rushed in to stake claims in the Swiftcurrent and St. Mary valleys. Luckily for those interested in the area becoming a park, mining efforts proved to be a flop in most cases. Only small amounts of copper, silver, gold, oil and gas were found. By 1901, most miners saw that they were wasting their time and left the area, leaving the door open for Grinnell and others to openly call for the area to be set aside as a national park.

On the west side of the Divide in what was to become Glacier, a somewhat different pattern emerged. It's been said that the decades preceding 1900 largely were years of attempted exploitation of natural resources throughout the area and that little had been done to cultivate appreciation of its scenic wonders. But one visionary man, mostly overlooked, saw and acted upon that opportunity, even though his main motivation may have been to make money.

Often dismissed as a drunk and an oaf, George Snyder stands as one of the first settlers to develop a tourist stop within the present boundaries of the park. In 1895 Snyder built a two-story hotel near the upper end of nine-mile-long Lake McDonald, on the west side of the Divide. He later told Doris that he had established a small stop there as early as 1892, a contention backed up by early Apgar resident Eddie Crugar's accounts. Considering the remoteness of the area and its location well into the interior of the present park, this represents a stunning accomplishment. But because no road approached even the lower end of Lake McDonald from the nearest railroad siding at Belton, Snyder had a problem: How would tourists reach his hotel?

Always a doer, and not one to check with authorities first, Snyder recruited a few men and built his own wagon "road," the first within the present boundaries of the park. The track wound through magnificent old growth forests of western red cedar from Belton to the site now known as Apgar at the foot of Lake McDonald, where a few cabins had been established by Milo Apgar, Charlie Howe, and others. To get the tourists nine more miles to his hotel, Snyder purchased and had shipped by rail a 40-foot steamboat, the F.I. Whitney, which had operated on Flathead Lake, about 40 miles to the south. When the steamboat arrived at the Belton railroad siding, Snyder and others floated the boat across the Middle Fork of the Flathead River, loaded it on a wagon and with sheer determination hauled it to the shore of Lake McDonald. Snyder's tour boat was the first powered craft on a park lake.

Another man, Ed Dow, started a stage line from Belton, where he owned a hotel, to the foot of Lake McDonald. The tourists were ferried across the Middle Fork of the Flathead from Belton to Dow's stage. Later, fringe-topped surreys, or "tally ho wagons," transported visitors to the foot of the lake. The regular flow of tourists had begun on the west side in what would one day become Glacier Park.

Early park visitor Genevieve Walsh recalled a trip she made on the stage to Lake McDonald in 1900. She described the three-mile road from Belton to the foot of the lake as a "slender ribbon, the trees so close together that my father, standing in the open coach, pulled white and brown moss from the trees for me. My dolls all became blonds with the wigs I made them from this moss. The wagon trip was so deep with needles and moss and leaves that the hooves of the horses made only a gentle clop-clop as they sped along." She also recalled that Snyder's "funny old steamer" showered passengers with sparks as the boat plied McDonald Lake.

Frequent passengers on Snyder's tour boat included famed cowboy artist Charlie Russell, who had established his retreat, the Bull Head Lodge, near Apgar, and the area's first ranger, Frank Liebig, who arrived about 1900 and assumed his duties as ranger of the Forest Reserve in June 1902. Liebig's wife complained that the boat's below-deck cabin was too hot, and that sparks burned holes in her clothes if she rode on the top deck. Liebig patrolled all of what is now the northern portion of the park. He worked out of a small ranger station at the head of Lake McDonald, on the opposite shore from Snyder's Hotel.

Liebig and Snyder would both be touched by the life of a girl born in Iowa about the same time the two men met. Doris's birth, the beginning of the organized movement to establish Glacier Park, the end of the mining "boom," and the first tourist trade all roughly coincided. Although Doris did not know Snyder until late in his life, they would have a profound influence on each other.

Many people would argue that James Hill and his son Louis of the Great Northern Railway Co. did more than anyone to help establish Glacier Park

McDonald Lodge circa1920. John Lewis acquired George Snyder's hotel complex in 1905 and completed the lodge in 1914. NPS Photo, Marble Photographer

and develop its potential. James Hill began extending his rail line west from Minneapolis towards the Pacific in the mid-1880s and by 1889 he had hired John F. Stevens to find a suitable pass through the Rocky Mountains. Such a pass was rumored to exist in the southeastern part of the Glacier Park area.

Stevens set out in December from Blackfeet Agency with a Flathead Indian guide. As the story goes, the guide became exhausted during a blizzard before reaching the summit. Stevens crossed the summit, now known as Marias Pass, and explored it through the early evening, assuring himself that rails could be laid over the pass. He spent the night walking back and forth in a snow-packed trail to keep warm, as the temperature dropped to 40 degrees below zero, before starting back to reunite with the Flathead guide. Stevens had accomplished the first documented discovery and official recognition of the pass.

Later, Stevens boasted that his discovery meant "the saving of more than one hundred miles of distance, much less curvature, and an infinitely better grade, together with the lowest railway pass in the United States north of New Mexico."

Railroad survey and construction began the next year and by September 1891, crews completed the line over the pass. The rails reached Kalispell by late December, just two years after Stevens explored the pass. The line offered the quickest railway route to the Pacific. In 1925, during Doris's first summer in the park, Great Northern erected and dedicated a monument to Stevens on Marias Pass. The railway continued to be the only transportation over the pass until a road was completed in 1930; for later residents like Doris and Dan, the railway remained the only passable winter travel link between East and West Glacier for years beyond that.

Great Northern had opened the transportation route to Glacier from both sides of the Divide. Now James Hill set out to establish the park as a "playground" and draw visitors from across the country. By 1905, George Grinnell and others had urged Hill and the Great Northern to use their influence to gain national park status for Glacier. Hill asked Montana Senator T. H. Carter to introduce a bill into the U. S. Senate to accomplish it. Carter introduced the bill in 1907, revised it, then introduced it again in 1908. The Committee on Public Lands approved the bill and the full Senate passed it that year. Montana Representative C.N. Pray carried the legislation through a House committee, but no action was taken and the bill died. In 1909 the bill was brought up in both houses of Congress again, and by early 1910 it finally passed.

The February 11 edition of the Kalispell Inter Lake carried a 10-line story announcing that the Senate passed a bill on February 9, 1910, providing for the "establishment of the Glacier national park in northern Montana." The May 14 edition of the Inter Lake ran a story dated May 11 from Washington announcing that the bill would be signed by President Taft within two days and that Senator Carter would ask Congress to appropriate $10,000 for "preliminary surveys and building of roads and trails." The article mentioned that a road from Belton to Lake McDonald was contemplated. Apparently, they were referring to an upgrade of Snyder's original wagon road, which some described as a "quagmire."

As the tail of Halley's Comet entered the evening sky, Glacier became a national park. W.R. Logan, the park's first superintendent, spent the summer of 1910 dealing with one of the worst fire years on record. He appointed six rangers to patrol the area and prevent illegal grazing and poaching. One of the first rangers, patrolling the Middle Fork of the Flathead and the west side of the park, was poacher and bootlegger Dan Doody, husband of notorious Josephine Doody, whom Doris knew much later. Besides stationing a handful of rangers around the park, Logan by 1911 had arranged for a few miles of road and a headquarters site.

Development of Glacier by the private sector was much more extensive. Louis Hill, son of James Hill and now president of Great Northern, took personal charge of a campaign to build tourist facilities around the park and draw visitors to them. One month after President Taft signed the Glacier Park legislation, railway crews began building the first chalets at Belton. Planning was also under way to build a complex of chalets and hotels on the east side of the divide, along with a road to connect major points. Great Northern acquired 60 acres of land near East Glacier from one of its first residents, Horace Clarke, another man Doris came to know later. Louis Hill

The Glacier Park Hotel, Louis Hill's showplace, in 1911 or 1912. Note that construction in nearly complete. NPS Photo, unknown photographer.

planned to build the Glacier Park Hotel on this beautiful site between Mt. Henry and the Two Medicine River.

Construction on this showpiece of Glacier's hotels began in 1912. Louis Hill personally designed the mammoth lobby, featuring sixty huge, 50-foot long cedar and fir timbers shipped by rail from Washington and Oregon. No expense was spared and the project cost $500,000, an incredible sum for that time.

By June 1913, the lodge was ready for its grand opening. The Blackfeet called it the "Big Tree Lodge" because of the huge trees, with bark still intact, extending upward from the lobby to support the ceiling timbers. Hill hosted a celebration for 600 Great Northern employees at the lodge to honor the 75th birthday of his father. Many former Blackfeet chiefs stayed in te-pees erected on the hotel grounds, beginning a popular tradition and tour-ist attraction. Over the next few years, Swiss-style chalets were completed at Cut Bank, St. Mary and other locations, and tent camps sprang up at strategic points. Hill designed the facilities to provide comfort at the big hotels, with adventure in the backcountry chalets available to those who wished to see the park on horseback.

Transportation of tourists eager to see Glacier's spectacular mountains and accommodations became a lucrative business. W.A. Brewster started the first tourist transportation company with three horse-drawn stages. By 1915 Great Northern completed the lavish Many Glacier Lodge on the shores of Swiftcurrent Lake and a road connecting these east-side attractions. To transport visitors, Glacier Park Transportation Co. brought in the first White Motor Co. tour autos, predecessors to Glacier's tour buses, which Dan Huffine drove when he arrived in the park.

On the west side, John Lewis had by 1914 completed the Lewis Hotel at the site of George Snyder's original hotel at the head of Lake McDonald. Lewis had acquired the land and original building from Snyder in 1905. Lewis's new hotel featured 65 rooms and an attractive, rustic-alpine style lodge. Later called the Lake McDonald Lodge, it was not up to the grandeur and luxurious standard of the east side hotels but it did offer fine accommodations to visitors who wished to see the west side of the park. Cowboy artist and storyteller Charlie Russell and his wife became close friends with the Lewis family. Lake McDonald residents viewed the Lewis Hotel as the backcountry community's gathering place and looked forward to Russell's stories around the lodge fireplace.

Boat transportation kept pace with the development of the park. By 1915, four boats operated on Lake McDonald, with George Snyder still involved along with several other men. From the beginning, Snyder gave park officials fits with his sloppy attitude and his disregard of their authority. Two boats operated on St. Mary Lake, transporting passengers to Going-To-The-Sun Chalets on Sun Point. The boat tours gained popularity as visitors saw the value of reclining in comfort while enjoying views of the glacially carved lakes and mountains. Most importantly, boats offered the only transportation to the upper ends of Lake McDonald and St. Mary Lake.

Great Northern's literature now boasted a complex of nine chalets, the luxurious mountain lodges, tent camps, and means of reaching them. Hill coined the slogan, "See America First," featuring it across the top of each page of the Glacier Park travel magazine. He referred to the Great Northern route as the "Glacier Park Line," and to the Blackfeet as the "Glacier Park Tribe." He added the Great Northern Mountain Goat as his company's trademark.

Year after year, Hill hosted well-known writers, like James Willard Schultz and Mary Roberts Rinehart, to help promote Glacier's charm. Hill also contracted with a young photographer, Tomar Jacob Hileman, to take photos of Glacier's stunning scenery for the Great Northern promotional brochures. Hileman specialized in photographing Glacier, and had tied his fortune to Glacier as early as 1913 when he and his fiancee became the first couple to wed in the park, near Lake McDonald. Hill's hiring of the young photographer began a long and productive business relationship between them, and Hileman became Glacier's best-known photographer. Hill's public-relations genius, his ability to judge people, and his investment of millions of dollars in development soon resulted in skyrocketing numbers of visitors to the park.

Once officials began to see the potential of Glacier, many called for the construction of a "transmountain road" to link the east and west sides of the park. Logan and Steven Mather, who became the National Park Service's first director in 1916, pointed out that such a road would allow tourists who did not hike or ride horses to see the park's interior. Mather pointed out that cross-country motoring was gaining popularity and that national parks

Louis Hill contracted with photographer T.J. Hileman to provide pictures for his promotion of Glacier. Hileman became Glacier's most well-known photographer, and his photos became an integral part of Hill's public relations campaign to build interest in the park. Here, Hileman is at Fifty Mountain Camp at the Continental Divide. NPS Photo, August 1925, unknown photographer.

must prepare to accommodate it.

After much debate about proposed routes of the transmountain road, government surveys confirmed that the route along Lake McDonald, McDonald Creek, and across the Divide at Logan Pass was the most feasible. At his own expense, J.E. Lewis constructed the first three miles of road along Lake McDonald in 1919. By 1921, the Park Service contracted with construction companies to extend the road six more miles to Lewis's Hotel, then east and north along McDonald Creek. By the time Dan and Doris arrived in Glacier in 1925, the road had been extended to Avalanche Creek on the west side and partly along St. Mary Lake on the east side. Crews from the Bureau of Public Roads had begun the detailed survey, in which Doris and Dan would play a part, of the route over Logan Pass.

By 1925 roads and autos had begun to change the complexion of Glacier, but it was still largely a "saddle horse park." The tourist business was booming, and the Glacier Park Hotel Company — a subsidiary of Great Northern — was enjoying terrific success with its lodges and chalets. W. F. Noffsinger's horseback concessions featured 1,000 saddlehorses and real cowboys, transported 10,000 tourists each year, and by some accounts comprised the largest such operation in the world.

Great Northern and the Park Service had worked together to develop

In Great Northern's campaign to draw tourists to Glacier National Park, no amenity was overlooked, from the best food to the finest music. Here, musician George Barton of the Glacier Park Hotel orchestra poses in a 1925 photo.

Glacier's potential, and each seemed appreciative of the other. But relations between the two were not exclusively positive. On a family visit to Many Glacier in August 1925, Park Service Director Mather noticed that Great Northern's park director Howard Noble had not removed the unsightly saw mill which had been used to cut lumber for constructing Many Glacier Hotel. Previously, Mather had asked Noble to get rid of the mill and saw-dust pile and he was enraged to see it still sitting along the shores of beautiful Swiftcurrent Lake. After inviting the hotel guests to watch, Mather ordered a trail crew to set dynamite charges around the mill and personally lit the fuse of the first charge. When visitors asked him about the explosions, he replied that he was celebrating his daughter's birthday. Hill threatened to sue when he learned of Mather's act, but relations soon smoothed. Great Northern and the Park Service needed each other too badly to risk a breakdown in relations. 1925 was also the year that President Calvin Coolidge presented to George Grinnell, now 76, the Theodore Roosevelt Medal, calling Glacier Park Grinnell's "monument."

During the same year, Great Northern bankrolled James Willard Schultz on a summer-long camp with Blackfeet elders along Two Medicine Lake, a few miles from East Glacier and the Glacier Park Hotel. Schultz was gathering stories from the tribal members for his upcoming book, "Signposts of Adventure," which covered the Blackfeet's early days in the Glacier area and the Blackfeet names associated with Glacier's peaks and rivers. Schultz's earlier books on Glacier and the Blackfeet had yielded so much good publicity that Louis Hill and Great Northern also provided free rooms at the Glacier Park Lodge for Schultz each year.

East Glacier had now reached the status of a "village of the storied West," with a wild West dance hall at Mike's Place, celebrities galore, bronco busters on nearby dude ranches, bow-legged guides, and "real Indians."

So it was during this exciting year of the park's eclectic early days that Doris and Dan first arrived in Glacier. Doris stepped off the west-bound Great Northern Train at East Glacier and Dan drove in a broken-down car from Bozeman; they both arrived at Glacier Park Hotel at about the same time. The two were part of the summer flow of more than a thousand of the country's best and brightest young people seeking romance, adventure, and low wages in one of America's newest national parks. Dan came on a lark, seeking the "Land of the Shining Mountains." Doris came to forget, and to seek a new life. Each of them immediately became involved in Glacier's development during its golden age.

Doris at work, Glacier Park Hotel, shortly after arriving in 1925. She also held jobs at the Hileman Photo Shop in the basement of the Hotel, and at Mike's Place in nearby East Glacier.

6
Maids and Jammers, 1925-26

"That was the first time I met Dan and I was so mad at him that I just liked to never get over it. I saw him off and on the rest of the summer but I wasn't going to speak to him."

In early June of 1925 Doris Weaver and her cousin Helen rode the Great Northern train from Minneapolis to Glacier Park — it was 24-year-old Doris's first trip to the western states. "Helen had worked at Glacier Park Hotel in East Glacier the year before and told me it was fun and an opportunity to make some money, although not much," remembered Doris much later. "I thought it sounded like an adventure so I went with her." The trip west appealed to Doris as a way of leaving behind the bad memories of her young husband's death.

Because Doris had finished college, she was able to come to the park earlier than most of the workers, so she helped open the dorms and prepare the rooms for the influx of "cheap help." As a maid, Doris earned a dollar a day. To maximize her pay Doris shared a room with Helen and several other young women in the dorm.

When Doris arrived in Glacier Park, tourism was booming. The 1920s were literally the "golden years" for the Glacier Park Hotel Company, a subsidiary of Louis Hill's Great Northern Railway. Hill had retired from his position as president of Great Northern so he could devote more time to promoting Glacier Park. Groups of Blackfeet were paid to travel in special trains to cities back east to promote the park and the hotel. Hill's campaign proved effective. In 1925, for instance, 52 special trains brought 8,000 tourists to the park, on top of the normal railroad traffic.

The hotel provided tepees and food to Blackfeet families in return for

Glacier Park Hotel across from the train station in 1925. A number of tepees were set up on the hotel grounds, but as Doris noted, "no one lived in them." They were for show.

dancing and entertainment for hotel guests. Blackfeet nobles like Charles Bull Child, Wallace Night Gun, and Wades in the Water spent summers on the hotel grounds as part of the arrangement. At times, more than 200 Blackfeet lived on the hotel grounds, partly drawn by the large tips given by well-to-do hotel guests.

The area near the hotel formerly served as ancestral camping grounds for the Blackfeet. Close by, the clear-flowing Two Medicine River provided water and a site where the Pikuni tribe held their annual Okan', a religious ceremony. One year the Bloods, another of the three tribes of the Blackfeet Confederacy, held their Okan' on the nearby banks. Afterwards the river carried the name, Two Medicine Lodges or Two Vision Lodges River. Later, whites shortened the name to Two Medicine River.

Doris enjoyed the rich history of the area, the spectacular mountains such as Never Laughs, Appistoki, and Rising Wolf, and the deep, turquoise water of Two Medicine and other glacial lakes. She settled into the eclectic atmosphere of East Glacier Park, and set out to enjoy herself and forget about the tragedies which befell her in Iowa. Early in the summer she began collecting animals, starting with a pet ground squirrel. "The cute little thing would ride around in the pocket of my maid's apron and sleep under the bed in our room," Doris recalled. "We'd feed him scraps from the hotel kitchen and teach him little tricks." Doris and the other workers also fed a variety of animals around the hotel grounds.Occasionally, a black or grizzly bear could be seen in the area, drawn by garbage. To Doris and the other hotel workers, the opportunity to see a bear was a treat. Bears were routinely fed and generally not feared. "There is only one thing to do if a bear takes a sudden dislike to one," wrote novelist Mary Roberts Rinehart in her book "Through Glacier Park" — "It is useless to climb or to run. Go toward it and try kindness. Ask about the children, in a carefully restrained tone. Make the Indian sign that you are a friend. If you have a sandwich about you, proffer it. Then, while the bear is staring at you in amazement, turn and walk away."

Consistent with her work ethic and her need to be frantically busy, Doris found two other jobs in East Glacier. "I liked to make money, you know," remembered Doris. "In those days you couldn't get very much but when I could get it I got it."

Doris's shift at the Big Hotel started at 5 o'clock in the morning. If she worked hard she could finish by 11 in the morning. Doris helped the maids, swept and mopped the halls, and did whatever else was needed for the day. After her morning shift, she worked at the photography shop of Tomar Hileman, also in the Big Hotel, for several hours or "whatever it took to print the pictures that day."

T.J. Hileman was now under a contract with Great Northern that provided him a monthly salary. Called "Mountain Goat Hileman" by some, he was known for hauling around a heavy, large format camera through Glacier's backcountry to capture breathtaking angles for his photos. He took news, promotional, and scenic photos for the company, which paid him on a per-print basis. In addition, Hileman established a photo shop in the Glacier Park Hotel, selling thousands of his prints to tourists. He was known as a perfectionist and was very demanding of his employees. His choice of Doris and others reflected his standards of hiring educated young men and women with demonstrated talents. Doris's artistic flair helped her perform quality finishing work and "colorization" — tinting black and white photos with transparent, color oil paints.

It was at Hileman's shop that Doris met co-worker Otto Bessey, the intelligent, intense young man who became her hiking partner. In addition to being a star athlete, Bessey majored in chemistry at Montana University, making him a natural for work at a photo developing shop. Otto had a bad case of the "little guy syndrome," which had driven him to the javelin championship of the Pacific Coast conference. He timed everything, including his hikes with Doris. After their hike to Squaw Peak, Doris noted that "never again" would she go on such a "wild, neck-breaking hike, over logs, through

East Glacier in 1926, Mike's place in center. Mike's sported a pool hall, fountain, dance hall, and cafe. The grade school is at the far right; John Lindhe's Glacier Park Trading Post is near the left side of the photo.

Looking at Mike's Place from under the Great Northern Railroad viaduct. Courtesy of Otto Bessey Jr.

Mike's Place fountain, about 1925. Mike's was a popular gathering area for the area ranches, small communities, railroad folks, and Glacier Park workers.

Here is a group shot of the 1925 bus drivers. Dan is third from the left among the men standing and is wearing a cap. Also notable is Fred Noble, the Glacier National Park Transportation Co. manager, who is squatting second from right.

creeks, up rocks." But Otto and Doris went on a number of other hikes together, including one to the summit of Mt. Henry. Otto went on to become a professor at a medical college after his years in Glacier; in Otto and Doris, Hileman had chosen his employees well.

Doris's work for Hileman provided her inside access to important events in the park. She attended a pow-wow where the Blackfeet adopted into the tribe the son of Mr. Simpson, president of Chicago's Marshall Field and Company. She mounted dramatic photos of Blackfeet chiefs performing the ceremony. She also mounted a photo of Lone Wolf, or Hart Schultz, the Blackfeet son of James Willard Schultz. Doris probably met Lone Wolf at the art studio he maintained near the hotel during the summers. She also met Lone Wolf's father and many of his Blackfeet friends when she visited their camp along Two Medicine Lake during the summer of 1925. Doris's sister, Maxine, remembered that Doris was excited to meet Schultz because, like many of the park employees, she had read his books about Glacier. However she had a mixed reaction to Schultz's stories about the Blackfeet, thinking that some of his portrayals didn't match with what she had heard from other tribal members.

After her afternoons at Hileman's, Doris walked the half-mile into East Glacier and went to work at Mike's Place in the restaurant. She worked in

Doris (left) and hiking partners from the Glacier Park Hotel, 1925. Hiking along Glacier's trails was the number one pastime of young workers in Glacier Park's hotels and concessions.

51

Doris with best friend, co-worker and roommate Marie Stepan.

Doris with a friend (probably George Barr) from the Glacier Park Hotel, 1926.

the fountain area, receiving $2 per shift. Sometimes she worked 12 hours for $2.

"And no tips in those days," remembered Doris. "I worked until they closed and lots of times I'd get back to the Big Hotel at 5 in the morning ready to go on my next maid shift. No sleep, no nothing."

Mike's Place drew crowds from Babb, Browning, and ranches all along the east side of the park. Doris's upbringing on the isolated Iowa farm hadn't prepared her for rough-and-tumble 1920s frontier Montana.

"They had a dance hall at Mike's," Doris remembered. "The dudes from all around and the cowboys came in. Sometimes they had gang fights. One morning when I went to work I had to step over a big puddle of blood to get in the door. A lot of times when I had to go home at 2 or 3 in the morning the deputy sheriff would say, 'Don't go alone tonight because there's a gang in town. We'll take you home tonight.' Those kinds of things made you shiver."

Doris became well known at Mike's for her wit and she enjoyed visiting with tourists, local residents, and Blackfeet tribal members. James Willard Schultz and other guests of the Great Northern stopped in from time to time.

Meanwhile, 21-year-old Dan Huffine, who had been raised in Bozeman, several hundred miles southeast of East Glacier, also saw the park for the first time that June of 1925. "My mother's cousin came to the ranch and he'd been working in Yellowstone, and wanted me to go there with him," remembered Dan much later. "But I said, let's go to Glacier. All I knew about Glacier was what I'd read in geography, how it was called the land of the shining mountains."

"When I first came out in 1925 there were some of those burial beds up on stilts," remembered Dan, describing his trip through the Blackfeet Indian Reservation on his way to Glacier. "I was surprised to see those when I came through; the Blackfeet buried their dead right on top of the ground and covered the bodies with rocks and boulders. There was a hill north of Browning where they buried quite a few of them; we went out there hunting arrowheads near the buffalo jump north of Browning on Cut Bank Creek and we'd see human bones lying around."

The next morning Dan passed through Browning, the center of life on the Blackfeet Reservation, and arrived in East Glacier, where he looked up Chapie Chapman, a Glacier Park bus driver. Dan met "three or four guys from Bozeman who were driving the red tourist buses." The drivers con-

Doris, Otto Bessey (left) and another friend on a hiking trip to Mt. Henry, 1926.

Dan Huffine and Bus #57 in 1925. Dan hauled tourists around the east side of Glacier Park and pointed out the park's major features.

vinced Dan to join them rather than sign up on the trail crew as he had planned.

With park business booming, it wasn't hard for a young man to land a job. On top of that, the owner of the Glacier Transportation Company hailed from Bozeman as well and knew the Huffines. The next day Dan reported to the Glacier Transportation Company Garage and passed the driving test.

Dan's consistent journal entries traced his first summer in the park. He rented a room in the dormitory and had time to go to an evening dance. Over the next few days Dan's diary entries detailed the dances he attended at Mike's Place, the number of times he danced each night, and routine trips hauling supplies around the park. On June 22 he "deadheaded to Many Glacier," meaning he stayed there for the night, and on June 23 he did the same at East Glacier. On June 28 and 29 he made runs to Many Glacier, Saint Mary and back and took several hikes. On June 29 he "went to a dance after supper and took sorority girl home."

Dan's diary entries for July and August detailed the number of passengers on his runs to and from the destinations on the east side of Glacier Park. It was a job, as he related much later, that he relished.

"When you're driving bus you dealt with nothing but tourists — dudes, they called them," remembered Dan. "They were just like you and I. They were from sororities, Boy Scout groups; sometimes you'd have 30 or 40 busloads in. We had 80 buses in the summer of 1926. They were smaller than the buses they have now, which haul five or six more passengers. You'd have a string of buses going out from East Glacier, Many Glacier Hotel, wherever it happened to be."

Dan's bus, No. 57, was a 1924 model with 4-speed ball shift. It had a 4-cylinder engine, 32-inch tires and carbide lights.

Travel in the park in those days was much different from what it is today because no road traversed the park. Instead, many people looked at the peaks and glaciers from the back of a horse.

"Often you'd take busloads to Many Glacier and they'd take saddle horse trips out of there," remembered Dan. "Some people would be dropped off to take the boat across Saint Mary Lake to Sun Camp. Some of the horse trips would last two or three weeks and the people would travel north to Canada and swing down to Lake McDonald."

Another trail ride would start from East Glacier, ascend Sun Point, then continue on to Two Medicine and finally climb over Pitamakin Pass to eventually wind up at Cut Bank Ranger Station and Chalets. To cater to these mounted tourists, and promote tourism and travel to the area, Great Northern Railroad built a number of chalets, most of them in the backcountry.

Dan enjoyed hauling tourists around the park, but he never felt comfortable in the role of a tour guide. "I'd tell them, 'Oh, this is Triple Divide Mountain,' or 'That's where the water runs three ways.' I was never much of a talker. Some of the drivers would talk a streak from the time they left the hotel. They'd read those big manuals and they knew every flower, every weed, every creek and spring. I guess people appreciated a certain amount of that but if I was riding one of those buses I'd ask to go to a different one."

Dan never drove over the U.S.-Canada border into Waterton Park. Many Glacier was the end of his run. "Sometimes I'd drive up there and come back," remembered Dan, "sometimes you'd stay up there a few days or run

The "Gear Jammers," Glacier Park Transportation Company, 1926. They referred to themselves as the "Hey Hey Boys." Dan is second from left, top row.

up to Two Medicine or Cut Bank. Before the road was built over Marias Pass there wasn't a really long route to drive." Dan learned the Blackfeet history along the routes, which skirted the reservation, so he could answer tourists' questions.

"We had a lot of fun with the dudes, especially the sorority girls," Dan continued. "Those tourists, they were really spooky about riding the roads; they were afraid the mountains were going to fall down on them. Often when we'd reach the top of a pass I'd say, 'See that green down there? Those are trees, not grass.'"

As the summer of 1925 wore on, Dan wrote of the dances he attended at each of the park hotels, late evening walks with park workers such as Budge, Helen, Ruth, Audrie and Alvina, and occasional hikes to places like Trick Falls (now called Running Eagle Falls) near Two Medicine Lake. The dance place near Many Glacier was the "Puff and Blow," and Budge, who worked at the Many Glacier Chalets, was Dan's favorite companion when he was there. They often hiked to Appekuny Falls near Many Glacier. In East Glacier the night spot was Mike's Place, and different women accompanied Dan there.

During August and September Dan went out with a half dozen female park workers. Based on his diary, a Glacier Park bus driver's life consisted of hauling tourists around during the day, loafing during down time, going on an occasional hike, playing cards, rarely missing a night at the dance, women, women and more women. A poem by Dan, copies of which were filed in various places in his notebook, tells the gearjammers' story:

I long to be at Glacier Park,
I long to be with the boys;
I long to wheel old fifty seven,
I long to hear the noise
Of the old boat in third gear,
As up Divide she glides;
And hear the "Dudes" bawl out,
'Go Slow!,' as around the curve she glides.
I long to line up once again
And see Claude give the sign,
To load 'er up with Dudes again,
And start off up the line.
I long to stop at sixteen mile
And have a good old pill,
Before I start up twenty three
And then head down the hill.
I long to see St. Mary Lake
And the boat that goes to Sun,
Sometimes I long for Many,
When the day's work is done.
I long to see old Two Med Lake
And take on a good old feed;

St. Mary Chalets, 1926, one of the gearjammer stops. Dan Huffine is second from left.
In the foreground, center, is Fred Noble, Superintendent of the Glacier Park Transportation Company. He's standing near a 1913 White Touring Car.

But I don't want the race track
For the grub there is the weeds.
I long to go to Mike's at night
And dance with "Hashers" sweet;
Just a few waltzes and a foxtrot,
While they walk upon my feet.
I long to see those darling maids
The pretty little things;
Sure they'll all be angels,
If they can grow the wings.
I long to see the bell hops
With their faces full of moon,
And hear them try to sing a song
With their voices out of tune.
I long to see the "laundry queens"
And the gearjammers as well,
For they are the only guys
Who are really full of Hell.
It won't be but a short time now
Until we can meet the train,
And see the "Bunch" come back
To old Glacier Park again.

Doris posing in cowboy garb at an area dude ranch. She got to know dude ranch cowboys and trail ride leaders in the park and found them exciting.

Doris and another Glacier Park Hotel worker at an area dude ranch.

C. A. Beil's Christmas Card, 1926. Doris met him on an area dude ranch. The cowboy artist composed a poem and drew a mural on the last pages of Doris's 1926 autograph book.

A Western Xmas Greeting to you and my NewYears Wish is That You may shake your Troubles like this Pony 'shakes his Pack.

December 25th 1926

C. A. Beil

Glacier Park Hotel workers and others at a dance at Mike's Place, 1926.

Dan, raised on an isolated ranch, cherished the friendships he made with the other jammers and the hotel workers during the summer season. That summer in the park had brought out Dan's need for companionship and socializing. On September 7 Dan took Alma Pyka to a dance at Mike's Place in East Glacier, and on September 8, Dan "had lunch, came back...Neilly and I picked up Helen Schwab and another girl, came to garage and talked a while. Took girls to Dorm 2 and home at 11 p.m." On September 9 Dan took Budge to a dance at the "Grill" in Many Glacier, and on September 11 he and Budge attended the last dance of the season at the same place. Most of the park workers — including Doris, who had headed back to the family farm in Iowa — left by September 15.

"After the summer season I'd go to work for the company on anything that needed to be done," Dan said later. " You see, 70 or 80 percent of the fellows had to go back to college and study to be lawyers, doctors and horse thieves. So anybody who didn't have to go back home had a job for a while." That autumn, Dan helped carpenters build two large garages to house the tour buses. And he fished on his time off, catching 8 to 23 trout each day.

On October 1 he left East Glacier for Bozeman, stopping off for a fling with Helen Schwab in the little town of Conrad on the way. Dan spent the winter and the next spring working on the family farm in Bozeman and doing odd jobs.

During the summer of 1926 Dan returned to the park and resumed his cavalier lifestyle. He drove tourists to every nook of the park's east side in No. 57 or No. 55 and tirelessly attended every dance that he could. His favorite dates that summer were Minna Hansen and Prudence Ritter.

When Dan and the other jammers were deadheaded at East Glacier, they often visited the train platform for entertainment. There, one warm night

A gathering at the Glacier Park Lodge. Blackfeet dignitaries were on hand to entertain the tourists.

The son of Marshall Field and Company's owner Simpson being adopted into the Blackfeet Tribe, 1926.

in the summer of 1926, Dan and Doris, who had also returned for her second summer in Glacier, collided.

Doris and Marie Stepan, a co-worker from Minnesota who Doris described as a "wild kid," often strolled down to the train depot when the 9 o'clock train came in for something to do. They and other hotel workers watched the people get off and on the train. Blackfeet Indians in full costume performed for the people on the train platform, as part of their "tourism promotion" work for The Great Northern Company.

"That's where I first saw Dan," Doris remembered. "Some of the maids pow-wowed around with the bus drivers, and he was going with a girl that

Going-to-the-Sun Chalets, located at the narrows along St. Mary Lake. Doris and her friends called it "Sun Camp."

The boat to Sun Camp. The trip was popular with tourists and Glacier Park workers alike.

I knew. But I never paid any attention to him. If he was her boyfriend I didn't interfere."

Doris and Marie left the platform after the performance and walked down the boardwalk towards Mike's Place. Dan and another driver had ogled Doris's striking face and athletic figure, and Dan was determined to meet her.

The two men came up behind Doris and Marie, linked their arms together and lifted Doris from the ground, then ran on to Mike's Place, holding Doris between them.

"Oh, I could have killed them," Doris remembered. "There was poor Marie and she had to come along alone and she got mad. She was temperamental anyway. She should have known it wasn't my fault; I didn't leave her."

Marie ignored Doris at the dance and finally "sneaked home alone." But Doris knew quite a few of the hotel workers, and she "just told Joe Sullivan, 'You've got to take me home tonight, because I got left.'

"That was the first time I met Dan," continued Doris, "and I was so mad at him that I just liked to never got over it. I saw him off and on the rest of the summer but I wasn't going to speak to him. I didn't want anything to do with him."

As yearbooks, or autograph books, the park workers used the annual

Two Medicine Chalets, located on the shores of Two Medicine Lake. Doris and friends, below, enjoyed horseback trips from here.

Hart Schultz, son of writer James Willard Schultz. Hart and his father were regulars around East Glacier.

Blackfeet camp on Two Medicine Lake, probably in 1925. James Willard Schultz camped with his Blackfeet friends and collected stories for his books.

Doris takes a break on a hike along the Two Medicine River. The Blackfeet called this river, "Two Medicine Lodges River."

Glacier Park Hotel workers, 1926. Doris called them a "darn good gang."

magazine, "The Call of the Mountains, Vacations in Glacier National Park," published by Great Northern Railway to promote tourism. Mary Roberts Rinehart, a frequent visitor to Glacier, wrote the foreword to the magazine, which was filled with Hileman photos of peaks, glaciers and chalets.

In Doris's yearbook for her first year in the park in 1925, Helen Yost, describing life as a maid, wrote "Dear Doris, I will repeat the scrub girls' daily exercises so that you may not forget your summer in Glacier Park. 1,2,3, knock, slowly open door, peek, stoop, look for feet, bend, twist neck at wash bowls, yes, no, enter 1,2,3...."

Richard Larson wrote, "My dear Doris, I'll never forget the girl of all trades from Room 6 Dorm 2, and I want to wish you all the success in the world and here's hoping you won't be an old maid school marm, especially when George is around."

A number of entries mentioned George, cowboys and a red Chevrolet, all associated with Doris's and her friends' adventures with cowboys from local dude ranches and with the wranglers who hosted horseback trips for tourists. Next to a photo of Trick Falls, Minna Hansen wrote about the fun they'd had on horse rides, and Pearl Busman wrote, "This picture reminds me of the Chevrolet and our first climb — the beginning of the romance."

Helen Nelson, from St. Cloud, Minn., wrote, "Here's hoping you can have such scenery before you when you and George settle on that Ranch — Good luck."

Near a photo of the Continental Divide, Doris's sweetheart wrote, "To the lady of many fine points: Led a wild life, earned all I spent; Paid back all I borrowed, lost all I lent; Met a girl, that was the end; Get a good dog boys, he will always be your friend. George Barr, Glacier Park."

Doris and Marie resting along the Mt. Henry trail with a friend. A rigorous hike, Mt. Henry was one of the most popular destinations for the Glacier Park Hotel staff. Hikers could begin from the hotel door.

Doris (far right) and friend (left) in costume, pose with the "laundry queens in uniform," before a Glacier Park Hotel function.

Although Doris loved the romance and adventure she found at the dude ranches, she didn't view the cowboys as potential mates. Being from Iowa, she found it hard to identify with them. But according to the photos and yearbook entries, the cowboys were infatuated with her.

A new crop of cowboys signed Doris's 1926 yearbook. Buck Conners, of Hughes and Conners Outfitters, wrote, "Dear Gal, Yore old homey mug causes me lots of restlessness and many, many days of anxiety. I could naturally just lay down and die for you and never bat an eye. Yours as B4, Home Address, North America."

Another cowboy wrote, "Here's to the lads you have met my dear and here's to the lips you have pressed. But the lads and the kisses are like whiskey in glasses the last is always the best. First last, and always, Rusty."

Doris's photo album is filled with pictures of the cowboys and trips to

Marie and Doris on the "Rising Wolf" shuttle boat on Two Medicine Lake,

Rawlston's Ranch, the Bar Heart Ranch, Jennings' Dude Ranch, and Art Brash's Dude Ranch. Located on the east slopes of the Continental Divide where the prairie and mountains meet, the ranches were a jumble of rocks and cliffs, rushing clear streams, and rolling prairie. In every way, the ranches and the cowboys who worked them fit Doris's view of the West, which she acquired from magazines promoting the popular and romantic view of the cowboy.

Doris and some of her friends spent the Fourth of July at Rawlston's Ranch and took in a traditional Montana rodeo, including bareback riding and bull riding. Bull riders are considered by many to be the most daring and tough athletes anywhere, and they attracted Doris and her co-workers. Doris mounted many photos of herself and her friends with their arms wrapped around various cowboys.

Doris and friend fishing, summer 1926. Doris experienced periods of sadness as she struggled to leave behind her bad experiences in Iowa.

Doris wrote, "The N-Heart gang and me. Talk about silly looks!"

Doris poses in an old engine near East Glacier.

Near the end of the summer of 1926, Doris began to feel more optimistic about the future. Below this photo in her album she wrote, "brainless."

Among the smorgasbord of available men, Doris and the other workers were also attracted to the musicians in Glacier Park Hotel's orchestra. In her photo album, Doris mounted a photo of George Barton, the saxophone player in the orchestra. George had signed her yearbook, "Saxitively yours."

Doris's prowess in hiking, outdoor skills, and her striking face and eyes drew the attention of men. She seemed to be the perfect combination of outdoorswoman and feminine companionship. Doris often hiked 10 miles, climbing 4,000 feet in elevation, to scale Mt. Henry. Entries by many of her friends mentioned an especially exciting hike. Elwood Bud Johnson of Minneapolis wrote across the centerfold map of the park: "It was on the trip up Mt. Henry that I first learned of your speed, O Doris, O Doris, you're a terror in speed. The ascent was splendid, the descent was worse, when [Marie] Stepan and Johnson had started to curse... with Weaver still holding the lead."

The entries in Doris's yearbook reflect the joy and intensity that characterized the friendships of the close-knit group of park workers. Marie, Doris's roommate again in 1926 and a frequent companion, wrote, "Here's to the apple of my eye, once we were bunkings and worked very hard. At working and fun making you were a card, here's luck to you, love to you, and more than that..." In Doris's photo album are many photos of Marie and Doris together. Obviously, Marie had forgiven Doris for being left on the steps that night on the way to Mike's Place.

The park workers shared dozens of adventures on boat rides, and horseback trips to the most beautiful points in the park. Photos of Sun Camp, Lake McDonald, Baring Falls, Two Medicine Falls, Many Glacier, and other attractions cover the pages of Doris's albums. Other photos of social events, like masquerade dances, pow-wows, parties, and skits, reflect the fun and comradeship of the workers.

At the end of the summer of 1926, Doris still felt antagonistic toward Dan, going so far as to jokingly call him the devil. She claimed that she didn't speak to Dan the rest of the summer after he and the other gearjammer had carried her down the steps to Mike's Place; however, page six of Doris's yearbook contains the entry, "Dear Doris, Don't let ol' Hades get behind you. #57, Dan Huffine, R.F.D. no. 2, Bozeman, Montana."

The end of the park season was a melancholy time for the park workers, many of whom had made the closest friendships of their lives. On September 15, 1926, Dan noted the melancholy mood and wrote of hauling the "cheap help," including his steady date, Prudence, to the train station for departure. Dan's yearbook contained notes and signatures of drivers and other friends with comments like: "When days are long and nights are short, remember your days at Many Glacier. Mary Burlingham, just a laundry queen," or from Gertrude Tess, "Tess the storm of the laundry," and from Harriet Dahllary, "Here's to a beefsteak when you're hungry, a good drink when you're dry, greenbacks when you're busted, and an eyeful when you spy — The Laundry Pest." Just above a picture of Gunsight Lake, Dan wrote, "Doris Weaver, 4304 Bloomington Ave., Mpls, Minn." So either Doris spoke to Dan long enough to give him her cousin's address, where she planned on spending part of the winter, or he got it from another maid or a laundry queen who knew Doris.

Dan hadn't given up on Doris yet.

Glacier Park Transportation Company tour buses cross the bridge at the lower end of St. Mary Lake. After driving tour buses for two years, Dan became the ranger for the St. Mary District in the early fall of 1926. Photo courtesy of Otto Bessey Jr.

7
Lone Ranger, 1926-27

"I heard that Dan had become a ranger and was all snowed-in up at
Saint Mary. I wrote to him and we began to see eye-to-eye."

On September 17, after most of the other workers had left for the season, Dan submitted an application to become a park ranger. To meet the qualifications, applicants had to be between 21 and 35 years old, at least 5 foot, 6 inches and 135 pounds, of "good moral and temperate habits, intelligent, discreet, patient, tactful... Invalids and consumptives seeking light out-of-door employment are not qualified for the work and should not apply." At 21 years, 5-foot-11 and 180 pounds, Dan qualified, but he wasn't immediately accepted. He worked for the transportation company for a few more weeks and hearing no word from the park service, returned to Bozeman.

Dan had only been home for a few days before he received orders to report to park headquarters to assume the duties of the Saint Mary Ranger position. Paperwork sent to Dan later proclaimed he was a "Park Ranger (Grade 7) in the Glacier National Park, Montana, at a salary of $1,680 per annum less $180 per annum for quarters, heat and light, effective on date of entrance on duty..." Dan dropped everything, left his father's ranch, and rode the train to East Glacier.

"I went up to the Park Service office and asked them if they had a job, and they said, 'Sure, we've got two of them,'" remembered Dan. "That was always my trouble, I could never keep out of work."

He spent the winter at Saint Mary, where he "wrassled the wind," patrolling a huge area extending south to the Hudson Bay Divide, the boundary of the area the Cut Bank Ranger patrolled. Dan's area encompassed hundreds of square miles and extended north to Sherbourne Lakes, nearly to Many Glacier.

St. Mary Ranger Dan Huffine and his dog, Stubby, early in the winter of 1926/27. Dan's district comprised hundreds of square miles of backcountry sprawled around 10 mile long St. Mary Lake. At this point, Doris still considered him the "Hard boiled Satan at St. Mary."

Saint Mary Lake, called by many the most spectacular in the park, dominated the area. Its clear, frigid waters reflect a line of steep-faced mountains with names like Red Eagle, Mahtotopa, Little Chief, Almost a Dog, and Citadel to the south, and Goat, Otokomi, and Going to the Sun to the north. The Blackfeet called the upper and lower Saint Mary lakes the "Walled in Lakes" or the "Lakes Inside."

Upon seeing the area for the first time in 1883, James Willard Schultz, traveling on the great north-and-south trail running along the base of the mountains, remarked, "[We] were soon looking at a scene so tremendous, so beautiful that I felt I could gaze at it forever...the mountains rose in grandeur to great heights. It was no wonder the Blackfeet named them the 'Lakes Inside.'"

Nearly 50 years later, the area was little changed and its beauty fascinated Dan as it had Schultz. Along with Dan, seven other rangers patrolled the east side of the park, which the federal government had purchased from the Blackfeet in 1895. Those other rangers were Lee and Whitcraft, Waterton Lake District; Heimes, Belly River; O'Brien, Swiftcurrent Valley; Hanson, Cut Bank; Paige, Two Medicine; Best, Lubec. On the west side of the Park, Ranger Fauley patrolled the Paola District, DeFord patrolled the Lake McDonald District, and Schoenbereger, Lorence, Sullivan and Fleming patrolled the North Fork, Logging, Polebridge and Kishenehn districts respectively.

"You ran around by yourself and did what you wanted to," remembered Dan. "Nobody ever told you to do anything. I'd patrol to Red Eagle Lake every once in a while to see if anybody sneaked in to trap marten, which they had done over the years. You'd just visit with the Indians, run into Babb for your mail."

On October 14 of 1926, Dan moved into the Saint Mary Ranger Station, which lies within a mile of the Blackfeet Indian Reservation, and near the shore of glacially formed Saint Mary Lake about 30 miles north of East Glacier and 10 miles south of Babb. The two-story station, one of the most elaborate in the park, measures 30-by-30 feet with a front porch covered by a roof extension. Dan hauled $128 worth of groceries to the station along with a .38-caliber special he'd just bought and plenty of ammunition.

On October 17 Dan began his patrols. He examined the phone line on the old Saint Mary Divide Road and according to his diary, "saw fresh elk tracks and an old grizzly bear track, 7 inches by 10 inches." He also remembered years later that one of his duties was to kill coyotes:

"The park furnished the ammunition if you had the gun. There weren't

The Blackfeet called St. Mary Lake the "Walled in Lake" because of the spectacular mountains which surrounded it. Dan took this photo just before he became ranger at St. Mary.

too many coyotes around Saint Mary, and ones I saw were too far to even think about shooting. The chief ranger would ask what was wrong with me, why didn't I kill more coyotes."

Over the next few weeks Dan hauled a lot of wood and patrolled into the Red Eagle Lake area, which was named by Schultz, an adopted member of the Blackfeet Tribe, after his uncle, a Blackfeet Sun Priest. "Packed two horses with supplies for Red Eagle Cabin...," Dan wrote in his diary. "In to Red Eagle at noon, saw 12 or 15 head of elk... Back to station at 4 p.m., changed clothes and left for Browning..." On a trip into Red Eagle on October 29, Dan packed in 200 pounds of salt for the elk and he often packed in hay as well. At that time, park officials believed that feeding wildlife was good management.

During November, as heavy snows covered the high country, Dan maintained trails, led packhorses to haul hay, and rode into Roes Creek (also called Rose Creek), Flat Top and Sun Camp on his horse, Peaches. It was not all bucolic bliss, however. There were moments when Dan's position as a lone voice of authority put him into real or perceived danger. On Thanksgiving Day, for instance, Dan "heard shooting down at the river. Rode down, saw two fellows from below bridge in the park. Went down to the ford and across, got on their trail, but was a few minutes late. They rode over the line just ahead of me."

Seeing elusive animals like this pine marten was just one of the rewards of being a backcountry ranger. Dan snapped this photo along the trail to Red Eagle Lake. Dan patrolled the area to ensure people didn't sneak over the park boundary to pursue marten and other valuable furbearers.

The bighorn sheep herd at Many Glacier, winter of 1926/27. Rangers around the park were concerned when more than one-third of the herd succumbed to lungworm and pneumonia. Rangers tried to help the herd by feeding them hay and moving feeding sites frequently, but it apparently did no good.

As Dan patrolled the backcountry, he often thought of Doris. He had dated many park workers in the previous two summers but none impressed him more. It was her eyes, her hiking abilities, and her no-nonsense attitude that distinguished her. She had pretended to be upset with him, but he could see a change in her feelings in letters she wrote to him. Doris had spent part of the winter in Iowa, where she taught part-time at schools near the family farm, and then visited her cousin in Minneapolis over the holidays. She couldn't get Glacier Park, or Dan, out of her mind. Many of the park workers who lived in the Twin Cities area gathered for parties, and the talk centered on Glacier and Montana.

"I heard that Dan had become a ranger and was all snowed in up at Saint Mary," Doris recalled. "I wrote to him and we began to see eye-to-eye."

Indeed, part of Doris's attraction to Dan stemmed from his new stature as a Glacier Park ranger. Park workers and visitors alike held a romantic view of the rangers, as reflected by Mary Roberts Rinehart's 1916 book, "Through Glacier Park," which Doris had read. "The rangers keep going all winter," Rinehart wrote. "...There are poachers after mountain sheep and goats... bad men from over the Canadian border. Now and then a ranger freezes to death. With a carbine strung to his shoulders, matches in a waterproof case, snowshoes and a package of food in his pocket, the Glacier Park ranger covers unnumbered miles, patrolling the wildest and most storm-ridden country in America. He travels alone... Generally he takes his man in. Sometimes the outlaw gets the drop on the ranger first and gets away."

St. Mary Chalet was within Dan's district in 1926/27.

In Doris's album a photo of Dan in his ranger garb is pressed between the pages. On the back of the photo Doris had written, "Hard boiled Satan at St. Mary, Feb. 1927." Obviously, Doris still had a ways to go before she completely trusted and forgave Dan, but she found him exciting and began to set her sights on reeling him in.

Back at Saint Mary, Dan had no inkling his destiny was taking shape. He plodded on snowshoes through deep drifts and across frozen lakes; he rode his horse, often along Divide Creek; he checked cabins at Red Eagle and Roes Creek. He also helped feed the bighorn sheep at Many Glacier, but signs were emerging that this practice concentrated the sheep and wasn't good for the herd. Dan and the other rangers reported a major die-off of bighorns in the Many Glacier area when the sheep contracted pneumonia, and 36 of the 88 sheep in the herd had died by the end of January.

Dan and the other Glacier Park rangers communicated during the long winter through an informal newsletter put together by Park Superintendant Charles J. Kraebel. In "Glacier Park Nature Notes, No. 1," dated January 19, 1927, Kraebel noted the die-off of bighorns at Many Glacier. Writing in the persona of the patriarch ram, he described the coughing and weakness displayed by the members of the band. Kraebel also described how rangers Lee and Whitcraft found a large golden eagle which had "met its death in combat with a small goat." He noted that after the battle, the goat limped off only to be killed and eaten by coyotes. In cases like this, rangers studied signs in the snow to interpret wildlife activities in their districts.

On his patrols along the reservation boundary, Dan often stopped at a few isolated ranches for visiting and an occasional meal. From time to time, he traveled by both snowshoes and horse 10 miles to Babb to pick up mail. For Christmas, Dan received a letter from his father and stepmother, Lena, mailed with a two-cent stamp, and received letters from Doris and other friends from the park. The letters and the faint hope of pursuing Doris helped ease Dan's loneliness. On New Year's Day,1927, a local woman cut Dan's hair, his first haircut since October, and on January 22, Dan observed his 22nd birthday.

In the second edition of "Nature Notes," dated February 18, 1927, Kraebel reported that the sheep die-off had been caused by lungworm and pneumonia. He noted that the skulls and hides of some sheep would be preserved by the Glacier National Park Museum Society under the supervision of its president, Morton J. Elrod, who served seasonally as park naturalist. In the same newsletter, Dan reported that while on patrol, he had counted 60-70 elk in the Red Eagle Valley and noted that he'd seen a number of lynx tracks.

The winter at Saint Mary was cold and snowy. Dan's notes show that temperatures ranged from minus 26 degrees to just above freezing during January and February. Snow piled to great depths in the high country. On one patrol in January Dan had to turn back before he reached Red Eagle Lake because his snowshoes would not support him in the deep powder. By March five to six feet more lay on the ground near the Red Eagle Cabin. In late May Dan reported 10 to 12 feet of snow on the Hudson Bay Divide and five to seven feet at Saint Mary.

Though Dan was settling into his life as a ranger, a seemingly innocuous letter that he received late that winter would prove to have an unsettling effect on him — and set the tone for a feud that would have a significant impact on Dan's chosen career. During spring of 1927, Chief Ranger F.L. Carter issued a terse order to the Glacier Park rangers to investigate trout spawning in each of their districts. "This is very important and must be attended to," Carter wrote. "No matter if you have other work, you will have to leave some one in charge...But I believe you will have plenty of time to do this work with out any trouble." Carter went on to instruct the rangers to catch fish in all waters and examine them for spawn.

Carter ended the letter in a rigid manner that would continue to characterize his dealings with Dan. "Do not put this work off or do not over look it, but make the investigation and make it thoroughly. I will be looking for reports on this matter the first part of June."

F.L. "Nic" Carter had transferred directly from the U.S. military to a post in Yellowstone National Park. He had served as chief ranger in Glacier Park beginning in 1925. Accustomed to rank and to delivering orders, Carter demonstrated no tact in his dealings with subordinates. He and Dan seemed to butt heads at every turn in the road. This letter about trout spawning was just one straw of many that Dan felt burdening him down with bureaucratic rigmarole.

Dan certainly didn't see how he could accomplish everything that was expected of him, particularly since he was preparing to move to a different ranger district for the summer. He ignored what he considered to be Carter's poorly thought-out orders on fish spawning and concentrated on the basic duties of his position. It was not the first direct order he defied, but so far he had gotten away with his insubordination.

Rather than worry about Carter, he started thinking more and more about Doris. He had received word that she would be returning to the park in May and began plotting ways to endear himself to her.

When Doris returned to Glacier in May 1927, she again worked at the Glacier Park Hotel. The train station where she and Dan first met the summer before is shown in the photo at bottom.

8
An Interesting Match

"Dan and I bummed around Bozeman that day and that's when Dan said to me, 'Bet you don't have the nerve to get married,' and I said, 'Bet I have.' "

When Doris returned to the park in May of 1927, her romance with Dan Huffine unfolded, although it was often shaky at the beginning, and years later they had contradictory recollections.

"I went out with him two or three times," Doris recalled. "I worked nights at the restaurant so I didn't have much time off. But every once in a while, I'd get another girl to fill in for me."

Sounds like a rather casual relationship, but Dan's diary entries help put the story in perspective, and it turns out to be the story of a rapidly escalating romance. On June 5, Doris helped Dan to pack his things for the move to the Sherbourne Lakes Ranger Station. The next day, he wrote that he "took Doris Weaver to Mike's" in East Glacier. On June 9, Dan took Doris to Mike's again, and on June 13 he went "out with Doris in the p.m." At this point, they were seeing each other nearly every day.

On June 16 Dan moved again, this time to the Many Glacier Ranger Station, which stands not far from the shores of Lake McDermott, or Swiftcurrent Lake. Dan stayed there for the rest of the summer, and at first he split his time between Doris and his old flame, Prudence Ritter. Reluctant to tell Prudence the full story of his romance with Doris, Dan went out with both women over the next few weeks. On June 26 he hiked with Prudence along the Belly River trail to Moran's Bath Tub and caught 12 grayling. That same evening, just after Prudence left, Doris came to visit him.

Lake McDermott (now called Swiftcurrent Lake) and the Many Glacier Hotel. In June of 1927 Dan took over the Many Glacier District and was stationed at the ranger station near the shores of Lake McDermott.

Dan's Many Glacier ranger district during the summer of 1927 included the spectacular Swiftcurrent Valley. Dan took this photo from just below Swiftcurrent Pass. Lake Sherbourne is in the distant right.

If you put any stock in the Indian lore, Dan was flirting with danger by seeing two women in the vicinity of Jealous Woman's Lake, the Blackfeet name for Lake McDermott. According to Blackfeet legend, two women of the west-side Kootenai Tribes, twin sisters Marmot and Camas, once camped by the lake with their Kootenai husband to hunt with the Blackfeet. The

Horse pack trips leaving from Many Glacier were still very popular in 1927.

fast-talking Marmot became convinced that the husband favored her sister after he procured an otter hide for Camas but could not get one for her. Marmot demanded a fight with her sister, but having no weapons, Camas proposed that they swim the lake across and back until one of them drowned. The two women rushed to the lakeshore, tore off their clothes and jumped into the water. After several times across the lake, Marmot tired, sank below the surface and drowned. Her death was mourned by Camas and her husband and ever after, the lake was known as an unhappy place.

Luckily, Dan soon explained things to Prudence, concentrated his attention on Doris alone, and avoided the potential danger of a battle between the two women.

During the rest of summer, Dan divided his time between work and romance. Sometimes he could combine the two. He made high country patrols in the Many Glacier area to Grinnell Glacier, Ptarmigan Lake, Morning Eagle Falls, Lake Josephine, Iceberg Lake, and other places — often accompanied by Doris.

Even though she held two jobs — at Glacier Park Hotel and at Mike's Place — Doris made time to see Dan. Indeed, she curtailed her participation in Glacier Park Hotel social activities so she could focus on him. A teacher and college graduate, Doris helped Dan prepare for his upcoming exam to become a permanent ranger in the park. In his notebook, Dan kept pages of sample exam questions provided to the temporary rangers by F.L. Carter. Doris helped Dan wade through the confusing math of government survey methods, firefighting nomenclature, and silviculture. In other areas, such as wildlife, horsemanship, and packing, Dan felt more comfortable. Doris and Dan grew closer as they shared a common goal.

As the summer wore on, Dan juggled his time between Doris, studying

The tour boat Altyn on Lake McDermott (now called Swiftcurrent Lake) in 1927. According to one Blackfeet legend, the lake was called "Jealous Woman's Lake" by the tribes.

for the exam, and his ranger duties at Many Glacier. Among his duties was stocking hatchery trout in park lakes, so Dan's contribution to the park's long-term ecology can still be seen today. The fisheries policy of the Park Service then amounted to stocking large numbers of fish in selected lakes in an attempt to keep dudes happy. Rangers and others, using milk cans and pack stock, planted millions of fish each year. On July 24, Dan and Lou Hanson stocked 300,000 grayling in Lower Kennedy Lake; on July 2 Dan planted 150,000 rainbow trout in Saint Mary Lake; on July 28 he planted 250,000 rainbow trout in Josephine Lake. In August Dan planted eastern brook trout in Lake McDermott and 150,000 rainbow trout in Lake Josephine.

As he patrolled, Dan also recorded all the wildlife he observed. On one patrol, Dan hiked from Many Glacier to Morning Eagle Falls and saw, "7 goats and one grizzly eating on a goat; 3 to 20 feet of snow the last 2 miles." During the 1920s, the big bears were not seen often. According to some accounts, this was because of the systematic shooting of grizzlies by sheep ranchers along the edge of the park. This is the only mention Dan made of seeing a grizzly in his patrols of the area, but that didn't mean there wasn't plenty of excitement for him that summer.

In those days the backcountry of the park was little used, and Dan often found or helped pack out injured hikers, or greenhorns, as Dan called them, who had tested their endurance, and found it wanting.

"Started out at 1:30 a.m. to find two fellows who were lost on Grinnell Glacier," Dan wrote about an incident on July 19. "Got to bed at 6 a.m...."

Doris and fellow park worker Myrna, who was Doris's main hiking partner in 1927.

HUDSON BAY
DIVIDE
ALT.
607GFT

About another rescue, Dan recalled: "One fellow on trail crew cut across the wrong gully, slipped and rolled about 100 yards and broke his shoulder blade. Three or four of us got him onto my saddle horse. After we got him out we loaded him in a car and drove him to East Glacier in time to catch the night train to Kalispell. We got to Kalispell by about 1 a.m. The next morning I went up to the hospital to see how he was, and they hadn't even looked at him yet. It made me so mad I could have killed them."

Dan's tolerance for bureaucratic bungling was almost non-existent.

His interest in history, however — a driving force behind his decision in later years to start a museum — was growing. Along with Doris, he explored old cabins and looked for Indian artifacts. One of the reasons that the Many Glacier area fascinated Dan was that it had attracted early oil and mineral exploration that ultimately proved unsuccessful. "They had an oil derrick right there within a quarter mile of Sherbourne dam with oil seepage on the surface, but they never got anywhere with it," Dan remembered. "They tried mining up at Cracker Lake. There's machinery that you couldn't believe they were able to get up there and buildings that were still standing (then)."

Doris and Dan grew closer as the summer wore on. On August 9 and 10, Dan went out with Doris to Mike's Place. These dates must have been a form of celebration, because on August 8, Dan had learned he had passed

Dan rescued more than one park visitor who had underestimated the rugged terrain on the east side of Glacier Park.

his written exam to become a permanent park ranger. Now he only needed to pass an oral exam, normally considered just a formality. Dan and Doris went to a masquerade dance on August 19. On the last day of August, Doris and Dan went on the train across the Continental Divide to Belton, near West Glacier, so that Dan could take another civil service exam. As the summer progressed, they must both have been thinking about the future, and about whether they would be separating again or finding a way to stay together.

In September, Dan patrolled and maintained trails to Cracker Lake, Swiftcurrent Pass, Granite Park, Piegan Pass, and other trails in the Many Glacier District. Once her duties at Glacier Park Hotel and Mike's fountain were done, Doris came to visit Dan, but only for a few days. She arrived on September 6 and left on September 9 for a waitress job in Great Falls, about 100 miles east of Many Glacier. Doris's decision to stay in Montana rather than return to the Midwest after the park season closed was significant. Now a widow for about 2 1/2 years, she had committed to a relationship with Dan.

Dan prepared to leave the Many Glacier Ranger Station for his next assignment, which was to spend the winter at the Cut Bank Ranger Station. On September 22 as Dan packed his things, he and rangers Joe Heimes and Tom Whitcraft listened to the famous Jack Dempsey-Gene Tunney heavyweight championship fight on a crackling radio. What they thought of the famous "long count" that let Tunney escape being knocked out by Dempsey in their Chicago battle, is left unrecorded. On October 14 Dan left for Great Falls to see Doris.

Dan's arrival stirred Doris and she later remembered that Dan had requested and received leave from his ranger job to visit his family in Bozeman.

"He asked me to come with him," she recalled. "I'd never been to Bozeman so I thought that was a big deal. In fact, I'd never traveled around Montana at all so I thought, OK, I'll go to Bozeman."

Dan and Doris went out together in Great Falls that night, passed through Helena the next day and reached Bozeman at 1 a.m. "Doris went to the Baltimore Hotel," Dan wrote in his diary. Dan went to his father's ranch and had dinner. The next day Dan toured Doris around town and Doris met Dan's relatives; he and Doris watched a show that night.

Dan's family made Doris feel welcome. "By gosh, we got over there and he took me to his grandmother's house and I'll bet his grandmother thought, 'What am I going to do with her,'" Doris remembered. "But she was real nice to me and I slept in her bed with her. And the next day she showed me how to make a bed. I'll never forget that — she showed me how to turn the covers back square, no rounded edge, oh no. She told me everything she could. She was quite a talker. I met Irma, Dan's little sister. She was just a sweet kid...

"So Dan and I bummed around Bozeman that day and that's when Dan said to me, 'Bet you don't have the nerve to get married,' and I said, 'Bet I have.' I don't know whether he just said it on the spur of the moment and didn't think I'd do it... We just went to the Justice of the Peace office and got it done. Dan didn't tell his folks we got married until later. "

Dan's version of the marriage was surprisingly matter-of-fact. "Went to town, bought a tube radio," he wrote in his journal on October 17. "Doris and I rode around until 3 p.m., stopped at the court house, got marriage license then went down and had Judge Axtell marry us with Sheriff Frank Slaughter and Doctor for witnesses. Then to see Aunt Fronia. Took Doris to Ma's, and went to the ranch. Had supper, went to town to Beech's place till 11:30 p.m...went to bed at 1 a.m."

On October 18 the newlyweds awoke at 3:30 a.m. and took the train back to Great Falls, where Doris stayed to get her things together. Dan returned to Glacier Park and spent the next few days hauling supplies to the Cut Bank Ranger Station, where the couple would spend the winter. On October 22, Dan drove the 1922 Dodge touring car he'd just bought to Browning, picked up Doris, and returned to the station.

A Great Falls Tribune article on summer workers in Glacier mentioned the wedding: "Probably the most interesting match last summer was when Doris Weaver, a graduate of the University of Iowa, became Mrs. Dan Huffine, and took up her wifely duties at the Cut Bank Ranger Station."

As it turned out, Doris's "wifely duties" extended way beyond those implied by the Tribune's article. She was about to find out how much of a greenhorn she really was.

Cut Bank Ranger Station, winter of 1927/28. That's Dan and Doris's 1922 Dodge coupe parked near the station. The spectacular peaks of the upper Cut Bank drainage rise in the distance.

9
Winter at Cut Bank Ranger Station, 1927-28

"The temperature dropped from 10 degrees above zero in the morning when Dan left, to 34 degrees below zero by nightfall. I loaded the stove and went to bed but in the middle of the night gunshots woke me. Someone just kept on shooting and shooting."

Dan and Doris had no time to think about a honeymoon after their impromptu marriage in Bozeman. In fact, as Doris related later, she contracted a moderate case of cold feet that lasted for the first weeks she and Dan spent at the Cut Bank Ranger Station. But Doris thought of her marriage to Dan as another job, and she was determined that it would succeed.

During that winter of 1927-28, park rangers began keeping journals at each ranger station. The library at park headquarters in West Glacier houses the journal for the tiny, isolated Cut Bank Ranger Station for that year with entries written in Doris's strong, flowing hand. Doris wrote her personal account of events in a four-inch by three-inch journal with "First National Bank, Minneapolis, Minnesota" emblazoned on the cover. She created a design from porcupine quills on the first page of the journal.

Two days after their marriage Dan bought supplies for the winter at Cut Bank. According to his journal, he paid $125 for a five-tube, dry cell radio, $15 for a Hudson Bay Blanket, $7.50 for skis, $8 for snow shoes or "webbs," $6.50 for a fishing pole, $15 for a Victrola and records and $100 for "grub." The Park Service reimbursed him for food, but he had to buy everything else, including a $43 uniform, out of his temporary ranger salary of $1680 a

East side of the ranger station, 1928. During winter, icicles connected the snow on the ground with the snow on the station roof.

year.

In the last week of October, Dan and Doris drove the dirt track to the ranger station in their 1922 Dodge coupe, which they had purchased for $125. The station, about 50 miles west of the town of Cut Bank, was perched in the foothills at 5,200 feet above sea level on the eastern slopes of the Continental Divide where the prairie and mountains suddenly confront each other. To the west lay more than a million acres of wilderness; to the east sprawled the 1.5 million-acre Blackfeet Indian Reservation.

The area was rich in Blackfeet culture and history. Cut Bank Creek, or Punak'iksi Ituktai, so named by the Blackfeet for the cliff-like banks on its lower reaches, flowed past the station and spilled onto the high plains, between 8,797-foot Kupunkamint (or "Shakes Himself") Mountain to the north and 8,341-foot Mad Wolf Mountain (named after a famous Blackfeet chief) to the south. North of Kupunkamint Mountain stands White Calf Mountain, which the Blackfeet called "Wonderful Child Mountain," named after the last of the Pikuni Chiefs, who was famous for his bravery in battle with the Cree Tribe north and east of Glacier.

The ranger station was about 20 miles from Browning, the nearest town, and 22 miles from the village of East Glacier, site of Glacier Park headquarters in those days. About 15 miles to the north stood Saint Mary Ranger Station and Chalet. In 1927 the snow-covered road into the ranger station was impassable by car after November 11. The only way to go back and forth to town was on snowshoes or skis.

"I began to wonder what I'd done," Doris said. "I had written to my dad that I had married Dan. I found out later that he was worried that I was in Dutch, that I was forced to get married."

Dan and Doris had to climb over piles of snow to enter the front of the ranger station.

Front of ranger sta. in 1928

By the time the letter reached her father, Doris was at the ranger station and could not be contacted directly. "He left word at Park headquarters for Dan to tell me that If I had gotten into something I wanted out of, that he would help me. Papa thought that I wouldn't ask for help, because he had always told us that we were on our own, and if we got into any jackpots not to come running to him.

"I don't know," continued Doris. "Part of me probably wanted out. But I figured I took on a job and I would finish it. We were raised that way."

The harsh winter temperatures and powerful winds of the Cut Bank valley shocked even Doris, who was used to the severe winters in Iowa. "I was a greenhorn, that's for sure," she recalled.

In her leather-bound photo album near a summer picture of Glacier, Doris wrote, "The good old summer time, when the air is full of sunshine and the park is full of cheap help." And near a winter photo of Cut Bank Creek she wrote, "But oh what a change in just three months!"

Doris described the Cut Bank Ranger Station as a "ranger's winter igloo," or "the shack." The station occupied a meadow with a sweeping view of the upper Cut Bank Valley and Bad Marriage and Mad Wolf mountains. A sign nailed between two posts read "Cut Bank Ranger Station — Information — File Complaints here."A small grove of quaking aspen grew behind

Doris and Dan look cold in these photos they snapped of each other in front of the ranger station.

the station, which was built of large, chinked logs and measured about 25 feet wide by 50 feet long, with an alcove attached to the back. The small front porch faced south. There were two windows on the east wall and two on the west wall, each divided into eight panes. Three log poles propped against the east side supported the cabin against the wind. The roof was steeply angled to allow snow to slide off during winter. Outside, a canvas tent housed the winter firewood supply. Dan covered the Dodge with canvas, too, and parked it behind the east side of the station.

Inside, the station was dark during the winter. Snow built up to the top of the windows on each side. Dan shoveled often to keep the windows and doors free. On the west side of the station, ice bridged the snow on the roof with the snow on the ground. The living area had a perpetual smoky smell from the wood stove, which puffed each time the door was opened. Water piped from a spring supplied a small sink.

From this humble but livable headquarters, Dan was expected to patrol areas around his district regularly, regardless of the weather. On December 1, Dan attempted but failed to complete a patrol along the steep trail that crosses into the South Fork of Cut Bank Creek, later called Lake Creek on National Park maps.

"Chief Ranger Carter ordered Dan to cross into the South Fork and stay in a snowshoe cabin," remembered Doris. "It was blowing so hard when Dan got on top that it knocked him down and he slid backwards down the slope. He took off his snowshoes and jammed them into the snow to keep from being blown clear off the mountainside. While he was lying there, a

Dan arrives at the station after one of his three-day trips to East Glacier for the mail and to report in to park headquarters. If the snow was set up, Dan could make the 22 mile trip one-way in about six hours.

Dan coming in after 22 miles — a long trip for the mail. 1928.

piece of snow as big as a wash tub broke off and slid down the mountain and crashed into him.

"He was scared," continued Doris, "and so mad that the Park Service expected him to make that patrol over the top under those conditions. He felt that no one could have made it; he couldn't even stand up. So he backed down the mountainside and returned to the station."

About once a month Dan snowshoed 22 miles into East Glacier for the mail and supplies, and to check in at park headquarters. According to entries in his personal diary, Dan covered the distance in 5 1/2 to 6 hours in good snow conditions. Dan usually stayed one day in East Glacier so the entire trip required three days.

"It was a toss-up between East Glacier and Browning as far as the closest place," remembered Dan. "The Indians went in to Browning. It was easier; you just headed right down Cut Bank Creek, pretty easy going. If you went to East Glacier, you had to go up over the hill, over Looking Glass. The old road that used to come out of East Glacier was a crooked, winding narrow road."

Of course, when Dan was out on patrol or gone to East Glacier, Doris was on her own. That year, on December 5, Dan left the ranger station for East Glacier and, according to his diary, "got caught in a hell of an east storm; couldn't see six feet at times." Doris remembered the storm vividly, too:

The area along the east side of the Continental Divide where Dan patrolled. Dan complained about the fierce winds of the Cut Bank Drainage.

"The temperature dropped from 10 degrees above zero in the morning when Dan left to 34 degrees below zero by nightfall. I loaded the stove and went to bed. In the middle of the night gunshots woke me. Someone just kept on shooting and shooting."

Doris climbed into the attic and hid under some saddle blankets.

"I was scared, you better believe it. I'd fall asleep but would wake up from the cold or the gunshots. The next morning I went back downstairs and looked outside, but couldn't figure out where the shots had come from. There was no sign of anyone, and I didn't hear any more shots."

The storm stranded Dan in East Glacier for an extra day.

"When he finally got back two days later, I told him about the shooting," Doris said. "He figured out right away that the bangs were made by the cold, not gunshots. That was the first time I'd seen temperatures drop so fast and so low that the trees and cabin logs cracked and snapped.

"I felt embarrassed, I'll tell you."

Doris remembered that temperatures were below zero much of the time from December through February, but records that Dan kept of morning and evening temperatures don't fully support her recollection. Temperatures were below zero on three days in November, 15 days in December, two days in January, and four days in February. Her memories of constant snow were correct, however. According to Dan's diary entries, snow fell every day in November (total 84 inches), and January had 25 stormy days.

On the day before Christmas, Dan and Doris left the ranger station to visit friends at Saint Mary Ranger Station and Chalet. Dan wore snowshoes and Doris wore heavy, wooden skis.

"The trip from the ranger station to Saint Mary was tough for me," said Doris. "I barely handled the climb up to Hudson Bay Divide with those

Timbered foothills rise to the high ridges in the Cut Bank Valley. Doris accompanied Dan on some of his patrols of this area.

heavy skis. But when I got to the top I knew we had covered nine miles and it was only six more, downhill.

"We got to the chalet long after dark. Boy were we wet and tired, especially me. I don't think a bed ever felt better, even if it did sag in the middle."

Doris and Dan spent Christmas Day at the chalet with caretaker Gaston Varis and his wife. They enjoyed the decorated tree, visiting, and dinner. Then they slept in preparation for the long trip home.

"We left for the ranger station before dawn the next day," remembered Doris. "The wind was blowing like sixty and the snow fell blinding and thick. When we finished the 1,500-foot, six-mile climb to the divide, I'd had enough. I told Dan that I was through, and that I wouldn't go another step, then I lay down in the snow.

"Dan didn't know what to do for a while, just kept saying that if I stayed here I would die. I told him I'd just as soon stay here as go on. Finally Dan took off his belt and threatened to hit me with it. That brought me to my senses. After that we ate lunch, rested, and kept going. We got back to the ranger station well after dark."

Dan's entry in his personal diary gave no hint of the conflict. On December 26, he wrote, "St. Mary to Cut Bank, 15 miles; left at 9 a.m., home at 5 p.m."

In her journal, Doris recorded the routine of their winter. "I made the first decent bread since coming up here," she wrote on January 15. "Wind is blowing — read a lot." Most of her journal entries addressed those subjects: chores around the cabin and the weather.

"Finished my felt scarf," Doris wrote on January 20. "Slid on skis — swell sliding. Baked bread, but not so good."

"We had a problem with some of our flour," remembered Dan. "When

Cut Bank Creek, winter of 1927/28. Doris enjoyed observing the many beaver which lived along the banks of the creek.

they took the winter's grubstake in they put the extra flour in the back room in a box they had there for meat. Along about the first of February or so, we opened that sack of flour and here it was all tasting of kerosene. Some darn fool had put the kerosene can in there. So I went to the first Indian place down the road and asked him to get us some more flour next time he went to Browning.

"I got along well with the Indians," continued Dan. "I'd met a lot of them when I was driving bus, a lot of the Crees." The Crees' ancestral home was north and east of Glacier in present-day Canada, but they occasionally entered the park through northern passes or from the plains to the east. They had contact with the Blackfeet through trading of weapons and had occasionally fought the Blackfeet in raids and skirmishes through the years. After the Blackfeet Reservation was established, some of the Crees took up residence there.

In her diary Doris mentions baking bread about once a week, and making taffy and prune Jell-o. She played solitaire, embroidered, sewed, and read. In one entry, she described Dan returning from a snowshoe trip from East Glacier loaded down with dozens of National Geographic magazines.

Doris sewed all winter. She worked on a silk rug for months. In one entry she wrote, "Am working on rug every day. Got to get that done." On March 11 she wrote, "finished the silk rug. Awful pretty, worth at least $25. Dan helped a lot."

She also spent a lot of time mending. "I patched socks, nine pair, and one shirt," she wrote on February 8. "Made moccasins out of some old sheep skin," she wrote March 30. She also finished a beaded belt and crocheted various items.

Doris's entries in her diary seem to show that she grew more fond of Dan as time went on. On January 9, she wrote, "Dan looked in the stove — it puffed out and now he has bangs, no eye lashes and singed hair: 'Chief-Look-In-Stove.'" In another entry, on May 14, she wrote, "Dan fixed the truck, I patched his socks. Went down to see ducks on the creek. Dan fell down in the middle of the road. Sure fierce how he falls for me — ha, ha!"

Dan wrote in his diary that Doris met him four miles from the station with hot coffee on December 21 when he was returning from a trip to East Glacier.

Dan often patrolled Cut Bank Ridge, the South Fork of Cut Bank Creek, and Milk River Ridge, paying particular attention to the boundaries of the district near the Blackfeet reservation. "The park had only been established for about 16 years," recalled Doris, "and people were still hunting and trapping inside the park boundary." According to Dan's diary, he patrolled 150 to 200 miles each month on snowshoes and on foot.

"That was an awful area to patrol," remembered Dan. "That old wind would sweep the snow off some places and pack it hard in others. You'd carry your snowshoes in some places and chop holes in the snow to step in. Sometimes that wind would blow so hard you'd come right out of your tracks. You'd have to just lay down and let her blow."

Several times, Dan saw people trapping or hunting within the park's boundary but they managed to make the boundary before he could reach them.

"I patrolled the area from Cut Bank to the Hudson Bay Divide," he remembered. "Then the line ran over to Sherbourne Lakes; occasionally you had to go along the reservation to see if anyone had sneaked in to trap marten. They told me to patrol the border, and if I saw any tracks, go in and

Doris and Dan checked on the Cut Bank Chalets as part of the routine patrols during their stay at Cut Bank Ranger Station. The main Cut Bank Chalet building is pictured here in a 1933 NPS photo.

Doris called the Cut Bank Ranger Station a "ranger's winter igloo, where longings are many... ."

get them."

According to Dan, Chief Ranger Carter told him not to get friendly with the Blackfeet because they would take advantage of him.

"Carter was afraid I'd turn my head while they got themselves a deer or a sheep," said Dan. "After I got out of the Park Service, a couple of the boys told me, 'We sat up on the ridge up there and watched which way you went. If you went that way we'd go over on the mountainside and get ourselves a sheep.' Sheep, deer or elk, whatever got in their road. They liked their wild meat. They figured why kill one of their cattle when they could kill a sheep. I never did actually catch someone poaching.

"I believe the Blackfeet pretty much accepted the park being there, although they felt it messed up their hunting grounds a little bit. It brought quite a little money to Browning because of the tourists, furnished some jobs. They're a pretty easygoing people, easy to get along with. If they didn't want to talk to you, they acted like they couldn't talk English."

During the 1920s the Blackfeet, who earlier had dominated the expansive, buffalo-rich plains east of the park, resented their captive existence on the 50-by-60-mile reservation. The three tribes which made up the Blackfeet Confederacy — the Bloods, the northern Blackfeet, and the Piegans or "Pikuni" — traditionally existed by hunting buffalo, and by raiding the tribes to the north and west to hold dominance over the plains. They had very little tie to the mountains of Glacier Park and rarely if ever hunted the mountain-dwelling animals. They viewed the area with awe as a spiritual place, not a place to hunt or dwell.

The Blackfeet were particularly resentful that many of their traditional names for features in the park were wiped out. James Willard Schultz re-

Snow piled so high around the station that the couple had to shovel to keep the windows free.

Us in 1928 beside the ranger sta.

lated what his friend, the Blackfeet Chief Tail-Feathers-Coming-Over-The-Hill, said in 1915:

"It is true that, nineteen winters ago, we sold to the whites this Back-bone-of-the-World portion of our reservation. But did we at the same time sell to them the names that we — and our fathers before us — had given to these mountains, lakes and streams? No, we did not sell them!"

Perhaps Carter wasn't entirely wrong in his concern about Dan. After all, Dan was certainly aware of the feelings of many of the Blackfeet whom he had come to know, and said later that he felt lenient toward those who might drift over the park boundary from time to time. Indeed, although Dan enjoyed some aspects of being a ranger, he never felt fully comfortable in the job for many reasons.

"It often seemed like you weren't accomplishing anything on that ranger job," Dan remembered. "You couldn't go out in the morning, come back in the evening and say you did anything. You'd just snowshoe up the ridge or somewhere. I was raised on a ranch and used to getting things done."

Doris went along on patrol with Dan a few times each month and often took pictures. Near one picture in her album she wrote, "A willow tree all ready for Christmas, all gnarled and knotted, windblown and weary, up on Cut Bank Ridge."

From time to time, Dan and Doris checked on Cut Bank Chalets, which were boarded up for the winter, a few miles up the valley from the ranger

By late winter, Dan and Doris appear happy and comfortable with each other. Dan traveled on snowshoes but Doris preferred skis.

station. The Great Northern Railway had completed the chalets and camp in 1913. One two-story, six-room chalet, two one-room chalets, and a dining hall occupied the camp site. At about the same time, Great Northern built chalets at Saint Mary, Gunsight, Many Glacier, Sun Camp, Two Medicine, and Sperry. Management of the chalets was turned over to the Glacier Park Hotel Company in 1917. The chalets served as layover points for extended horse trips in the park.

On January 20, Doris recorded a typical work day for Dan: "Pretty windy for traveling in the morning. It got better in the afternoon, so put on webbs and made a patrol up towards the chalets and back by way of Amphitheater Mountain, northwest of the station. I was looking for elk tracks as I thought that the elk might come down along the base of the mountains from the Milk River country. Saw a large track — resembled a big wolf. Made eight miles in all — snow was rather crusty in places."

Dan often patrolled along the base of Amphitheater Mountain, called Three Horns Mountain by the Blackfeet for a member of the Pikuni tribe who killed a Nez Perce, captured the man's woman and horses and brought them across the mountains to the buffalo plains.

Based on their diaries and recollections, Dan and Doris saw little sign of deer or bear during any season in the Cut Bank valley. They mentioned seeing elk or elk sign six or eight times. Several entries in Doris's journal mention coyotes howling, and Dan saw a few on patrol. Dan mentioned seeing lynx and otter tracks occasionally. This was in sharp contrast to the descriptions of the area by James Willard Schultz just 50 years earlier.

"We followed up the Marias," Schultz wrote one April, "then its northern tributary, the Cutbank River, until we came to the pines at the foot of the Rockies. Here was game in vast numbers; not many buffalo nor antelope just there, but elk, deer, mountain sheep and moose were even more plentiful than I had seen them south of the Missouri. As for bears, the whole country was torn up by them." Schultz then described an encounter with a grizzly on a ridge above the Cutbank River, which included a high-speed horse chase.

In the ranger station journal on February 20, Doris recorded one of Dan's typical "game surveys":

"Commenced the game count today. Got up real early and went up the valley to the South Fork trail, then cut off across the ridge into the first valley to the right of the trail. Followed the ridge up above timberline into the rock slide. Saw sheep tracks and later located seven head of sheep farther up the valley and to the left. Had to use webbs all through the timber. Made eight miles in all. Saw two coyote tracks and millions of rabbit tracks."

Nary a bear anywhere in this late winter survey, or in later surveys as spring approached.

According to Doris's diary, it snowed at least half of the days in March and April, but by late April, Doris was getting outside nearly every day. On April 26, she wrote, "I went up to the chalets and saw a snow slide. Sure is oodles of snow between here and there. I made a flower bed in front of the shack." Doris tried fishing in Cut Bank Creek, but had no luck. "All the fish we caught this year were might have beens," she wrote.

"Real summer weather," Doris wrote on May 9. "Lots of ducks and beaver down along the creek. All kinds of flowers. Saw first yellow lily." Doris often visited the many beaver dams along Cut Bank Creek near the Ranger station. She found it fascinating to watch the animals work on their dams and lodges. The Blackfeet considered the beaver the most intelligent of all quadrupeds because they worked in the summer, had a warm lodge in the winter with plenty of food, and did nothing all winter but eat, dance, sleep, and sing. If Blackfeet mythology is correct, the beavers Doris watched in Cut Bank Creek were descendants of great beaver chiefs.

The area along the creek where Doris stood, a popular Blackfeet camping spot, supported large concentrations of beaver in Blackfeet times. According to tribal legend, beavers or "tree biters" represented strong medicine and could sometimes take on the shape of men. White Fur, a beaver chief, once lived in these ponds with his wife and their son, Loud Slap, who gained his name from his ability to slap the water loudly with his tail to warn the gens, or clan. As the legend goes, the clan had eaten nearly all the young aspen and willow around the ponds, so White Fur sent his son down the Cut Bank drainage to search for a new home. Loud Slap found a wonderful place in an adjacent drainage to build new dams and lodges, and the clan moved, intending to return to their home when the young trees regenerated. In the interim a rival clan, led by Strong Dam, took possession of the clan's old ponds and when White Fur's clan returned, a fierce battle between the beaver warriors ensued. According to legend, White Fur's clan regained their old home and he and Loud Slap lived long lives in the Cut Bank Valley. Doris, who had read about the legend, wondered if the beavers she watched were descendants of the mythical beaver chiefs.

As grass began to grow on the little flat around the ranger station in early May, other animals held Doris's and Dan's attention, too. "One night the biggest racket you ever heard woke us up," remembered Doris. "About 10 porcupines had moved in to feed on the green grass. They were whining, scraping, and gnawing all around the porch. The rest of that spring I kept knocking them off the porch with a broom, but it did no good — we were stuck with them." Dan wrote on May 19 that he "killed three porcupines today. They are barking all the young quaking aspen around the station."

Dan shoveled snow drifts and drained water from the access road and opened it for travel by May 12. On May 16 Doris and Dan drove into East Glacier to rent a house for the summer and see about summer jobs, then returned to the station. During the rest of May, Doris hiked along the area's trails, enjoying the flowers and views.

On the last day of May, Doris and Dan left the ranger station and the Park Service. They had found out earlier that Dan would not be granted permanent status as a park ranger. Doris claimed it was because Dan failed to complete the patrol to the snowshoe cabin on the South Fork of Cut Bank Creek those many months before in a raging blizzard.

"We didn't know the Park Service like we knew it later," remembered Doris. "We should have kept our mouths shut. But Dan told Carter he didn't make it over the top and into the snowshoe cabin. Carter was a military man from Michigan. He told Dan that whenever he gave an order, he expected it to be followed, or else."

"Carter and about five others, including (assistant superintendent) Vincent, came over from Yellowstone, where they had soldiers, not rangers," remembered Dan. "They were allowed to go over to Glacier without losing their seniority. Those Army guys, they liked to fiddle-faddle around but they wanted the rest of us to work."

Doris blamed Carter for Dan's problems: "Dan wasn't allowed to pass his oral test to become a permanent ranger. He passed the written test just super, but Carter wouldn't let him pass the oral test." Indeed, Dan received word that he had failed the oral examination he'd taken earlier, even though he thought it had gone well. In a letter from the district secretary of the 11th U. S. Civil Service District, he was informed that he "did not possess the qualifications required in this particular position... ."

"So late in May we left," continued Doris. "Dan was through with the Park Service. Two years later, Carter apologized to Dan, said that he had the same thing happen to him when he tried (to reach the cabin in a wind storm). But it was too late by then."

"I always told Carter how bad the wind was on that stretch," remembered Dan, "and so did Lou Hansen, who'd rangered there before me. Carter just laughed, thought it was a big joke. But after he tried it, he said, 'Don't ever go across there when the wind's blowing. Those guys told me all those years how bad it was but I thought they were just talking through their hats.'"

Dan wrote the last entry in the ranger station journal on May 31: "Leaving the park service today. Couldn't talk fast enough to the civil service examiner. Started in with the park service on October 7, 1926 at Saint Mary — moved to Sherbourne Lake for 10 days, then to Many Glacier, then to Cut Bank for the winter of 1927/28. F.D. Huffine, Ranger."

Years later, Doris painted a picture of the outhouse located in the back yard of their East Glacier home. It was at this outhouse that Doris had her hilarious run- in with a Blackfeet woman who made the mistake of stopping one time too many.

10
Indian in the Outhouse, 1928-29

"So then Dan got up and here the outhouse was still rocking and he said, 'What's going on out there?,'" and I said, 'Dan, you've got to go out there and let that Indian woman out of the outhouse.' And he said, 'No sir, I'm not getting in on this deal at all. You got her in there and you'll get her out.'"

As the snows melted on the east slope of the divide, swelling the streams above their banks, Dan and Doris turned their backs on Bad Marriage Mountain and left the Cut Bank Ranger Station. An article in the Great Falls Tribune mentioned the couple's stay at the Cut Bank Ranger Station and marked their exodus, noting, "Mrs. Huffine was 20 miles from the next ranger station and 30 miles from the nearest woman. A few days ago she came to town for the first time in six months."

On the last day of May 1928, Dan and Doris moved their belongings to the little village of East Glacier Park, which was to become their home for the next four years. Doris's sisters and brothers and her Aunt Eva and Uncle George were out from Iowa to help clean up at the ranger station and prepare the little home Dan and Doris had rented in East Glacier. Doris was pleased to see her relatives and she was entertained by her sister Maxine's description of their trip west.

"We had a heck of a time getting out there in the old touring car," remembered Maxine. "It had a canvas top that came up in the back and went up to the front windshield, then it was open all the way around the sides. We drove all the way with a top speed of 30 miles per hour — it took us four hours to come up one of the hills. We had flats and you had to jack the car,

Because of prohibition, the dancehall business boomed at Mike's Place and continued strong through the early 1930s.

Considered the heart of East Glacier, Mike's had burned in the mid-1920s and was quickly rebuilt. Doris was one of owner Mike Shannon's favorite employees. (Photos courtesy of Otto Bessey, Jr.)

Doris (back row, 7th from left) worked in the Glacier Lodge Hotel kitchen for $35 a month during the 1928 and 1929 summer seasons.

take the tire off the rim, patch it, then pry the tire back on just right."

Uncle George and Aunt Eva, unaccustomed to children, struggled to keep order on the trip. "We kids — Frank, Shirley and I — were getting on their nerves one day," continued Maxine. "They made us get in the back, which was a mistake. Frank pecked and pecked at Shirley until she got up to tell Aunt Eva about it, and as she did, Frank grabbed me by the hair and pulled my head down on the seat. Shirley sat down on my head.

"When Shirley got up, my jaw was over here and I couldn't shut my mouth or open my mouth. Eva got George to pull over and as he did, Frank said, 'There's nothing wrong with her,' and he hit me on the side of the jaw. My jaw went back in place and George said, 'Eva you're always fussing. I don't see anything wrong with them. Now you get in the back.'"

After helping Dan and Doris move, Eva, George and the kids accompanied them on tours around the east side of the park. After spending about a week in Montana, the Ashleys left for Iowa.

Dan and Doris had moved to East Glacier during an exciting time for the town and for the country. The town, bolstered by tourism promoted by the Great Northern Railroad Company, was booming. That November, Herbert Hoover would win a landslide election to become president. Amelia Earhart would beat out Mabel Boll, known as "Queen of Diamonds," and three other women who died trying, to become the first woman to fly in an airplane as co-pilot across the Atlantic Ocean.

The town of Glacier Park, formerly known as Midvale, and later known as East Glacier Park or East Glacier, represented a melding of railroad people, hotel company workers, Park Service employees, ranchers, tourists, homesteaders, and Blackfeet Indians. The town supported about 400

Doris described their house in East Glacier as a "cracker box." The couple supplemented their income by purchasing and renting out another home, and by selling chickens and eggs.

year-long residents during the '20s and '30s; this number swelled to about 1,000 during the summer, when America's wealthiest families such as the Rockefellers, Roosevelts, and Vanderbilts visited dude ranches and the Glacier Park Hotel. East Glacier Park was a hub for railroad travel to the park and the home of Glacier Park's administrative headquarters.

East Glacier sprawled in the classic fashion of a town on the western frontier. False-front buildings faced the mountains of Glacier Park; behind the buildings lay the rolling prairies of eastern Montana. The Glacier Park Hotel and Great Northern Railway complex across the tracks added a worldly and aesthetic air to the community. No churches stood in East Glacier, but people held church services in the lodge and in the school. The railroad men boarded at the classic inn, the "Frozen Dog," named for the temperature of its sleeping rooms.

Like most residents, Dan and Doris easily found jobs during the summer season, with the influx of tourists. In his diary the day after they moved into town, Dan wrote that he started work with the Glacier Transportation Company at $135 per month and mentioned that he loaded 4,000 pounds of lumber for a construction project at Many Glacier. He received a check from the Park Service for $135, and sent a $1,000 check "for 20 shares prepaid in the Security Building and Loan Association." Dan sold the 1922 Dodge touring car for $34 and banked the money. The couple was accumulating investments at a surprising rate considering their youth.

Doris went to work for the Glacier Park Hotel Company again for $35 a month, this time in the bakery at the big hotel kitchen. Because she was married, however, she no longer took part in the single employees' social activities like dances at the hotel and group hikes. This time it was a job, not a way of life.

Doris also returned to her old night job at Mike's Place, the center of Glacier Park culture, for $2.50 a shift. Mike's had burned in about 1924 and was rebuilt by Mike Shannon, whom Doris had come to know well, into a large dance hall which often attracted crowds of up to 200 couples from a radius of 60 miles. Mike's quietly served as the bootleg capital of the area during this period of illegal booze and also featured gambling and roller skating. Doris, who had developed a reputation for wit, occasionally talked with James Willard Schultz and his son Lone Wolf when they visited Mike's. She read Schultz's books and enjoyed them, but disagreed with some of his interpretations of Indian life. She knew Browning almost as well as East Glacier; it was the closest real town and the home of many of her Blackfeet friends.

Most of East Glacier's year-long residents, including Dan and Doris, supplemented their income by bootlegging in the summer, cutting wood in the fall, and cutting ice on Two Medicine Lake in the winter for shipment by rail to the east. Because of prohibition, the town was occasionally visited by "revenuers," but these men never seemed to notice anything unlawful there. Newspapers carried stories of bootleg busts in nearby northern Idaho such as the 1929 arrest of the mayor, chief of police, and entire board of trustees

Dan worked for the Glacier Transportation Company during 1928 and 1929. He hauled supplies to every corner of the park using this 1922 Dodge truck.

of Mullan, Idaho, for "a widespread conspiracy to violate prohibition laws," but in the towns along the edge of Glacier Park, bootlegging was ignored, maybe because of the influence of Great Northern's president and chief Glacier Park tourism promoter Louis Hill.

With their vibrant youth and somewhat rebellious ways, the Huffines quickly integrated into the community. They bought the house they were renting and directed their energies to making it livable.

"Our house on the edge of East Glacier was really just a little cracker box," remembered Doris. "It had one long room and two little teeny rooms. It didn't have any doors on the inside, just openings. No one had lived in the house for a long time."

As history buffs, Dan and Doris enjoyed East Glacier and its rich mix of cultures, and they learned that the house they'd bought had an interesting background. Early resident Horace Clarke had once been shot in the face and left for dead by the Blackfeet, leading to the massacre of a Blackfeet camp along the Marias River. Clarke was granted 160 acres of land near what became East Glacier under the Federal Indian Allotment Act of 1887. Around 1910, he sold 60 acres to the Great Northern Railroad Company, which become the site of the Glacier Park Hotel and nine-hole golf course.

Horace's sister, Isabel, married Thomas Dawson and in 1893 they established a ranch along Midvale Creek, about a mile west of what became East Glacier, on land that adjoined the Clarke homestead. Dawson Pass and Isabel Lake in Glacier Park bear the names of these early residents. In the early 1920s the Clarke-Dawson Cemetery was established on a piece of Horace's land. Horace eventually married Blackfeet Margaret Full Kill and they had several children, including John Clarke, who became famous working with wood. Dan and Doris's little house stood on the edge of East Glacier behind John's studio.

Because the house had been vacant for some time, townspeople became accustomed to cutting through the yard on their way to work. At times, these trespassers would use the outhouse, too. This practice continued even after the Huffines took possession of the property, and nothing seemed to dissuade the offenders. One day when a Blackfeet tribal member, a frequent "visitor," came through the yard, Doris finally did something about it.

"It was early in the morning, nobody was around, and I looked out and there she came, across the back of our place," remembered Doris. "Our house was right on the front of our lot. There was a cabin on the back of our lot and this outhouse sat in the middle. She walked right up to the outhouse and went in; it wasn't locked. Well this had been going on too long, so I just decided that that's enough. I just didn't like her using our outhouse as she pleased."

Doris strode up to the outhouse and without warning hooked the padlock across the door, then ran back to the house. Soon the woman realized she was locked in and began lunging at the door.

"That door just bowed out like it was going to burst out of the hinges," remembered Doris. "I just can't imagine to this day how she could shake the house like that; she was a powerful woman. The darned old building would rock like it was going to fall over frontwards, then it would settle back in, and here it would go again."

"So then Dan got up," continued Doris, "and here the outhouse was still rocking. And he said, 'What is going on out there?' and I said, 'Dan, you've got to go out there and let that Indian woman out of the outhouse.' and he said, 'No sir, I'm not getting in on this deal at all. You got her in there and you'll get her out. I won't have anything to do with it.'

"That was true, I sure got her in there," Doris admitted years later.

Finally, she formulated a plan and worked up the courage to see it through. She walked over to the outhouse, unlocked the padlock, undid the hinge, and opened the door. She looked in and said, "Good gracious, are you in here? How did you get in here?" The woman replied that she was cutting through the yard and just had to stop.

Doris replied, "Boy, you better not do that again, or else I might go to work and leave you in there forever."

The plan apparently worked, though the Indian woman was by no means the last stranger to make an unscheduled stop at the outhouse.

Despite such occurrences, Dan and Doris found they liked owning property and within a year the couple had bought from Jessie Paul another house for $675. In his diary, Dan noted that he "ordered a new $54.85 range from Sears in Spokane and $12.00 of linoleum from Ward's in Great Falls." Later, Dan built yet another house on the back part of one of their lots. They rented out two of the houses and lived in the other and spent a lot of time trying to make the homes more livable. There was certainly a lot of room for improvement. The house in which Dan and Doris lived was not secure, for instance, and Doris often worried at night. Indeed, Doris's apprehension, coupled with Dan's propensity for shooting first and asking questions later, nearly resulted in tragedy.

"The window above our bed had no screen, it was just open all the time," remembered Doris. "One night I woke up and said, 'Dan, somebody just now went by the window.'

"You know he just grabbed that old six shooter and bang! out the window. He shot so quick it scared me. Here it was an Indian kid from down town and he'd been sent to deliver a message to someone who lived in behind us. And instead of cutting through where he should he missed and cut right through our yard, right under our window. That pretty near scared the kid to death when Dan shot.

"So the kid went back down town and said, 'Oh boy, I'll never go near there again. That Huffine will shoot you before you can think.'"

In Dan's work hauling freight for the Glacier Transportation Company he traveled to all the same locations along the east side of the park that he had visited as a ranger and tour bus driver. His job with the company kept him busy. On one typical day, Dan noted that he "Drove to Saint Mary in #16, moved out all machinery, 18 slips, 2 wagons, 2 road plows, and gobs of

Doris and Dan enjoyed the outdoors summer and winter during their years at East Glacier.

odds and ends. Cleaned out about 1 ton of loose hay and moved 65 bales back to the north wall."

Because of his disappointment in not becoming a permanent ranger, it was hard for Dan to accept his role hauling supplies to ranger stations and trail camps. Although Dan often claimed he didn't care about being a ranger, each year he took the ranger exam and privately longed to secure a ranger position. One February Dan traveled to Kalispell on the Empire Builder train and took the oral exam for park ranger. "Nothing to it," he wrote. "Two fire questions, two first-aid questions and some reprimand for past favors. Will pass if it pleases them to pass me."

That April, Dan accepted a job with the Park Service at $4.48 per day hauling hay, oats, gasoline, grub, lumber, and other supplies to Many Glacier, Saint Mary, and various trail camps. He wrote a note to R. Vincent, assistant superintendent of the park, noting that he accepted the job "with the provision that I be free to accept the Ranger position I have taken the Civil Service exam for, if I should be appointed." The appointment never came. Dan's sister, Irma, believed that, even though Dan and Doris gave other reasons, Dan wasn't able to get a permanent appointment because of

Chalets at Sun Camp. One spring Dan drove a company boat to check on the camp and found that a grizzly had wrecked a Glacier Transportation Company cabin located near these chalets.

his lack of education.

Ironically, Dan encountered more grizzlies in his jobs hauling for the Transportation Company and the Park Service than he did in his former job as backcountry ranger.

One spring Dan traveled across Saint Mary Lake in the transportation company boat to get some powder to blast snow drifts on Hudson Bay Divide. When he reached Sun Camp, he stopped in at a transportation company cabin near the chalets. The cabin consisted of an office and kitchen with a pit down under the floor for food storage.

"I got up there," remembered Dan, "and went to the cabin, which was about 200 yards from the lake, to eat my dinner but there wasn't much of a cabin left. An old grizzly had knocked the window out, pulled the wall down, went in and ripped everything to pieces. He'd taken a big old army ranger cabinet and tore it apart. He'd found the flour and sugar that had been kept in the oven to keep it away from mice, ate all of it he could hold, then spread the rest all over. Before he went out he pulled all the bedding down that was hanging down from the rafters and ripped it to pieces."

The grizzly had torn down a stovepipe that extended up at least as high as Dan could reach toward the eaves of the building. Dan felt nervous because it was clear that the bear had just left. "He must have been a monster," remembered Dan. "He couldn't find his way out so he bashed the back wall down and made himself a door. And me with only a .38 special. I wasn't in any hurry but I got out of there pretty fast."

On the cruise back down along the lake that same day Dan saw a grizzly

During the winter of 1928/29, Dan and Doris managed the Donaldson's Bakery in Bozeman for Dan's uncle.

and three cubs north of the mouth of Red Eagle Creek. Dan slowly drifted towards the grizzlies until he'd approached to within about 100 yards of them across a shallow bay. Remembered Dan, "That old sow decided that If I wanted to see her she'd come out to meet me, so I left there too."

Overall, however, Dan's experience with grizzlies was typical of the earlier time period in the park when bears rarely clashed with people. "I've met very few grizzlies face to face and when I did, they went their way and I went mine, and both of us hurried right along doing it," he said.

Dan spent plenty of time outdoors. He had been a fisherman since boyhood and enjoyed it as a sport and as a way to obtain food. He and Doris often fished the Two Medicine River, only a short walk from their house. In one journal entry Dan mentioned catching several fish up to two pounds in the river. The couple also enjoyed fishing the other streams and lakes along the east side of the park.

"I often helped Frank Harrison haul whitefish caught in Saint Mary Lake for the restaurant. One morning Frank came in, madder than a wet hen. A big mackinaw trout got in his net and whipped it to a frazzle, just tore it all to pieces but still didn't get away. That fish weighed about 35 pounds.

"That's a lot bigger than anything I ever caught with a rod. I was raised flyfishing on small streams around Bozeman, so I often fished all around the park. I'd fish those little holes on the stream below Many Glacier and did well. Swiftcurrent Lake was good fishing but sometimes I'd go with

While in Bozeman, the couple finally had professional portraits taken by a local photographer.

those Scandihoovians out there in a boat and they'd pull fish out and pull fish out, but I'd never get a bite. But then I'd take them down to where I fished and they couldn't catch fish there; they were too fast for them."

Although Dan never got another ranger position with the Park Service, he did land a job as a fire guard. During the severe fire season of 1929, Dan worked for the Park Service as a fire guard for $4.42 a day. During the first few days, Dan noted that he "Made and filled pack boxes with grub — took truck out for try out, trying to loosen clutch on Ford and dropped screw-driver in transmission case so had to take transmission cover off. Loaded up Ford truck #10 with grub, tools, pump and hose ready to go any time a fire starts. Nothing to do so slept for a while this P.M."

In his notebook, Dan kept a typed guide to firefighting issued by the Park Service. The guide, which Dan studied thoroughly, describes the direct, two-foot, parallel and indirect methods of digging fire lines. It also lists advice on crew size and choosing the method of attacking the fire. Dan had little firefighting experience before becoming a fire guard but he had studied firefighting techniques each time he prepared to take the Civil Service exam for park ranger.

"Fire broke out at Summit," Dan wrote on July 24, and on July 25 he wrote that the fire was still going good. On July 27 he met and received advice from the assistant superintendent of the Lewis and Clark Forest, Mr. Moore. On July 28, Dan "went to bed at 8:30 p.m., Morris called me at 11 p.m. to go out on fire on Mt. Henry trail. Took truck 3/4 mile above saw-mill, walked 1/2 mile found fellow and girl from Hotel with campfire just out. Home at 1:00 a.m." Dan had lost a little sleep over a false alarm on that occasion, but there were other instances where his presence helped make a difference.

On August 23, 1929, for instance, Dan received notice of a fire above Lubec. He "went out with truck 8 1/2 miles took pump and hose one mile up on speeder, had fire along RR. Checked at 8 p.m. left man on pump and fire going good in brush and scrub timber east and south. Men busy all night — no water there for pump." Dan mentioned fires around Nyack and McDonald Lake. He mentioned that it was "hot as blazes." The fire situation continued to get worse. On August 26 a 50-man crew came to help, and on August 27 Dan took a telegram to Superintendent Moore which ordered more patrolmen stationed at strategic points and closed the forest to all travel.

Dan finally got to see Doris when a fire broke out near their house in East Glacier, along Midvale Creek. "We put one pump down to the creek — it was only about a quarter of a mile from our place," Dan remembered later. "We didn't have anything to eat for 24 hours. Finally the ranger, Tom Whitcraft, came down and I said 'Hey, when are we going to get something to eat around here. We haven't eaten since last night at supper.' I'd been there all day listening to those pumps roar, getting a splitting headache. Doris had listened to the pump running in the creek and she thought about bringing me something to eat but she thought, 'Oh there isn't any use doing that, they always feed men on a fire line real well.'"

On August 30, Dan and the crew fought an unusual fire that was burning underground. "We had our pumps sitting by a peat bog," he remembered. You could run your hoses eight feet deep and put the fire out, turn around twice, and there was fire coming out of that hole again."

As the fire danger worsened, most of the men and equipment were sent to West Glacier. A fire near Columbia Falls, 10 miles south of Glacier Park, swept northeast, jumped the Middle Fork of the Flathead River, burned

In the late 1920s, the eclectic town of East Glacier drew park workers and visitors, residents from ranches, hamlets, and the Blackfeet Reservation.

into the park and rushed across the Continental Divide. The fire had begun on August 16, entered the park on August 21 and raged out of control. The fire burned thousands of virgin western red cedar and hemlock in the Lake McDonald area. Large numbers of men attacked the fire, but it was the weather that finally snuffed it out and put an end to the fire season, too. Snow fell on September 2 and continued for several days. Dan lost his job on September 6.

During that summer, 50,000 acres burned in the park compared to an average of 5,000 acres per year during the previous eight years.

Each fall in those early years, Dan and Doris scrambled for odd jobs. It didn't get any easier starting in 1929 when the country entered the Great Depression. "We were always out of our summer jobs by early September, because they were tied to the park season," remembered Doris. "We raised chickens on the side and butchered them out. We'd order hundreds of chicks at a time." In one diary entry, Dan noted that Doris got in 311 heavy mixed chicks from a mail-order house. They sold butchered chickens for $.75 a piece and eggs for $.25 a dozen.

"During the winter there just weren't any jobs, unless you were very lucky," recalled Doris. During the winter of 1928-29, Dan's uncle and aunt asked the couple to come to Bozeman to run the bakery while they went to California. As Dan and Doris made plans to leave for Bozeman, Dan got word that his stepmother, Lena, had died, just a year after Dan's half-brother Curtis's death. Dan had now lost his mother, stepmother, and five brothers, leaving only himself, his father, 7-year old Irma, and his infant sister Jackie.

The couple boarded the train bound for Bozeman the next day.

"She willed herself to die," remembered Dan's sister, Irma, describing Lena's death. "Her mother had told Lena that Curtis would go to hell because he wasn't being raised in the church. So Lena said Curtis needed her more than her two living daughters did. When company would come over, Lena would just shove Jackie into Dad's arms, run into her room, and wail." After arriving in Bozeman, Doris and Dan cleaned up at Dan's father's ranch and helped out where they could.

The couple started an apprenticeship at Beech Huffine's bakery two weeks before Christmas. The bakery, known as Donaldson's, advertised "Donaldson's Big Boy Bread, just like Mother's." The bakery promised "special orders filled promptly."

Dan's uncle and his wife left for California and left them in charge. On an average day Dan and Doris took in about $20. On January 9 Dan wrote, "$20 today, every one quit eating. Have 140 loaves of bread left tonight." Dan and Doris often went to dances, getting home at 2 a.m., and they watched movies at the Ellen theater. On January 20 they watched "Companion Marriage," and Dan, who had begun to refer to Doris as Dorothy or Dody, noted in underlined script as if it were a big event, "Dorothy took a bath". On January 22 Dan noted his 24th birthday; he received a "fine leather billfold from Dorothy," and on the next day noted that the temperature dropped to 40 degrees below zero. On January 30 the couple watched "Forgotten Faces" at the Ellen, and made 12 dozen cupcakes for a special order. On February 1 Dan noted "Dody's birthday." Doris downplayed her birthdays, often ignoring them as part of her attempt to cover her past. She represented herself as Dan's age, four years younger than she actually was. On February 2 Dan wrote, "Ground hog day — yes he saw his shadow. This was the big day of our season, $54.50; had a special sale of coffee cake and sold 28 of them at $.20 each. Sold 40 cakes and 500 loaves of bread — had 25 loaves of bread left this evening."

In late March, after the successful stint at the bakery, Dan and Doris rode the train back to East Glacier. They stopped in Great Falls on the way and went to the "first talking movie — real good. Cost $.50 each."

That summer the couple returned to their jobs with the Glacier Park Hotel Company and Glacier Transportation Company. They attended dances often, hiked the trails on the east side of the park, and enjoyed visiting with the tourists and young park workers. More of the same until the summer ended in a rush. In late September of 1929, the season ended and Doris lost her jobs at the Glacier Park Hotel, Mike's Place and at the Post Office, and Dan finished his job with the Glacier Transportation Company. The couple resigned themselves to an uneventful winter. Then, according to Doris, came the offer that made them part of the famous, trans-park, Going-to-the-Sun Road's history.

"A man came to the door one day," remembered Doris, "and said to me, 'Can you cook? There's a job open in the crew surveying the trans-park highway, and I can give you $100 a month. I'll let Dan go with you too, and he can flunkie.' The man didn't tell me why they needed a new cook. I found that out later."

Doris said later that $100 a month was a big sum for a young woman to earn then, so she accepted.

Earlier that fall, Dan had asked about work on the survey crew. According to Dan's diary, the chief engineer, A.V. Emery, had told him that he had enough men on the survey line and that he already had a good cook. So Dan and Doris were not expecting the offer. On October 17, however, Dan wrote, "We took jobs at Sun Camp with Emery. Dody to cook at $100 per month and me to work on the line at $75 per and board."

But the next day a disappointed Dan wrote, "Emery couldn't get permission to take out man and wife on payroll. OK for Doris to come and cook. I can help cook and help around camp for board."

Dan drew his wages from part-time work with the Glacier Transportation Company and the couple prepared to leave for the surveyors' staging area, Sun Camp.

Engineers faced tremendous challenges during the construction of the trans-mountain Going-to-the-Sun Road. Tunnels and arch culverts were required to traverse the steep cliffs on either side of Logan Pass.

11
Bull Cook, 1929-32

"Why, while we were sleeping against the outside of the tents, the grizzlies were digging right under our noses. The surveyors were getting nervous, I'll tell you."

"Bears, bears, and more bears. They were everywhere, running around like mice."

That's how Doris described the situation at the camp along Reynolds Creek, where she and Dan cooked in the fall of 1929 for the crew surveying the east portion of the Going-to-the-Sun Road, originally called the Transmountain Highway.

The road, probably the best known feature in Glacier National Park, winds 51 miles east to west around glacier-carved peaks of the Lewis Overthrust. The road climbs to 6,664 feet where it crosses the Continental Divide at Logan Pass, named Misum Oksokwi, or "Ancient Road" by the Blackfeet. According to legend, west side tribes like the Snake and Kootenai crossed the Backbone here into buffalo country. Road engineers, after looking at several east-west routes including Swiftcurrent Pass, Gunsight Pass and a torturous route up the cascading Logan Creek, selected the route as difficult but possible to build and a good choice to provide views of the park's glaciers and mountains.

"The grandeur of the east side will be tempered by the more smiling and equally lovely western slopes," wrote novelist Mary Roberts Rinehart about the route in the 1918 book, "Tenting Tonight." "And when, between the east and the west sides, there is constructed the great motor-highway which will lead across the range, we shall have, perhaps, the most scenic motor-road in the United States..."

Pack trains carried supplies from the Roes Creek area (site of present-day Rising Sun Campground) to the survey camp on Reynolds Creek. The hard-working surveyors had immense appetites, according to Doris, and Bureau of Public Roads Foreman A.V. Emery insisted on the best quality foods.

Many who have seen the road, opened for public travel in 1933, call it an engineering feat equaled by few. In 1924, Park Service Director Stephen T. Mather called for the survey and major construction to begin. Frank Kittredge of the Bureau of Public Roads was assigned as the locating engineer, and he was frankly in awe of the area and of the task before him.

In a later report, Kittredge wrote: "On a beautiful fall day (September 16, 1924), Superintendent Charles Kraebel drove me to the beginning of the proposed operations — along the shores of beautiful Lake McDonald fringed with dense forests of evergreens, stately tamarack and clusters of already coloring quaking aspens; thence, along McDonald Creek with its falls and tumbling white water as it cascaded through the canyon. And rounding a bend in the road there, squarely across the canyon, stood the great wall, the backbone of the Continental Divide, here called 'The Garden Wall..' How to carry into the roadbuilding these great, intangible values for the inspiration of people without sacrificing the very values we came for

The Reynolds Creek survey camp consisted of a line of 16- by-16-foot and 16-by-24-foot tents. Doris said that she and Dan lived in the first tent on the left. Black bears and grizzly bears fed on the camp's garbage dump in the timber behind the tents.

Heavy snows and grizzlies forced the crew to move down to Sun Camp in early November.

was the problem of the engineer.

"The task was a little bit terrifying, inasmuch as it was already fall and the winter closes in very early in this high altitude and far northern climate. But neither Director Mather nor Dr. Hawes [Kittredge's boss at the Bureau of Public Roads] said anything about wanting the survey if convenient. I was sent there to make the survey, period. Mr. Mather wanted a survey which would enable the Park Service to let a contract for construction the following spring."

By the fall of 1929, construction was just beginning on the eastern portion of the approach to Logan Pass. Dan wrote on October 19 that he and Doris had caught a ride at 1 p.m. to the end of the Sun Road in packer Bruce Wert's truck earlier that day. Wert brought supplies to the construction crew every few days, but he and his truck could only go so far — since the construction crew was even then building the only road that would ever cross that intimidating terrain. In the meantime, it took a string of pack animals to get supplies in.

"There weren't any roads," remembered Doris. "You either had to walk the trail or go by boat across Saint Mary Lake to Sun Camp, then up the

It was common practice to feed bears such as these black bears along road-ways and around Going-To-The-Sun Road survey and construction camps. Doris believed that feeding garbage to the black bears was good policy, and allowed humans and bears to coexist.   Park Service officials condoned the policy around the camps. Grizzlies, however, were a different matter, as Doris and the survey crew learned.

trail to the survey camp at Reynolds Creek."

Doris was wary of boats, knew the nature of the winds on Saint Mary Lake, and had heard stories of terrifying trips across the 10-mile long, 289-foot deep glacial lake in the barge. "I wasn't about to cross the lake in that scow," she said later.

Doris's concern was apparently justified, based on a description by Kittredge of a fall ride across the lake in 1924. Kittredge and his crew crossed the lake by boat to pack out the camp of a marooned survey crew who had been snowed in after they crossed the divide from the west side.

"As we left in the bright sun of early morning," Kittredge wrote, "the watchman's parting advice was that if we felt any wind to pull for the shore at once; that the storms came up suddenly and the lake could be very rough and dangerous in a few minutes.

"It was a superb boat ride through a rugged winter setting, we taking turns rowing and steering," continued Kittredge. "We rowed past the nar-rows and past the little island and within perhaps two miles of our destina-tion, when all of a sudden I, being warm from rowing, felt a cool breath of air on my neck. I remarked to Jim that I felt a little puff of air and he had better steer us toward shore. We took a diagonal course, but it wasn't five

St. Mary Lake is known for its dangerous waves formed by powerful winds sweeping along the Continental Divide.

The Bureau of Public Roads scow transported the surveyors and their equipment from Sun Camp when the crew finished work in mid-November. Doris wrote on the back of the photo, "It was cold and I refused to ride in the scow, so I walked the bank."

Line showing the Going-to-the-Sun Road survey route on the east side of Logan Pass, with Going-to-the-Sun Mountain in the background. The photo was taken just below the present east tunnel and looks east towards the Reynolds Creek Survey Camp. (Glacier National Park Photo, from the final report of the location survey, transmountain road, 1929/30, Bureau of Public Roads.)

minutes before we were shipping water from the waves. We knew we could not get into the trough without being swamped. We knew we could not go straight forward against the obviously increasing wind without being swamped. Our only choice was to try to turn and go with the wind and hope that we could reach the shelter of the island and then the headlands of the narrows. This we tried to do by rowing as hard as I could and Jim bailing water as fast as he could and by good fortune we reached the shelter of the island and then made the promontory at the narrows."

Kittredge and his companion then floundered along the water's edge through snow, rowing at times in quieter bays, until finally in the late afternoon they reached the landing place near Sun Camp.

Doris was not willing to repeat any such aquatic adventure , so she and Dan walked along with the pack string about three miles to the Sun Ranger Station, arriving about 6:30 p.m. They were up early the next morning and packed the three miles to the survey camp along the clear, rushing waters of Reynolds Creek, called Beaver Woman Creek by the Blackfeet after a noted natoyi', or sacred woman.

"At the camp there was a line of 16-by-16 [foot] and 16-by-24 [foot] canvas tents," remembered Doris. "We cooked in a tent with a dirt floor. The tents were on the edge of this thick timber with logs criss-crossed on the ground. You could barely get through it. The tents were set up right along Reynolds Creek so we could have the water to use in the tents. You had to cross a little foot bridge to get from the trail to the tents."

It didn't take long for Doris and Dan to discover that their new job was not going to be easy. They rushed to get lunch and dinner for 22 men the first day and worked long into the night to clean up and get organized. Dan remembered that the big eaters included the four or five Cree Indians among the crew.

"You couldn't imagine what those guys could eat," said Doris. "Once, the boss decided that he wanted to have a big 20-pound ham for supper, all spiced up with cloves and all that stuff," remembered Dan. "We figured we'd have meat enough for sandwiches for tomorrow. Well, those guys ate up that whole ham, licked it up right down to the bone."

At another meal the men ate several whole hams, a turkey, cans of vegetables, and more than a dozen loaves of bread. Doris rushed to keep up with their appetites, cooking on a primitive folding wood stove and oven. Supervising engineer A.V. Emery insisted on excellent meals for the surveyors, including fresh fruit pies, eggs, and as much food as they wished to eat.

As much as they might grouse about it later though, the two camp cooks had it pretty easy compared to some of their earlier jobs. As Dan put it: "Doris and I had all day to fool around. We'd wrap up the workers' sandwiches the evening before. They'd stop in, eat their breakfast, grab their sandwiches and take off. Then they'd be back about 5:30 or 6:00. We'd usually hike around, go to Saint Mary Falls."

There was certainly much to see. The camp stood at the base of magnificent Going-to-the-Sun Mountain, regarded by the Blackfeet as, next to Chief Mountain, the most beautiful of all the mountains in the area. James Willard Schultz claimed to have named the mountain on a winter hunting trip to the "Walled in Lake" with his Blackfeet friend, Tail-Feathers-Coming-Over-The-Hill, as they sat near a fire eating cuts from a bighorn ram they had killed on the cliffs above the lake.

The road surveyors' jobs on the steep route were hard and dangerous, which probably led to their big appetites, as well as to their sometimes erratic behavior. "One day, an axe man returned to headquarters in mid-day," wrote Kittredge about one incident. "He said he couldn't take it; that while on the line, he looked down immediately below him and saw the tree tops going round and round in the breeze; and he began to go round and round; he got down on his hands and knees and crawled back to where the slopes were not so steep and just came right on in for his pay."

In another incident, Kittredge described how a resident engineer's request for a raise for his crew was turned down by his supervisor. Later, the supervisor accompanied him to a work site.

"Upon turning around, the resident engineer observed his boss clinging to the wall, knees trembling, and in fear of falling. This seemed like an opportune moment, so the resident engineer, while steadying his chief, quietly remarked, 'How about that raise for the boys?' The response from the boss, grand man that he was, was quick and effective, 'Give them anything you want.'"

In addition to the sheer altitude, bears posed another danger to the survey crew. "When I got to the camp, I found out why they needed a new cook," remembered Doris. "The bears just got too thick. The woman who was there before me was making pies one day on the work table against the side of the tent. A black bear came along, ripped a hole in the side of the tent, and stuck its paw into the pie dough. That woman got desperate and said she'd had enough. So that was that. She took off and walked the whole six miles back to the road."

The Park Service issued 14 pages of regulations covering the camps. Among other things, the guidelines called for landscape preservation, clean tents for cooking, dining, and sleeping, and proper sewage and garbage disposal.

Workers ignored the garbage disposal guidelines, however. In his diary, Dan noted that black bears stayed around camp, feeding on garbage discarded by the crew. Doris had no fear of black bears and considered it natural to allow the bears to range close to the tent.

"The blacks never bothered us to speak of," remembered Dan. "We just took them for granted. They'd be around all afternoon and early evening. One of the rangers at Belly River had a malamute, and we borrowed that dog to help keep the bears away from the tent."

"The men would go into the raw timber behind the tents and just dump the garbage every day," remembered Doris. "We didn't have to haul it away like people have to now. We didn't have to fuss at all, we let the animals have it. There were lots and lots of black bears and they always fed on the garbage, day and night. We didn't think anything of them. All they did was eat the garbage; they never bothered us around the tents at all. The boss, Mr. Emery, had a police dog that was supposed to help keep the bears away from the tents. The dog, Mollie, wasn't afraid of black bears."

"The black and brown bears [cinnamon-colored black bears] were not so bad after it was found that they could be best handled by being plentifully fed," Emery wrote later in his engineering report. "Since the harming of animals within the park is prohibited, many schemes were devised to prevent depredations by the bears. Meat houses and kitchens had doors and sidewalls studded with nail points.

"Finally, the cooks and flunkies found that systematic feeding of the refuse to the bears kept them from pillaging," Emery continued. "At the tunnel camp it was usual to see 10 or 12 large bears hanging around the cookhouse at meal times, waiting to receive their share. One bear's special place was against the jamb of the back door of the kitchen where he sat perfectly at ease, and more afraid of other bears than of the men.

"However, in the case of the grizzly bears an entirely different animal had to be dealt with. When, in the late fall of 1927 they began to invade the camp of the Russian stationmen at Logan Pass, the park ranger was required as a guard to keep the bears away and to quell the fear of the workmen."

In a passage deleted from an engineering report, Frank Kittredge described a similar situation at the camps in 1924. "The bears were something of a problem as well as amusement around the camp. At first, they were a little timid, but they soon lost their fear and assumed quite a dictatorial attitude with respect to the cook and anyone else who got in their way." Kittredge then described an incident of a bear charging a cook, and added, "That, together with other incidents, was a little too much, so authority and a rifle were obtained from the park superintendent and bear trouble was ended so far as he was concerned."

At Doris's camp, grizzlies began causing problems in early November.

"All of a sudden one evening we looked out and we saw grizzlies, eight or nine of them, eating the garbage." remembered Doris. "You couldn't imagine how close they were — no more than 30 yards from the tents. Once the grizzlies moved in, the black bears moved out. We never saw a black bear after that.

"Mollie, Emery's dog, lost her nerve right away; she knew the difference between black bears and grizzlies. She wouldn't bark at the grizzlies or chase them."

Doris continued: "In the morning when you went outside and looked around you could see where the grizzlies had dug around the sides of the tents where the dog had buried bones. Why, while we were sleeping against the outside of the tents, the grizzlies were digging right under our noses. The surveyors were getting nervous, I'll tell you."

Dan too had his share of bear tales: "Once, a grizzly dug right under our double cot we slept on in the cook tent. That was bad enough, but when they got to rattlin' around the boss's tent why that was too much. He said, 'We're getting out of here.' Once in a while we'd get out there and shine a flashlight out toward the garbage pit, just a short distance away. An old bear would just stand up and snort at you, then you went back where you belonged. It was kind of crazy."

In his diary entry on November 5, Dan wrote, "Bears tore up everything outside. Even dug up bones Mollie had buried. We're going to move the camp." Then in big letters, he wrote, "TWO GRIZZLY BEAR OUT AT THE GARBAGE PIT."

Doris remembered the incident that sapped the courage of most of the camp members.

"One night we were woken up by the worst clatter you ever heard," she recalled. "Somebody screamed, 'Bears, bears, big and better bears!' A grizzly had charged and rammed into the side of a tent, knocking a couple of sleeping surveyors out of their cots and knocking over the tin wood stove.

Dan is seen here driving a Fordson tractor in his job at the East Glacier golf course located near the Glacier Park Hotel.

After that night, some of the men just wanted to leave." Doris said that the anxiety of the crew increased as fast as the snow depth during the next few days.

On November 6, Dan wrote, "Saw two grizzlies tonight. One started toward Emery and me. We sure kicked dust in his face getting away." Probably not by coincidence, the crew abandoned the camp at Reynolds Creek the morning after Emery and Dan had been charged by the grizzly. Emery had decided that the grizzlies were a threat to enter the tents at night.

"I thought that the men were jumping the gun," Doris said. "I felt that as long as we fed the bears, we'd be all right. But Emery was the boss."

Doris knew that once the camp was moved, it wouldn't be long before she'd be laid off and lose her coveted wages of about $3 a day. "The bears really weren't a problem as far as I was concerned. In those years [of the Depression], you weren't afraid of anything if they would give you something to live on."

The surveyors must have been impressed with Doris's bravado among the bears at Reynolds Creek. According to an entry in Dan's diary, the surveyors dubbed her "Bull Cook." Nonetheless, caution prevailed and the camp was moved.

"We loaded everything up and hauled it all down to the ranger station at Sun Camp," Doris remembered. We set up our headquarters there, cooking operation and all. The men had to walk the extra miles to the job each day."

Dan described Sun Camp as "a beautiful place, right down along the mountainside, close to the lake. There was a big hotel and chalets. It stood

Dan drove this 1924 White truck and hauled supplies for the Glacier Park Transportation Company. He also stocked fish in the park's lakes and streams.

near Sun Point."

Doris, as usual, looked to animals for entertainment. "That stay at Sun Camp was something," Doris remembered. "The weasels seemed to have their headquarters at the ranger station, too. There was a tiny hill, like a little mound, in front of the ranger station and it was undermined by weasels. I never saw so many weasels in my life; there must have been 20 or 30 of them at one time perched on that mound. They would just come out of there, sit up, and look around.

"Dan and the packer thought it would be a big joke to see if they could snare the weasels," Doris continued. "So they'd lay out there and try to jerk snares they had set around the little holes when a weasel stuck his head out. The first one they got, they didn't want to let go because they thought it was such a feat to catch it.

"They brought him into the washroom of the ranger station, but after they let him loose in there, no one would use the room because the weasel was in there. So they had to try to get him out. When they opened the door and went in, he'd disappear; they just couldn't find him at all. They finally figured out that the weasel went through the toilet and got in the pipe gooseneck. That's where he would hide. One toilet was dry and he went down the empty pipe. How would he know to do that? They finally got him out of there."

According to Dan's diary entry, the crew spent only five days at the Sun Ranger Station before they finished work for the year.

"It wasn't long before the snow got too deep for the men to work and they had to give up," remembered Doris. "We walked out. I wasn't going to ride that scow across the lake for anything."

Dan and Doris met the crew at the foot of Saint Mary Lake. "We took the

Back home in East Glacier, Dan and Doris kept busy with chores around their home. For several winters, Dan painted trail and ranger station signs for the Park Service.

scow out of the water and turned it over," wrote Dan on November 12. "Dody and I came in to East Glacier with Emery. We got a flat tire on the Hudson Bay Divide." Dan noted the following day in his diary that the crew had given them about $50 worth of food left over from the camp.

In the back of Dan's diary for 1929, Dan and Doris summarized their income for the year. Doris had made about $150 in wages working at Mike's Place and at the post office throughout the year, and about $100 cooking for the survey crew. So, as it turned out, the cooking job was an important part of their income. Between them, they'd made $1,567, a good sum when hamburgers cost just a dime. Dan did very well selling shirts, coats, shoes and hosiery and often noted in his diary commissions of up to $5 in a day. In his job hauling supplies around the park he doubled as a traveling apparel salesman.

By Christmas of 1929, it had snowed six feet in East Glacier according to Dan. Goose was the main attraction for Christmas dinner; old friend Lou Hansen visited. On the last day of December, Dan wrote, "Another year gone. Did well, lived well and have been well. Have two houses and lots, 1 Ford and the first place pretty well fixed up. Hope 1930 treats us as good as 1929 has."

Life in East Glacier did have its hardships. The weather along the east slopes of the divide was extreme and unpredictable. One February a "chinook," a warm, fierce mid-winter wind, hit East Glacier with such force that Dan turned back in his attempt to walk to town. Chickens, dogs and other animals were seen blowing across the landscape like tumbleweed in the estimated 100-mile-an-hour gusts. Within a few hours, the temperature rose from below zero to 46 degrees above zero.

One March, Dan wrote, "Started snowing at 3 p.m. and what a snow — dirty! Melted a dish pan of it and the water was black with mud in the bottom of the pan. I say the dust was carried over from the east at a high altitude and dropped when it hit the storm." This "dirty snow" probably was tied to the great drought, which caused much of eastern Montana, the Dakotas and the Great Plains to be called by the new name of the Dust

Bowl during the Depression years.

The weather brought its share of illness to Dan and Doris, but it was usually taken in stride. Early in 1930 Dan and Doris left for Great Falls to take in two "talkie" movies and see about Doris's sore throat. On a Friday, doctors at Deaconess Hospital in downtown Great Falls removed Doris's tonsils. By Saturday Doris was feeling better and was able to eat a soft egg and a half-pint of soup. Dan paid the $10 hospital bill and the couple returned to East Glacier.

In the fall that year, after Doris and Dan lost their summer jobs in the park, Dan went to work for Joe Waring on the little nine-hole golf course that had recently been built near the Glacier Park Hotel. East Glacier seemed a strange location for a golf course, on the edge of a mountainous national park bordering the Blackfeet Indian Reservation. Ironically, the old North Indian Trail ran across the seventh fairway. Louis Hill, the "Godfather of Glacier," bankrolled the golf course and owned a summer cabin on the first fairway. Dan worked on equipment in the shop, hauled manure, worked on roads around the course and the hotel, and rolled the fairways driving a Fordson tractor.

In his summary for 1930, Dan reported that they sold 273 chickens for $158, and again did well on commissions for shirt and shoe sales. With his income from his job hauling for the Park Service and Doris's wages from Mike's, the couple earned a total of $1,937.43, a great deal of which they put directly into savings.

Members of the community knew Doris as an extreme tightwad. Her reluctance to spend a penny more than she needed to was one of the major reasons the couple did so well financially. John Lindhe, the operator of the Glacier Park Trading Post, East Glacier's mercantile, probably winced when he saw Doris enter the store.

Doris tried scheme after scheme to make money while they lived in East Glacier, and in 1931 she went in with another girl and ran a hot dog stand. "We were going to make ourselves some money," she later said. Dan wrote about building the stand and helping attend it but for some reason never noted any income from the enterprise in his diary. Doris also worked during the Christmas seasons at the post office.

Because of Doris's education and experience she was able to get an occasional job as substitute teacher at the Glacier Park Elementary Grade School. The school, built of brick in 1923, was a short walk from Dan and Doris's house. Conveniently located, the school was just five false-front buildings down from Mike's Place.

The couple continued to work occasionally for the Park Service. One winter Dan painted more than 46 signs for use at trailheads and campgrounds along the east side of the park. Rangers in each district gave Dan carefully written messages and sign sizes. For example, "Atlantic Creek," "Atlantic Falls," "Mt. James," and refuse and bathroom signs were ordered by the Cut Bank ranger. This must have been particularly distasteful to Dan who had gone from being the Cut Bank ranger to the person painting bathroom

The recently completed Going-To-The-Sun Road along St. Mary Lake, July 15, 1933. With the completion of the Going-to-the-Sun Road and the auto road over Marias Pass, East Glacier began to decline as the bustling hub of what had been a rail-oriented Glacier Park. Doris and Dan moved over Marias Pass about the same time to accommodate the auto tourists at a tourist lodge they purchased.

signs for the new ranger.

Dan continued his job hauling for the Glacier Transportation Company, and his job also placed him right in the middle of the Park Service's plans to encourage the planting of fish in as many lakes and streams as possible in park waters. In driving freight trucks, as well as in his occasional work for the fish hatchery, Dan hauled millions of non-native fish to every corner of the park. In his diaries for the period, Dan recorded each trip he made with hatchery fish. For instance, he noted that he planted 35,000 eastern brook trout in Two Medicine Lake on June 15, 1931. Then on August 13 he wrote, "Fish to the extreme end of Saint Mary Lake. Took the 'Little Chief' (a boat used by the park service and transportation company) into less than 3 feet of water." He also packed fish into Red Eagle Lake several times during August.

During the fall of that year he noted, "September 17: planted load of fish along Lake McDonald. September 21: took 42 cans of rainbow trout to Lake McDermott, old name, new name is Swiftcurrent lake; took 68,000 native trout to Kintla Lake. September 30: rainbow trout to Stump Lake at Many Glacier; October 2, fish to Lake Josephine. October 4, more fish to Lake McDonald, Ranger and packer took 24 cans to Trout Lake; October 5, fish to Fish Creek, Lake McDonald; 30 cans of rainbow trout to Lost Lake on road by Sun Camp; found instead of a barren lake there are lots of 16-20-inch native trout there." The year before, Dan noted that on one occasion he'd stocked 75,000 fish 16 miles up McDonald Creek from the lake, an incredible number of fish for such a small stream; the next week he planted about the same number.

With all the work they were doing, Dan and Doris steadily built their wealth during their stay in East Glacier. In March 1931, Dan wrote that he sent eight $500 bonds to Commercial National Bank to be sold. On April 7 he wrote, "Dody and I went to Browning right after supper to fix up Liberty Bonds for transfer and new issue on same. Had Smith Bonds paper fixed for Committee for the Protection of Bond Holders, got safe deposit box."

Their only bad investment was sinking $100 into a muskrat farm, a move vehemently opposed by Doris. They lost every penny, as Doris had predicted. The farm turned out to be a scam, and the couple never was able to contact anyone after sending the money. The last mention of the subject was an entry by Dan in his diary during March 1932: "Wrote Northern States Fur Farm regarding $100 invested, summer of 1930."

Very few entries in the couple's diaries reflected the hard financial times much of the country was experiencing during the period. Newspapers support the fact that Montana did not feel the full effects of the 1929 stock market crash and Depression until the early 1930s. However, records show that 20 Montana banks went under from 1929 to 1931, and numerous newspaper advertisements from the period urged Montanans to buy.

"Wake up, it's time to buy," one ad began. "Prosperity is not dead in America, it has simply been asleep dreaming bad dreams of depression."

Based on one account by an East Glacier resident, the village did not feel the Depression until 1931. That July, on a Saturday night with hundreds of people whooping it up at Mike's, a fire claimed many of the buildings in the town. This was a major blow and the beginning of the town's decline as a hub and gathering place.

After workers extended Highway 2 west from East Glacier over Marias Pass, Dan and Doris traveled more and more to the west side for fishing and other pursuits. "The road over Marias Pass was opened in 1930," remembered Doris. "The 1929 fires speeded up construction of the road. Before that if you wanted to bring a car from East Glacier to West Glacier you had to ship it on a flatbed train car and it cost you $32."

One August day the year after the new road opened, Dan, Doris, Ranger Whitcraft and his wife left East Glacier at 5:15 a.m. and drove over the Divide to Dickey Creek, a tributary of the Middle Fork of the Flathead River. In what must have been a record day for four people using the traditional method, they picked 17 gallons of huckleberries and returned home late that night. That day represented the beginning of Doris's lifelong affair with huckleberries. After having that kind of picking, she vowed to move to the west side as soon as possible.

One of the last chores the couple undertook at their East Glacier home was to establish a well. They wished to end their reliance on a surface spring on the back of their lot, but they nearly put an end to more than that.

"We tried to drill a well by hand on our place with a post hole digger and an extension," recalled Doris. "One day when we were drilling we hit a rock, so we put dynamite down there to blow it, and ran into the house because we figured it would kick rocks around when it blew.

"All of a sudden, the neighbor goes and peeks down the hole to see what was going on," continued Doris. "And this dynamite was ready to go off. Lucky for him the dynamite didn't blow. The fuse must have been too wet. We never did get any water from that well."

For more than a year, Dan and Doris had been looking for a tourist camp or land on the west side of the park. On April 17, 1932, they drove to Hidden Lake to look over the Sibley Tourist Camp, which was for sale for $3,000. Later in April Dan quit his job hauling for the Park Service. The couple traveled to Kalispell to complete the lease transfer with the State Forest Department for the land occupied by the Sibley Camp, and on May 2, Dan and Doris bought the camp for $2,850 in cash.

The couple left East Glacier just as the town began its decline from a bustling center for an eclectic mix of residents and visitors. In the next several years, Prohibition was repealed, the large dancehalls disappeared and many individual bars were built in small communities. Mike's Place no longer drew crowds of hundreds of people from homesteads and hamlets. With the completion of the road over Marias Pass, the Park Service reduced its operations at East Glacier and the Going-to-the-Sun Road diverted most of the tourist traffic — which now came in motor cars rather than by rail — around East Glacier. The park was now accessible to average Americans driving brand new Fords, which they could buy for $400 to $600.

"We had a chance to buy a tourist camp along the Middle Fork of the Flathead River, so we went into the dude business again," recalled Dan, likening it to hauling dudes around the park. "But this time it was tourists along the road, and they had their own cars."

The Huffines found massive snow depths and isolation at their new tourist camp at Hidden Lake, located on the boundary of Glacier National Park.

12
Huckleberry Hound, 1932-40

*"One dog got there first, tackled the bear, and the huckleberries
spilled out all over. The bear whacked the dog and
rolled him down the hill."*

In the shadows of the steep Middle Fork Flathead canyon on the west
slope of the Continental Divide, only one tourist camp stood along the sixty
miles of narrow road between East Glacier and West Glacier. The responsibilities at the "Huffine Camp" overwhelmed Dan and Doris at times, but
they enjoyed the idea of owning their own business.

"Dan didn't want to work under anybody," remembered Doris. "He was
always fighting a boss. So we decided to cater to tourists." The deed to the
camp entitled the Huffines to all the buildings including the lodge, cabins
and shop, but the land was leased from the state for $75 a year.

On May 8, 1932, Doris and Dan loaded 30 rabbits, 100 baby chicks, as
well as tools, clothes, and everything else they owned into an old Model A
coupe and drove the newly completed mountain road from East Glacier to
the remote camp at Hidden Lake, a railroad siding near Stanton Creek.
The camp stood at the mouth of Stanton Creek on the Middle Fork of the
Flathead River. Stanton Lake, glacier-scooped and nearly a mile long,
straddles the drainage 1 1/2 miles upstream on Stanton Creek. Above the
lake rises spectacular Great Northern Mountain.

The steep ridges of what is now the Great Bear Wilderness bound the
camp to the south, and just to the north of the camp the far bank of the
Middle Fork of the Flathead River forms the boundary of Glacier Park. Six
miles downstream Nyack Creek enters the Flathead, issuing forth from a
yawning, U-shaped canyon carved by glaciers and traveled by tribes cross-

Great Northern Trains sometimes stopped at the Hidden Lake Siding. The railway represented the only link to the outside world from November to May.

ing the Continental Divide. At the head of this canyon over the east side of the backbone lies Pitamakan Pass and Amphitheater Mountain, some of Doris's stomping grounds from four years before.

At the camp, Doris, then 31, and Dan, just 27, hosted tourists traveling in the Glacier Park area, fishermen from both sides of the divide, and hunters using the backcountry areas south of the Middle Fork. According to Doris, the work load at the camp was daunting.

"We were pumping gas all the time," she recalled, "and we were fixing tires, selling groceries, everything you can think of. Not only were we running the service station, but we ran a big dining room and did all the cooking. It was a bad deal! We rented 12 cabins, did all the cleaning on our own, all the washing, everything that needed to be done. Nowadays, I don't know that anybody could do it. They'd just quit. But in those days, a nickel was a nickel and we needed it." Doris began feeling some of the strain of her hard life. Her teeth bothered her constantly and she required her first pair of glasses, which she hated wearing.

In addition to working at the camp, Dan maintained ties to the park by driving tour buses for the Glacier Transportation Company, which sometimes called on him to transport either Civilian Conservation Corps members or tourists around the park's east and west sides. With such a busy schedule, Dan wrote only sporadically in his diary as the couple readied the camp and hosted their first tourists. On July 9 he wrote, "Nine cabins rented, calls for eight more. Plenty busy all day from 5:30 a.m. to 12 midnight."

Doris complained about the work but she welcomed the business. Be-

Dan and Doris continued their love affair with animals at the Hidden Lake Camp. Here Dan feeds the baby chicks the couple transported across Marias Pass to the camp in the spring of 1932. The Huffines kept dozens of skunks, several bears, badgers and coyotes around their property.

cause she loved animals and to help attract more guests, Doris kept badgers, skunks, bears and other animals as pets behind the camp.

"We had two young couples staying at our place," Doris remembered. "They wanted to see the bear we kept out in the shed. Our kitchen window looked right out on the shed so I could see them while I was working.

"The two guys went first and looked in through the door. It was a low door and they had to stoop to get through it. The girls were right behind them. Well that bear was crouched in the dark in the back of the shed and he let loose a big woof, like they do if something gets too close. The woof just scared those boys silly. They turned and knocked those girls flat; ran right over them. That was funny. Those girls had to get up and run away after the boys left.

"Another guy that came to stay in our cabins had two of those English bulldogs," continued Doris. "You know, those mean-looking dogs that seem like they're ready to eat the world. He took those bulldogs on chains up to peek at the bear.

"The bulldogs looked in the door and the bear woofed at them. You should have seen those bulldogs. They tried to get away but their paws just dug dirt like spinning tires."

When she was not having fun at the tourists' expense, Doris found plenty of other ways to keep occupied. She did the accounting for the couple's business and wrote most of their diary entries. She began writing in the 1932 diary in August. Each day she recorded the amount of money they took in at the restaurant. Sometimes she mentioned the number of cars that passed

Doris and Dan spent a lot of time on snowshoes during the winter. They hauled wood using a toboggan, checked their Pelton Wheel generating plant on Stanton Creek, and mushed into the Great Bear Wilderness.

The "V-Plow" finally opened Highway 2 to auto travel by May each year.

the camp, and she often wrote about huckleberrying.

On August 24 she wrote, "$1.40, restaurant. It didn't rain last night. Everyone went berry picking today but me. Dan hauled sawdust from Nyack. Took up some plants today so I can bring them in for winter. We are varnishing the dining room."

On August 26 Doris noted that she "Went huckleberrying — one mile straight up and 1+1/2 ahead — got 3 gallons. It sure is hard coming down. Dan met me part of the way up the trail." When they reached the camp, Doris found that she had left her glasses in the huckleberry patch. She turned around and jogged the 11/2 miles back up the mountain, retrieved the glasses, and returned to the camp just at dark.

"Not much doing — cold and damp," she wrote on August 29. "Started to rain at dark. Sold 14 gal. huckleberries today at 75c/gal. Dan worked on water line from Stanton Creek. I canned pickles and made jelly."

Often, Doris, Dan, or their guests hiked to Stanton Lake, perched about two miles up the Stanton Creek canyon directly behind the tourist camp. Doris and her sister, Maxine, a frequent visitor and helper, sometimes went huckleberry picking above the lake with George Snyder, their nearest neighbor, whom they called "old Snyde."

"That fat old guy," remembered Doris. "He was so bulky! He was too lazy, see, to bend and pick so he would get up on that mountainside above Stanton Lake to the west and then he would just sit down — he weighed 250 pounds at least — with his pail and he'd slide right down through the huckleberry bushes. He'd just pull off the bushes as he went, pick what he wanted and throw the rest of them away."

According to Doris, it was hard to tell "if he was a bear or a man."

On one berry picking trip above Stanton Lake, Doris's sister Maxine, then about 20, and Dan's sister Irma, about 12, ran into a bear. Maxine dropped their packsack full of huckleberries and shoved Irma up a tree while the bear went for the berries.

"We had two dogs," remembered Doris. "One dog got there first and tackled the bear, and the huckleberries spilled out all over. The bear whacked the dog and rolled him down the hill. The other dog got there about that time, then it took over and chased the bear.

"Our dogs were mean; they knew bears and they could rip hide right off them. In fact, I was surprised that dog got rolled by the bear, because they usually didn't get hit. I felt sorry for the bear many a time because there would be great hunks of hide ripped loose."

Maxine and Irma collected their huckleberries and headed down the mountainside. "I felt sorry for that poor kid," remembered Maxine. "She was just all scratched up from being shoved up through the branches of that fir tree."

On another berry-picking trip, Doris and Maxine drove Dan's brand new

Dan often fished the Middle Fork of the Flathead River near their camp, supplementing their diet with fish and game. Across the river from Dan is Glacier Park.

Ford, one of the first pickup models. They drove to the top of the steep ridge west of Stanton Lake via a road that was just being put in from the back side of Crystal Creek. The road was nicely graded. Doris wouldn't park next to the hillside because she was afraid that the men working on the road would come around the corner and scratch Dan's new car. So she parked as close as she could to the outside bend of the road.

Maxine remembered that she and Doris "went picking, came back, and here sat three of the road men on the inside edge of the road. They had driven their equipment past our truck and shook all the dirt and rocks out from under the outside wheels."

The truck perched on the outside edge of the road with two wheels hanging over the side, resting on a tangle of logs and sticks. The two inside wheels held most of the weight of the truck on the steep mountainside. The men wouldn't look at the two women because they felt embarrassed that they'd created such a dangerous situation and didn't know what to do about it.

Doris, never one to be gotten the best of, looked at Maxine and said, "Well we can't leave it here. We've got to get it home. Get in, Maxine, get in. Dan will be mad if we scratch his new car. You have all the nerve in the world, now drive it off of there." Doris then grabbed the truck's door handle and said, "I'll hold it."

"I was in hysterics," remembered Maxine. "As if Doris could hold the car by the door handle. If I had gone to the bottom I would have laughed my head off all the way. So I got in, cranked it up and drove it along a log and back onto the road. We loaded the huckleberries and drove away." Doris was happy that they had avoided catastrophe but felt disgusted at the road workers who "never did a thing, just watched us, the fools."

Doris used huckleberries gathered during these adventurous trips in meals she sold at the restaurant, and she often sold the huckleberries to tourists as well, and to the men on the train.

"We could jump a freight in front of our place," she recalled. "They were pulling uphill with the old Mallets [powerful French-built helper engines] in those days and the trains weren't going very fast at all. We'd jump on the caboose, ride across Stanton Creek, and then jump off. The trains were puffing, they could hardly make the pull. So, we'd give these fellows on the train our huckleberries for 50 cents a gallon and they would take the berries over east of the divide to Havre and sell them."

In October and November, Doris made brief notes about the hunters they hosted and the coming of winter. By December the roads from East Glacier and West Glacier were snowed in and impassable. The railroad provided the only transportation. Dan and Doris used a toboggan to collect wood for heating. They also had a permit to dig coal along Stanton Creek, and they used coal for part of their winter fuel. The long winters were often without reliable electricity, however. At first Dan and Doris used a crude generator-light plant in a shed behind the lodge. Later, they operated a Pelton wheel generator or "light plant" purchased for $610 and installed on a pipeline in

Stanton Creek.

"We bought a big wooden water main from Columbia Falls and put it in the creek to power the Pelton wheel," remembered Doris. "Dan was carrying one section of it on his back one day, and as he came around a creek bend he looked up and saw a grizzly. The bear was so scared it tore out of there like a shot and ran up the mountainside. The bear grabbed a rotten stump and fell partly back down." Dan returned to the lodge, told Doris about the bear, and said, "I was ready to come home for lunch anyway."

Despite their investment, the light plant often malfunctioned, especially in winter. Doris told one story about such an occasion that demonstrated just how endearingly eccentric she could be:

"Once Dan was gone somewhere and all of a sudden our lights went out," she said. "I thought that maybe someone was on the creek, messing with our light plant. So I got the six-shooter, wrapped it in my apron and headed for Stanton Creek. We had a pair of coyotes that would travel with me, one about 100 feet ahead, one about the same distance behind. When I was heading along the road to the creek, a car stopped and a man asked if I needed help. He thought the coyotes were wild and that they were stalking me. I thought that was so funny! When I got over to the creek, no one was there. The screen was just blocked on the water pipe intake."

Of course, if Doris's story-telling made her seem like a 19th-century mountain woman, it should be remembered that she lived so many years in a region that is famed for its colorful characters. The Huffines quickly learned, for instance, that their overweight neighbor, George Snyder, had a picturesque past as an early settler in northwest Montana. He'd prospected in Glacier Park in the 1890s and built the first hotel on Lake McDonald. Snyder sold out to John Lewis in about 1906 for $1500, and built a small hotel just outside the west entrance to Glacier Park on the banks of the Middle Fork of the Flathead River. In spite of court challenges from the Park Service and area residents, Snyder opened a saloon there in 1912, beginning a long series of battles with the Park Service. Later, in violation of his permit, Snyder began operating tour boats between his hotel and the Lewis Hotel at the head of Lake McDonald; Snyder won a court case against the Park Service over the issue. Finally, in the early 1920s, while drunk and operating a tour car from his hotel into the park, he collided with a Park Service team of horses drawing a wagon. Snyder went to jail and the Park Service finally succeeded in getting his business shut down in the park.

Sometime after that, Snyder sold his place, moved to a tiny cabin along Stanton Creek, and drank up what little money he had left on high-priced Prohibition liquor. Because of all this, George had a bad reputation.

"We did an awful thing, the first winter," remembered Doris. "Old Snyde lived in a little cabin over against Stanton Creek. Everybody told us not to have anything to do with him, because he was a shyster and would take you for whatever he could get. We were dumb and green and we believed what they said. We didn't take any pains to get to know him ourselves."

Dan and Doris avoided Snyde; they never went to his cabin to visit that winter, and it was a long one, November to May. When Snyde would come down to the camp the Huffines didn't invite him into their lodge.

Finally in the spring, Snyde came to the back of the lodge and looked in the window. Doris had baked a pie that day and Snyde looked so pitiful she decided to give him a piece. She "took a piece out to him and he just grabbed it off the plate as if it might escape him, like he would die if he didn't get that pie, just shaking to get that pie. He just needed it so bad, something nice and good." After that, the Huffines helped him all they could, and according to Doris, Dan was "over at Snyde's place more than he was home."

Later, Dan and Doris learned that Snyde didn't have a nickel, and ate only flour and beans all winter. "We could have helped him," remembered Doris, "could have divided our food, but we didn't have the brains to judge for ourselves."

Doris remembered that the snow usually lay over six feet deep in the Middle Fork valley during the winter. They often had to shovel around the windows to let the light in. The snow piled high on the sides of the railroad track, forming a tunnel which hid the train. Often, Doris walked the tracks six miles west to Nyack for the mail, then either walked back or rode the train back in the evening.

When Maxine visited, the sisters often enjoyed the trip together. "I came in one Thanksgiving from Iowa," remembered Maxine. "The next day we got ready to walk to the post office. It was sunny, but Doris insisted on bringing coats, sweaters, parkas and extra socks. On the way down we took off all the sweaters and coats. The sun shone down into the tunnel formed by the snow along the tracks, and it was hot. We walked the last few miles in just our parkas.

"When we got to Nyack we couldn't believe the thermometer reading — 40 below!" continued Maxine. "Then we had to walk back instead of taking the train because we had to pick up our clothes we had left along the way."

The mile of road west of the Huffine camp usually melted off in late April. Dan and Doris often went on walks on sunny afternoons, and she recounted one particular Sunday afternoon when they set off down the road.

"We walked down to the Coal Creek curve, where the big hill takes off there up towards the mountains. And, my gosh, here was this big grizzly digging around at tree roots trying to find something to eat. Dan said 'That's a grizzly up there'. And sure enough, it was. Dan said, 'I'm going back for the gun. I'm going to have a grizzly!'

"He had to go back a mile up the road, and I stayed there to watch the grizzly. And when he got back to the house, instead of walking back down, he brought the car down. I was over on the railroad track, ready to run of course if the grizzly looked at me. So the grizzly wandered around this hillside while Dan was gone — it took him quite a little while — and finally the grizzly worked his way over the hill and disappeared over the top.

"So then," Doris continued, "Dan comes back down the road in the car, just in a hurry. I thought he'd know that the grizzly had gone over the hill, but he didn't. He got out of that car and grabs the gun, and there he starts

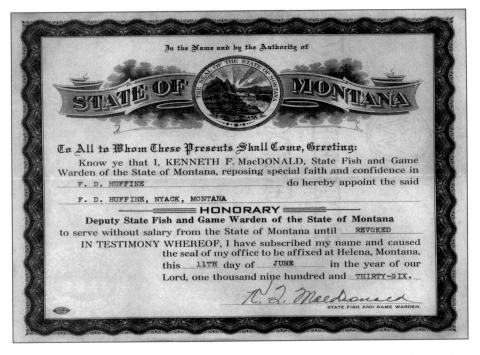

Dan Huffine was appointed an Honorary Deputy State Fish and Game Warden in 1936 to help watch out for poachers along the isolated Middle Fork. Dan retained the honorary warden status throughout his years in the Middle Fork despite the fact that he was at times on both sides of game laws.

shooting — up at that hillside. And I thought 'what in the Sam Hill ails him?' I just couldn't imagine why he was shooting at that hillside, up there where the grizzly was. He just kept shooting, shooting, shooting!

"Finally, I got desperate, because we didn't waste shells in those days, they were valuable. So I tore over to the car to stop him from shooting up every shell he had, and I said, 'What in the Sam Hill are you shooting at up there?' And he said, 'Why that grizzly, don't you see that grizzly up on the hillside?' I said, 'There isn't any grizzly on that hillside, that grizzly went over that hill before you got down here.' He said 'He didn't either. Why, can't you see it up there? I think I hit it!'

"Oh my land! I pretty near had to knock him in the head to get him to quit shooting at a stump that the grizzly had peeled yellow, looking for ants. I said, 'Yeah, you just about shot that stump to death.'"

Later that year, Dan bought a pair of eyeglasses.

Poaching was common in Glacier Park during the 1930s. Dan and Doris knew Hugh Buchanan, the district ranger for the park, and he often told them about his patrols. One particular trip he took with his wife, Madeline, much to her regret.

"Hugh and Madeline had been down here Saturday night and Madeline had some new boots," Doris wrote. "She was going to go with Hugh up Park

Stanton Lake country in 1935 looked vastly different from the timbered basin that exists today. Note Great Northern Mountain in the background. The 1929 fire swept most of the timber from the hillsides. Dan, Doris and Doris's sister, Maxine, often snowshoed across the lake and once nearly went through a thin area in the ice.

Creek, over a pass, and down and out Coal Creek. They started on their trip and had only gone a few miles when they came upon a man's tracks crossing the trail and heading up Park Creek. Hugh told Madeline to stay there and make sure he came out, then took off on the trail. Hugh overtook the man, and sneaked up on him. The man, (whose name was) Potter, finally saw Hugh and tried to throw his pack in the brush, but Hugh was too quick for him. He had six traps and bait for a lot more, so he must have had a cache somewhere but Hugh couldn't find it. Madeline had to wait four hours and said it nearly froze her." Potter received a $100 fine and sentence of 30 days in the Flathead County jail.

Dan agreed to help watch the area for poachers. Pressed between the pages of a notebook he kept during the 1930s was a certificate naming him an "Honorary Deputy Fish and Game Warden for the State of Montana," signed by the state game warden, Kenneth F. McDonald, on June 11, 1936. The document proclaimed that Dan held the title "until revoked."

In that remote stretch between East Glacier and West Glacier, there was much to keep an eye on beside the wild game, too. The road was narrow and dangerous and many cars crashed on the narrow bridge across Stanton Creek, about a quarter mile from the Huffine Camp. Doris spent more than one night tending accident victims until help arrived from Kalispell. Other times they could scavenge at accident scenes for anything of value left behind. One night they were returning from a dance in West Glacier and heard a report that a shoe salesman had crashed into Crystal Creek, several miles east of their camp. They drove to the creek to have a look and to see if any shoes were scattered around that they could pick up.

When they arrived, they saw the salesman's truck resting down in the creek gully. They made their way into the gully and looked through the boxes in the truck.

"All of the shoes were samples for the right foot," recalled Doris. "We couldn't think of anyone with just one leg, so we were out of luck."

Several times a month, Doris and Maxine visited their friend Josephine Doody, an older woman who lived in a little shack along the road about halfway between the Huffine Camp and West Glacier. Josephine was in her 80s, and about that time in the early 1930s she had been hurt in a car crash along Highway 2.

"We often loaded up some food for her in our Model A when we left Kalispell and dropped it off on the way back to our camp," remembered Doris. "We visited her mostly for the stories; she was fun to talk to. Once she brought out a trunk and showed us a finely embroidered quilt. It was beautiful. All the squares were hand-drawn and embroidered. She tried to give it to us but we wouldn't accept it."

Josephine told Doris and Maxine that she had come to McCarthyville, an abandoned railroad town west of Marias Pass, from the south. Doris said that although Josephine described herself as a dancer, it was widely known that she was a prostitute at one time. She certainly seemed to have a colorful life, at least the way it was told to Doris and other Middle Fork residents. While living in McCarthyville in about 1890, Josephine fell in love with Dan Doody, who went on to become one of the original six rangers of Glacier Park. Josephine reportedly told Doris that she had been addicted to opium obtained from the Chinese railroad workers, and that Dan Doody had kidnapped her and locked her in a small hideout cabin to dry out, later marrying her. Whether Josephine had embellished the story with scenes from a silent movie melodrama, or whether it really happened that way we don't know. Doris enjoyed a good story either way, and Josephine had plenty of them.

Dan Doody died in 1921, and until about 1930, Josephine had lived mostly alone on their 160-acre homestead located within the park across the Middle

Dan seems proud of his new pickup truck. On one huckleberry picking trip, Doris and Maxine nearly drove the truck over the edge of a mountain road.

The Doodys were one of the most notorious couples who lived along the Middle Fork. Dan Doody was one of Glacier's first rangers, and considered an outlaw before and after his ranger service. Dan Doody died before the Huffines moved to the Middle Fork, but Doris became good friends with Josephine Doody, here pictured with old-time McDonald Lake resident Charlie Howe years before. Howe operated one of the first boats on the lake. When Doris knew Josephine, she was a colorful old woman living in a tiny shack in Nyack Flats along a Middle Fork tributary, Deerlick Creek. (Photos courtesy of Betty Robinson Schurr)

Fork of the Flathead River from the shack. Many residents remember stories of Josephine's moonshine stills.

"The railroad workers would blow their whistle once for each quart of moonshine they wanted to buy, then wait," remembered Doris. "Soon, Josephine would row across the river and deliver their hootch. She used the hideout cabin sometimes to hide from the revenue men."

According to Doris, Josephine was "a spitfire kind of monkey. She was tough and I mean tough." After Dan Doody died Josephine lived alone on the isolated homestead until one of her hands moved her across the river. She possessed skill with guns and did all her own hunting.

"The park rangers didn't see it when she shot elk and deer in the park," Doris continued. "Some of them were afraid of her because she was worse than any man in cussing you out. She had a bad reputation; supposedly she'd killed a man in Colorado."

Charlie Holland, the ranch hand who'd helped her across the river, was an old drunk and moved in with Josephine for a place to stay. During January of 1936 Josephine fell ill with pneumonia, and Charlie was taking care

The Doodys lived in this homestead across the Middle Fork on 160 acres within the boundaries of Glacier Park. Josephine was known as the bootleg lady of Glacier Park. She regularly ferried hootch across the river to Great Northern Railway men. (Photo courtesy of Betty Robinson Schurr)

of her. Suddenly, Charlie got tired of providing care and decided to load her on the train to Kalispell; the road was snowed in from November to May, so the train was the only way to get her to the hospital. According to Doris, Josephine said, "Don't even think of moving me. I'll die as sure as shootin' if you move me." Charlie paid no attention to her, flagged down a train and put Josephine in one of the cars with the help of a stretcher and the train crew.

"It was so cold and snowy, way below zero," continued Doris. "She got chilled on the way as they had to change trains at Columbia Falls and take the old rattling dinkey down to Kalispell. She died in the hospital the next day."

Records show that Charlie signed the transfer of the homestead deed the day of Josephine's funeral, which he did not attend. Doris remembered that Charlie soon sold the homestead, spent the money on booze, and vanished from the area.

Another character, Monty Atwater, a writer and temporary employee of the state Game Commission, often stayed at the Huffine camp.

"We have always heard that Monty was a writer," Doris noted in her journal. "But we never saw anything he wrote so we thought he just wrote in his head like the rest of us.

"Once Monty needed to phone Kalispell while we were gone, and forced the front window up and cut a deep groove in the casing. I was mad, I can tell you. There's a railroad phone right out front that anyone can use in emergencies but that's Monty for you: no respect for anyone's property and

The Doody Homestead still stands on a small parcel of private land within Glacier. (photo taken by the author in 1989).

more nerve than two government mules.

"Another time," continued Doris, "when he was fixing up his place he would come down here and borrow pipe pieces and the cutter until I hid the cutter so he couldn't just walk out in the shop and get it. He borrowed a two-inch union and returned a 1-1/2-inch union and said he guessed it didn't matter what Dan had. The next day he came and borrowed that and that was the last we saw of either union. So you can see why I like him so.

"I heard his wife finally left him. She was half-decent and I sure don't blame her."

Monty wasn't the only character that annoyed Doris. "Talk about brainless men," Doris wrote in her diary. "This morning when I went in to Nyack John Robertson told me about loaning two horses to some men to pack out three deer they'd killed up Cascadilla Creek. Coming down they let one horse fall off the trail and roll end over end down the cliff until he wedged between some logs. Then they went down and hammered the horse's head with rocks until it was all smashed to pieces and then came back and wouldn't pay John for the horse.

"About 10 days afterwards here came the poor horse into Nyack," Doris continued. "He was in such bad shape that John killed him. If they had any sense they would at least have shot the horse or gotten him out because he was just knocked out and was not broken up."

One guest at the camp told Doris about a search for buried loot south of the camp in the Bob Marshall Wilderness. "Mr. White let some men have his mule to go looking for $144,000 that is hidden up the South Fork by Hole-in-the-Wall," Doris wrote in her diary. "The money was hidden by bandits who robbed a train. Most of them were shot at Coram but a few escaped and it is thought that they hid their money up the South Fork. They have

Near the end of their stay at Hidden Lake, Doris worked in the Nyack Post Office near the Red Eagle siding and depot, a few miles west of their camp.

found an old camp up there with some old shells just like they used in those days so they are going to do some digging to see if they can't find the money. Mr. White is to get a share of it for the use of his mule."

Doris probably referred to loot stolen by the Northern Pacific train robbers, caught near McCarthyville after lawmen chased them across Montana in 1893. Lawmen shot several of the robbers near Essex, and a citizen shot another near Coram. Records show that no robbers escaped. The loot, never recovered, only amounted to a few hundred dollars, but people in the area still held a more romantic view of the holdup.

In their constant search for free protein, Doris and Dan often fished in the nearby river and in Stanton Lake. In summer, they fished the inlet and outlet streams and the lake. In winter, they fished through holes in the ice. Doris remembered a particularly good fishing spot that Dan found.

"Dan fished the outlet, where the creek leaves Stanton Lake, that was good at times. He finally got on to going up the east side of the lake to some beaver ponds up along the east side. You had to go through quite a bit of brush to reach them. Nobody knew about these ponds, but Dan found them. He would just come home with the most beautiful fish. That was super!

"Every time he could get a chance to get in there without anybody with him he would go. He didn't want anyone to find out where it was, of course. Because the minute you let anybody find out in those years, just like now, your place was overrun by people. We knew enough to keep our mouths shut."

One spring Dan, Doris, and Maxine hiked up to Stanton Lake to see the elk in a basin above the lake and to check out Dan's fishing spot. "They were walking along right on top of the snow," Maxine remembered. "I don't know why but I kept sinking through the snow every time I took a step.

Doris occasionally substitute-taught at the Nyack Schoolhouse which operated during the 1930s.

They kept yelling at me to hurry.

"We started heading across the frozen surface of Stanton Lake to look over the beaver dams on the east side," Maxine continued. "Dan said it would be an easy hike across the smooth surface of the lake. Well we got a ways out on that ice and began noticing how honeycombed the ice was. We looked down and saw nothing but water under a thin layer of ice. Suddenly, we felt like we were floating on a chunk of ice and we could see ice chunks breaking up on the other side. We barely made it back to the west side." They called the incident, according to Maxine, "the day we walked on water."

In summer, the couple also fished the Middle Fork of the Flathead River for the "prettiest bull trout that ever were." Dan and Doris guarded their secret fishing holes on the river until, according to Doris, "some woman up above our place messed things up. She was catering to tourist parties, and to encourage them she would tell them where to catch bull trout. And it was only a few years before you just couldn't get a bull trout where you wanted to at all because she told everybody where to go, and she wrecked every spot that the natives had. We were quite disgusted with her, I'm telling you. Dan was very unhappy."

Doris and Dan also caught spawning whitefish from McDonald Creek in Glacier Park during the late fall. Whitefish could be caught in large numbers and the couple considered them excellent when smoked.

"The Park Service allowed us to dipnet whitefish at the head of Lake McDonald," remembered Doris. "We would blacken a lantern glass except for a little spot so the light would shine out in a beam on the water. Then we'd watch for the whitefish and dip them with a long-handled net. At first, in 1934 or 1935, we were allowed to take home all the fish we could get, but the next year the Park Service cut the amount down to 50 fish per day. This lasted about two more years and then none were allowed, so our fun was finished. It was great while it lasted and it is fun to remember all those bonfires and friends we met and visited with around them, and the many times we got home at 2 a.m."

The couple's winter meat supply consisted entirely of wild game. Doris hunted only occasionally, but Dan spent a lot of time hunting during the fall, often killing his elk on natural mineral licks on the park boundary along the river upstream from the camp.

"You had to wait until the elk put one foot in the river as the elk started to cross over from the park side," remembered Dan. "A lot of times I had to float the elk across the river, or chase a floating elk down the river." The elk and deer meat provided a big part of the couple's winter food.

As the years went by and Montana's economy improved, business at the camp increased. In summer, Doris and Dan regularly hosted 40 or more tourists at one time. Doris did most of the cooking and washing; her sister Maxine helped during the summers, as always, for no pay. During a particularly busy period over the Fourth of July holiday in 1936, Doris had an untimely accident.

"We had a great big door leading to our cellar where we kept our supplies. The door must have been five or six feet long and it weighed a ton. I was in a hurry, cooking for somebody, and I didn't quite swing the door open good enough. When I went down, I took hold of the edge to let myself down the steps and the door came down and smashed my right hand. It split open all my fingers. I got it pushed up with the other hand, so I got out quick enough."

Maxine didn't remember the incident as Doris had related it. She remembered Doris screaming, "Maxine, get me out of here! How am I going to get this door off my fingers? Get that food served. Don't let those things burn! Are you going to be all day getting me out of here?" Maxine remembers that she lifted the door from Doris's hand.

Doris said she "did what I always did when I got hurt and I thought the blood was running. I took my apron, rolled my fingers up tight, and ran into the timber. Dan had to cut my ring off because my fingers were smashed. I went into town and they bound the fingers together, because the bones were cracked lengthwise."

Later that day when Doris returned to the camp, she found a woman helping out, cooking hamburgers. The woman was "so slow, and such a fizzle cooking hamburgers, that I had to get right in there and take over, bandages and all, even though the doctor told me not to use the hand for several days."

The next day Doris and Maxine decided to go huckleberrying, but Doris couldn't pick huckleberries with the splints on her fingers so she "just took the splints off and picked huckleberries. And that's the way I got over that."

That was just her matter-of-fact approach to everything. In her diary on

The couple built the Huffine Camp into a tidy, attractive tourist stop. They dreaded leaving, but Doris's health and the country's upcoming involvement in World War II forced the move.

July 3, 1936, Doris wrote about the incident : "Lots in to eat. Smashed all four fingers in cellar door at breakfast time. Had to go to town for x-ray. One bone cracked."

On July 4, Doris wrote: "Worst yet and my two fingers in splints. Fed 55 — wow. Talk about work. 11 sets of bedding." July 5 was even "worse than the 4th — fed 65 and my hand sore. No one to help except Maxine. Had to wash 11 sets of bedding; out-cabins all full."

In spite of her status as an unpaid, indentured servant, Maxine enjoyed her summers with the Huffines at the Hidden Lake camp. As in the past, Doris looked to her for companionship and, of course, for free help with the chores. "We had a lot of fun at that camp," Maxine remembered. "One time Doris sent me down to wallpaper some of the cabins. I was supposed to unroll all these rolls of wallpaper and cut the edges off, then reroll the paper. I was working hard to get it all done."

But as always, Doris pushed Maxine to work even harder. "I went down to help Maxine glue the wall paper, and there she was laying stretched out on this bed reading these dumb romance magazines."

Maxine explained to Doris that she had popped off the perforated edge of each roll of wallpaper without unrolling it and finished the work in a fraction of the time.

"That's the height of laziness," Doris told her. "Lay there and read those trashy magazines instead of trimming that wallpaper right."

Maxine had other adventures at the camp, some of them involving dances in West Glacier, which she often attended. "One summer night I went down to West Glacier to a dance at Al Wright's hotel," remembered Maxine. "The fellow who brought me back to the camp turned right around and left because it was late. I went through the lodge to get to the outhouse in the back."

"That's when I heard something that scared me," Doris added to her sister's account. "I said to Dan, 'Somebody is going through this house.'"

Maxine picked up the story again: "I'd just about reached the outhouse, when zip! something went right over my head. I heard the bang, and then 'Who's there?', Dan says. He shot right over my head. I almost didn't make it to the little house.'"

Doris remembered that Dan only fired a warning shot and the bullet did not travel as close to Maxine's head as she thought. "But I do remember her telling me that she was so scared that she thought about crawling down the hole," Doris said.

Maxine, Dan, and Doris sometimes went together to dances at Wright's hotel along the Middle Fork near West Glacier. Maxine helped close the hotel bar some nights and remembered one particularly odd patron.

"This one fellow came down every night and just got so drunk on beer," remembered Maxine. "Then he'd buy eggs and throw them at the wall to watch them splatter. We got smart and we sold him eggs at a dollar apiece. The next day, though, I'd have to clean up the eggs — what a mess! So I got even smarter and boiled the eggs. The next time, I charged him a dollar a piece for the boiled eggs and let him throw them; he didn't know the difference, he was so drunk. I don't remember his name but he was some big shot who owned a cabin up on Lake McDonald."

Doris often dragged Maxine along to help if things went wrong around the camp. Once, Doris's huge badger, Mollie, who lived to be 23 before she died, dug under a section of wire in her pen, escaped, and immediately dug her way into the chicken coop.

"We kept trying to push this smaller coop over the top of the badger to catch her," remembered Doris. "That badger dug like a backhoe and then she'd stick her nose up to see where she was, then she'd tunnel some more. Finally we got her to dig her way back out of the chicken pen, so we saved the chickens."

It wasn't just hungry badgers that spent time at the Huffine camp. Doris remembered many desperate people passing through their service station, too. "Those were bad days, you know, during the Depression. There wasn't any work to be had and people were starving. They had big families and there was no welfare, nothing to help them. When they were building Fort Peck Dam everybody thought that if they could get to Fort Peck, they could get a job. They'd come through on rickety old cars. You couldn't imagine it nowadays — you think you've seen rickety cars, but you haven't seen anything. The cars were old, dilapidated, with no tops, and all full of kids. All their belongings were piled in there, hanging over the sides. They couldn't go any distance without breaking down or having a flat tire. Something would happen — the radiator would blow.

"They'd buy one gallon of gas. They couldn't afford any more at a time. It was so sad. But it was sadder when they would get over to Fort Peck and they couldn't get a job. The jobs were all gone. They would have to beg and limp back home again."

In April of 1940, two men in a Buick pulled into the camp late at night and parked by the gas pumps. They left the motor of the car running, saying that the battery was low. After Dan filled the tank they gunned the motor and sped down the road again without paying.

"Dan tore into the bedroom, grabbed the big rifle, rushed out and began firing at the car. But the car had gone too far and he missed. We described the car and gave the license number to the sheriff. But our nice, like a mule's hind end, county attorney said he couldn't bring charges against the men because we couldn't identify the men, just the car.

"Later, the mother of the boys that did it came to our place and turned them in. She paid us for the 15 gallons of gas. The boys got $25 fines and 30 days in jail."

Although Doris usually maintained her stoic attitide, some of her diary entries show the stress she felt operating the tourist camp. On June 8, 1934, for instance, her entry indicated that she felt trapped:

"Sunny," Doris wrote. "Dan moved light plant. If I could just get my money out of this place how I'd love to quit so Dan could run it like he wants to but I can see no hopes."

The hard work at East Glacier and Hidden Lake caught up with Doris when she developed a heart condition as she neared the still relatively young age of 40. "The doctor said it was my own fault," recalled Doris, "that I had tried to live my whole life in a short while. I couldn't work around the place anymore; I had no energy. So Maxine had to come and help out full time. I took a post office job at Nyack because I could lay down and rest there when it was slow. I commuted to the job in an old Model A. Dan wouldn't let me drive the pickup.

"Finally in late November of 1940 we sold the place and moved into Kalispell to run the bus depot during the war."

Odd bits of paper, bills, and other items are pressed between the pages of the couple's diaries from the 1930s at Hidden Lake. An envelope dated 1933 bore a three-cent stamp. Sales ledgers from October 1934 show that gas sold for 21 cents a gallon, kerosene 15 cents a gallon.

The camp was not a big money maker for the Huffines, but they netted reasonable profits. Their records show they took in between $104 and $667 per month during the busy months of June, July, and August. During the 30s when many people were struggling, they continued to sock away money in savings bonds, and collected rent from a house they still owned in East Glacier.

Doris wrote lots of sayings and tips on small slips of paper while at Hidden Lake. One of the rhymes suggests her attitude that perhaps life had more than its rightful share of drudgeries and toil:

Tis a hell of a life," said the queen of Spain.
Three minutes of pleasure, nine months of Pain.
Six weeks of rest
Then at it again."

At it again! That probably described Doris's feeling as she left her familiar life along the Flathead River for the next adventure in her life, one that she knew would be filled with more hard work and perhaps less of the pleasure she had come to expect of life near Glacier Park. She found it hard to leave her huckleberry patches; the clear, frigid waters of the Middle Fork of the Flathead River; and all the animals she'd acquired at the remote camp. Even before she had come to Montana, she had never lived in a real town, not even one the size of Kalispell, and she dreaded the confinement it promised.

Doris and Dan worked hard at the Hidden Lake Camp and thrived financially during hard times. Most of all, they were happy to be living on the edge of the wilderness and Glacier Park.

During the spring of 1945 Dan, then 40, visited Bozeman and told his father that he and Doris had purchased another tourist camp along Glacier Park's Middle Fork Flathead River, 200 yards from the Walton Ranger Station. After working at the bus station in Kalispell for almost five years, Dan and Doris timed their move back to the park with the end of World War II.

13
Bus Depot Operator, 1940-45

"I was on duty one morning and by Gosh if someone didn't open the bus depot door and say, 'Pearl Harbor has been bombed; we're in the war.' Then your whole life fell apart... It was just a madhouse from then on."

The Intermountain Transportation Company's bus depot in Kalispell was located at the center of town, on 17 Main Street. The depot featured a fountain, seating room for customers, ticket counter and bus garage. When Dan and Doris took over as managers in 1940, traffic was routine; the United States was still a year away from entering World War II and motorists could acquire tires and gasoline at a reasonable price.

Kalispell in 1940 featured about a half-mile of Main Street and 8,245 residents. The town centered around the junction of U.S. Highway 2 and U.S. Highway 93, just 30 miles south of Glacier Park and eight miles north of Flathead Lake, the largest natural freshwater lake west of the Great Lakes in the United States.

Doris and Dan decided to take the depot job because they thought it would give Doris an opportunity to get lots of bed rest, as her doctor had ordered. It didn't work out that way.

It was a friend of the Huffines, Carl Lassiter, a bus driver for Intermountain Transportation, who arranged the job for them running the depot. "He said that Dan could do it himself and I wouldn't have to help," Doris remembered. With that understanding, the Huffines sold the Hidden Lake camp and on the 22nd of November moved to Kalispell. The couple did not relish town life, and viewed the job as an interim move. Soon, they learned that the job was too big for Dan to handle on his own, and it was back to work for Doris.

"We bought the fountain with sandwiches, candy and all that," remembered Doris, who was 39 when she and Dan took over. "And you had to put out all the bus tickets and do all the baggage. It was too big of a job for Dan so I had to go down and help or we couldn't hold the job."

Even that wasn't enough. Doris found that she "could work a few hours in the morning and get things going, then we had to hire a girl to cover the fountain when I wasn't there."

As Doris worked more hours, she required even more rest to function. "I worked until noon, usually, then I had to go home and go to bed," she said. "Sometimes I couldn't get up again until 8 or 9 o'clock at night. Then I'd be up for a few hours and go to sleep again because I had to be at the depot early each morning."

The first year at the depot, Doris and Dan hired Peggy Brash, the daughter of old friend Art Brash from East Glacier, to work the fountain. "I worked from 9 a.m. to 9 p.m., six days a week," recalled Peggy, who had also worked for Doris during the summer at the Hidden Lake camp. "Dan paid me $10 a week which was pretty good money for a kid just out of high school." Dan and Doris had known Peggy since she was 4, and treated her like family.

Peggy said that people knew Doris as a worker bee and Dan as a practical joker who "would always say these crazy words to me, and I'd try to look them up but the words weren't in the dictionary."

Doris longed for the mountains of Glacier Park and found her weakness hard to bear. "Doris hated those years at the bus depot," remembered her sister Maxine. "She was too weak to do all the sewing and handwork she loved to do at home. She had to spend too many hours at the bus station."

Peggy agreed that managing the depot was not what Dan and Doris wanted to do. "They didn't like towns, they liked to rough it," she said.

Dan found it hard to learn the bus schedules at first and had trouble during busy periods. The couple nearly quit the job after the Christmas rush, but taskmaster Doris got them back on track.

"I had to learn the transportation part of it too," Doris recalled. "Because when the rush came and they were all boarding the buses there had to be two of us at the transportation desk and the hired girl had to handle the fountain. I can remember when it got going good, Dan came home one day and said, 'I can't do it; I've got to quit.'" Doris told him that others have succeeded at it and he could too.

Doris believed that Dan's problem stemmed from his lack of education. She believed that education "really helps train your brain."

"Finally," Doris continued, "after he learned more and got more confidence in himself he figured it was easy, just a snap. But the books were thick and there was a row of them you had to know, you can't imagine what it covered. You had to tell people how to get from Kalispell to anywhere they wanted to go, all over the United States. You had to know every change, every city; you had to be able to tell them whether they should go this way or that way, and quote prices. And you gradually learned it, but when you first looked, it seemed impossible."

While they were learning the ropes of the bus business, Doris and Dan settled into the small town life of Kalispell. They visited friends and talked about world affairs. Headlines from that first winter told of savage German air strikes on London, Greek and Italian campaigns, U.S. plans to increase production of war materials and increasing U.S. war aid to Great Britain.

The couple bought a small home about two miles from the depot. Dan also farmed a small place near Columbia Falls: He grew wheat and hay, raised chickens and sold eggs. Once their house nearly burned. Sparks exploded from a fire in nearby oil storage tanks. Doris was able to get out of bed, climb up on the roof of their house and, using wet blankets, put out the flames. In addition to her house, she had saved her precious collection of Glacier Park photos and memorabilia.

The couple soon became comfortable with the nature of their new job. The December 11, 1940, edition of the Kalispell Daily Inter Lake newspaper listed the Intermountain Transportation Company bus schedule. "Serving Montana — Connections Everywhere!" it proclaimed. Buses traveling the west shore of Flathead Lake south to Missoula left Kalispell at 8:30 a.m., 12:15 p.m., and 4:45 p.m. Buses traveling along the east shore of the lake to Missoula left Kalispell at 8 a.m. and 4:30 p.m. The bus traveling north and east across Montana to Havre left at 2:30 p.m, and the bus traveling west to Bonners Ferry, Idaho, left at 4:30 p.m.

Fares for the trips included $1.90 to Libby (90 miles), $2.35 to Missoula (120 miles), $4.75 to Butte (230 miles), $10.65 to Seattle, $22.65 to Los Angeles, and $26.25 to Chicago.

"We worked on commission," Doris remembered. "What we made depended on the tickets we sold. That way, you wanted to sell as long a ticket as you could to get your commission."

During the first winter Dan and Doris managed the bus station, anxiety was building over the war in Europe. In early 1941, the Inter Lake announced the election of Montana's 11th governor, Sam Ford. In the same, January 6 edition, President Franklin Roosevelt's speech to Congress was reported in which he warned of an "unprecedented foreign peril" and demanded a "swift and driving increase in our armaments both for defense and the use of fighting democracies abroad." Roosevelt asserted that the build-up was not an act of war.

After the couple had operated the bus station for about a year, everything changed.

"I was on duty one winter morning in 1941 and by gosh if someone didn't open the bus depot door and say, 'Pearl Harbor has been bombed; we're in the war,'" remembered Doris, who was 40 at the time. "Well, then your whole life just fell apart. That was like saying they blew up your own place."

On December 6, the Inter Lake carried stories on Britain's declaration of war against Finland, Hungary and Rumania, and of a Japanese proposal for a special commission for peace talks. The December 8 edition carried the headline, "Japanese Inflict Heavy Damage in Pacific"; it also carried the text of the president's message criticizing Japan for "attacking while conversations looking to peace were in progress" and asking for a declaration of war.

"After Pearl Harbor you couldn't get tires, you couldn't get this, you couldn't get that, everything was rationed, everything was short," remembered Doris. "It was all being put into war work. You had to have a slip of paper every time you bought a gallon of gas. You couldn't get any sugar without a slip of paper. You couldn't get flour."

"You may be eligible to buy a new Firestone war model bicycle," declared one advertisement in the Daily Inter Lake. "Come in, let us explain the new government regulations and help you fill out a rationing certificate," the ad continued.

"If you had an extra tire and didn't have it on your car you had to turn them in for the war surplus," Doris remembered. "Everybody thought that there would be secret police coming around to look and that you'd better not hide these spare tires. Everybody turned them in but all they did was ship them to Butte and somebody made money off them. I tried to talk Dan out of turning ours in; we had six good tires and he just knew that we didn't dare to keep the extra two. I wanted to hide them."

With these events, business at the depot skyrocketed. "People were all leaving the Flathead, heading to Washington, heading to Butte to go into war work," remembered Doris. "Everybody wanted to do their part. And so they just gave up things here and left as fast as they could. They couldn't get tires and gasoline so they had to ride buses.

"Then all the young guys were drafted. They came from Troy and Libby and Columbia Falls to travel to Butte, where they had to go to enter the army. They came from Browning, everywhere. Oh my land, that was awful to get those people through Kalispell. It was just a madhouse from then on."

Maxine, who was living in Seattle, remembered her visits to Kalispell. "When I visited Doris at the depot, it was so busy I'd have to talk to her over the counter. There were people everywhere and Doris made a big effort to talk to everyone and make them feel welcome."

One afternoon a number of Blackfeet draftees from Browning gathered at the station, waiting for their bus. The Blackfeet began fighting some of the other men and, as Doris remembered, "Dan got mad. He went over there in the middle of those fighters and grabbed some hands and twisted some thumbs." The fighters made peace. Doris and Dan had made many friends among tribal members during their years in East Glacier, and they were not about to allow the young men to be hurt.

Many young GIs on their way to war visited with Dan and Doris and later corresponded with them from all over the world. Dan, in his late 30s, had been classified 4-F by the local draft board. Doris spent long hours writing to soldiers she barely knew, sons of friends or cousins. It's clear from the letters that the soldiers cherished hearing from people in the states. She also corresponded often with her brother, Eldon, who served around the country, in Australia and in New Guinea. Doris kept a stack of War and Navy Department "V-Mail" (V for victory, of course) that was photographed and censored before it was mailed to her.

"Dear Doris," her brother wrote on July 9, 1943. "The censor loosened up today and put a note on the board saying we could tell we are in New Guinea. The natives here are very friendly and are always in camp trying to sell us something or other. I bought a grass skirt or two and was going to send them back there but they won't let me mail them so you will have to get along without one. They would probably be a little cool for Montana anyway."

A year later Eldon wrote that he was still battling malaria, mosquitos, humidity and heat. He wrote, "I saw Bob Hope and several other movie actors in a show so things are getting pretty civilized here." In later, uncensored letters, Eldon confided that his job had been to help build P.T. boat bases in Dutch New Guinea.

Eldon, with his farm background, considered the work he did in the Navy a joke. "He told us he only did one full day's work the entire time he served in the Navy," recalled Maxine. "And that was 10 hours of tossing sacks of sugar overboard near the end of the war. Sugar was rationed in the states and we all wanted it so badly."

"Dear Doris," Eldon wrote from a stop in San Francisco, out of the reach of censors. "There's no use of starting to tell about the inefficient way things are run or the waste and general mismanagement of the U.S. Navy because that would take too long but if everyone knew there wouldn't be as many war bonds sold."

Doris felt skeptical about the government in general, and Eldon's stories confirmed her feelings. She was opposed to the U.S. entering the war in the Pacific, thinking it unnecessary.

One of Dan's old gearjamming friends from East Glacier wrote from Iran, a country he described as consisting of "terrible heat, rain, mud and cold." Norman Gray, or "Hersch" had been in a base hospital for months with shattered vertebrae. He talked about learning to drink vodka, eating chicken fried in camel fat, and keeping the supplies rolling to "Uncle Joe Stalin." He talked about seeing Jack Benny at the USO. Describing the "women situation," he wrote "quite a few nurses here, but the army still reserves them for the officers. So you can see why we content ourselves with pictures and letters from the girls back home."

Another GI, addressing the letter to "Intermountain Wives" wrote, "Dan, if you don't write next time I'll write Doris and mark it personal and tell her not to let you read it. Of course that checked baggage keeps you busy but if you would do away with that after-dinner nap just once you'd have time to write."

Despite the escalation of the war and their busy schedule, the couple still found time to attend movies like "Buck Privates," starring "the screen's new comedy sensations" Bud Abbott and Lou Costello, and "The Maltese Falcon," starring Humphrey Bogart and Mary Astor. They also attended dances at "Jimmies," fished Lake Blaine occasionally, and went hunting for deer and elk. There was little time for the kind of extended adventures they had enjoyed in previous years when they lived closer to Glacier Park. Dan drove a taxi around Kalispell some nights. They went to card parties and attended Grange functions. Dan played his banjo at various gatherings.

At times, the weather was so bad that the buses couldn't operate. "Didn't go to work," Doris wrote on January 19, 1942. "Terrible blizzard and Dan had to walk; 9 degrees below zero." Dan and Doris followed the railroad tracks to town when visibility was poor.

In 1943 a man from Cut Bank offered to buy the fountain and take over the bus station, but Dan and Doris refused. It was hard work but they made a lot of money on commissions. Doris sensed they were in the right business during the war, and planned to re-enter the tourist business after vacation travel resumed.

Doris and Dan maintained their strong friendship with Carl Lassiter, a driver for the Intermountain Company, and his wife Julia, often visiting at each other's homes. Carl's daughter, Sandra, became a favorite of Doris's.

"Doris brought pies to the depot to sell at the fountain," recalled Sandra, who was 6 or 7 years old at the time. "I remember seeing the pies stacked on the hood of her car in pie carriers."

According to Sandra, Carl tried, always unsuccessfully, to keep Julia's Christmas present a secret. In 1943, he almost succeeded.

"My dad was talking to Dan over the ticket counter one day, waiting to leave on his route, and he had the idea to put mother's present in the depot safe so she couldn't shake it and find out what it was," Sandra recalled. "On Christmas Eve Dad and Mother were getting ready to go home so Dad asked Dan to get the present out of the safe. Dan took it out and, just joking around, shook it. The present started singing; it was a green musical powder box. So mother found out that time, too."

Doris and Dan prospered during their time at the depot. They collected commissions and continued to invest in bonds. Doris, though, remained a penny pincher when it came to dealing with her sister Maxine. In a January 17, 1944, letter, Maxine thanked Doris for some rationing points and meat Doris had sent to her, then went on to write, "About the money I owe you, how much is it to be exact? I will send you the check Papa sent me for the lambs." Maxine went on to ask Doris to let her know if that didn't cover it. Maxine was too polite to point out all the work she'd done for Doris and hadn't been paid for, beginning 20 years earlier with hawking sandwiches to the road construction crew in Iowa and continuing through her indentured servitude at the Hidden Lake camp.

By 1944 Doris began to feel stronger. She had worked hard, but she also spent a lot of time in bed, resting. She popped digitalis regularly and that helped her heart as well. The couple began looking for another tourist camp they could operate in the Glacier Park area, and luckily a camp in the Middle Fork Flathead drainage near Essex was for sale. Dan and Doris quit the bus station on December 1, 1944, and bought the camp, which was located near Glacier's Walton Ranger Station. Dan spent the rest of the winter fixing up and selling the couple's home in Kalispell and traveling back and forth to the camp to ready it for tourists in the spring.

"Left 9:20 a.m. for Essex 'Riverside Camp,'" Dan noted in his diary on February 27. Got there about noon, looked everything over, made coffee, had lunch. Brought curtains home to work on them; home 7:30 p.m.; 22 inches of snow at camp." The next day, Dan took a break from working on the camp and rode the bus 300 miles southeast to visit his family in Bozeman. Doris stayed in Kalispell to pack and organize their household items and the growing collection of antiques, Indian artifacts, and Montana memorabilia they'd acquired.

As usual, Dan took his sister, then 24, to several dances during the five days he was in Bozeman. "Irma and I to Farm Bureau Dance at Fort Ellis," Dan wrote on March 3. Blizzard started 11 p.m.; home 12:25 p.m., temperature 2 degrees."

"I remember dancing with him that night," Irma recalled. "He said to me, 'Hey Mickey, why don't you let me lead.' During the war there weren't many men around. I was used to dancing with other women, and I guess I was used to leading."

Dan continued working on the camp when he returned to northwest Montana. On March 12, he wrote, "Took another load to Riverside. Keith Jarrett went along to help shovel snow. Home at 7:30 p.m., supper and to show, "Arsenic and Old Lace" at the Liberty." The rest of Dan's spotty journal entries that spring concern moving supplies to the camp and doing various repairs there.

Doris's mysterious weakness and heart condition dissipated, although she continued to take heart medicine. Finally, she wrote that she "felt as strong as before. But it took four years in bed."

As World War II wound down, Dan and Doris opened for business at the Riverside Camp. In the summer of 1945, after victory in Europe and Japan's surrender, the mood of the country was upbeat, rationing ended, and vacation travel picked up again. The August 9 edition of the Inter Lake announced, "Second Atomic Bomb Dropped: Important City Nagasaki Hit." And on August 15, the headlines proclaimed, "World Enters New Era of Peace."

The couple demonstrated uncanny timing in their business move, and they once again landed at the Glacier Park boundary.

Doris lifted "Willie" each day of his life even when he reached a weight of 50 pounds. The beaver adored Doris but hated Dan; Dan liked him anyway. Willie often sunned himself and dozed on the back porch, but considered the bathtub his home.

14

Beaver in the Bathtub, 1945-52

"Some folks might have thought it odd that we kept a beaver in our bathtub, but it seemed natural to us."

"If you didn't feed him bread at dinner time Willie would amble over to the breadbox and clip off a few hunks of wood, just to show you what he could do," Dan remembered, describing the pet beaver Dan and Doris kept while operating a tourist camp at Essex from 1945 to 1952. "His headquarters was the bathroom; I believe he figured the bathtub was his." The beaver formed part of a host of pets the Huffines kept at the camp including a mountain goat, bears, skunks, and elk.

The Huffine Riverside Camp stood in a timbered canyon within a shout of a mineral lick used by mountain goats and served a tiny town surrounded by three million acres of wilderness. The Huffines' property crowded the riverbank just upstream from the Walton Bridge and consisted of a gas station and store, rental cabins, and a white frame house. The far bank of the river formed the boundary of Glacier National Park.

Essex lies about 55 miles east of Kalispell on U.S. Highway 2, just 15 miles east of the Huffines' old camp at Hidden Lake. In the 1940s, the town supported a school with about 20 students in grades 1 through 8. Doris reported that 105 people lived in the town according to the 1950 Census. Essex served the Great Northern Railroad as a major boost center for freights heading east over the Continental Divide at Marias Pass. Across the river and just upstream stood the tiny Walton Ranger Station.

Doris carefully recorded the profits and debts of the Riverside camp. During the fall of 1945 they took in only $1,057.55, while investing $2,058.79 in improvements and $667 in inventory. By 1949-52 they were taking in

The Huffine Camp, located across the Middle Fork of the Flathead River from Glacier Park, offered an ideal jump-off point for park visitors and people entering the Great Bear Wilderness. Elk hunting, fishing for bull trout, and huckleberrying drew people from both sides of the Continental Divide. The camp perched in one of the biggest snowbelts in Montana. One year, Doris reported that 123 inches of snow fell in January alone.

$6,500 to $9,000 dollars each year on the service station and cabins, which rented for $1.75 each night. But according to Doris's records, they never made more than $1,000 profit in any one year. At the same time, Doris made wages working at the Post Office, Izaak Walton Hotel, and writing a column for the Hungry Horse News. Dan earned money driving the red tourist buses occasionally in Glacier Park and working at a temporary gravel-crushing plant along the road west of Essex.

Besides being an important station for the Great Northern Railway, Essex was a stopover for automobile tourists drawn by Glacier Park to the east and the Great Bear Wilderness to the west. The winter snows often isolated the town, and communications were poor.

"Essex is really getting up in the world," Doris wrote in her news column on May 19, 1950. "The Great Northern installed a telephone in the Hotel this week. This is the first telephone ever for the Hotel, and in fact the only telephone in Essex. Sure sounds odd to hear a phone ring."

The Izaak Walton Hotel, built in 1939, formed the center of the Essex community. The Inn, as it eventually became known, hosted parties, served as polling place and provided a coffee spot. Doris worked as a waitress at the Inn's cafe from 11 a.m. to 6 p.m. during the winter. This job provided her with an opportunity to keep up on the local happenings for her "Essex News" column, a natural extension of her love for gossip and need for mental stimulation after a winter of cabin fever. Essex is perched in a snowbelt, with snowfalls of over 100 inches a month considered routine during the winter. The severe weather of the Middle Fork canyon often dominated local conversations, and Doris spent a lot of Hungry Horse News column inches

The camp consisted of a gas station, grocery store, rental cabins, a white frame house and this large shop. Dan and Doris kept many of their wild pets in the shop, which was heated by a wood stove.

complaining about it, too.

"Trouble, trouble," she wrote one January. "Such a blizzard in the Middle Fork country this week that even old timers are stumped to remember a worse one. We've had lower temperatures, but 30 below is cold enough. The state rotary plows and V-plow work day and night but can't keep U.S. Highway Two open.

"The Middle Fork country is slipping back," Doris wrote a week later. "Highway Two is still closed, and the report is that it won't be opened for a month." Snow slides covered the road east of Essex. One of the slides buried two maintenance workers, but they were extracted from the snow and revived.

During one January, 123 inches of snow fell. Students attended school for several days in the Izaak Walton Hotel: They could not get into the school because it was buried by snow.

During the winter the ladies of Essex met regularly as part of a sewing club, and Doris dutifully recorded each meeting in her column. More often than not they played cards instead of sewing. "Tuesday afternoon the sewing club met at Mrs. Ray Withrow's," Doris reported. "We had to use snowshoes right up to the door. The roads were all closed and a blizzard was blowing, but we sat around the warmest, friendliest fire and ate lunch."

Electric power lines had not been installed in the Middle Fork canyon, so generators supplied most of the electricity in Essex. In her news column, Doris led the fight to extend electric lines east to Essex. "A representative of the Rural Electric Association was here this week finishing the signing of easements for the electric line," she wrote. "We are sure glad to see work

Across the Middle Fork, the Walton Ranger Station is tucked against the base of the ridge. The ranger station can be seen through the frame of the Walton Bridge. Doris lamented that the 100 residents of Essex barely got to know the Park Service rangers stationed at Walton before they moved to other assignments. Doris's favorite ranger was Dave Stimson, whom she described as "a tough one."

begin on the line as it just doesn't seem possible that we will have lights after all this time. Wouldn't it be wonderful to turn on a light whenever you wanted it and have someone else worry when it goes on the blink."

Hunting season represented the biggest time of the year for Essex residents, and in both her column and journals, Doris often wrote of the sport. She had matured as a narrator and developed an uncanny skill for interpreting nature and life in great detail. She often sermonized about ethical hunting, yet she condoned and took part in breaking game laws as long as local people, or "natives," did the shooting.

"Hunting season opened on the Middle Fork with the largest number of hunters we have ever seen," Doris wrote in her column one October. "It was estimated there were 1100 hunters up here plus horses! We didn't realize that there were that many horses in this part of Montana. Many got their elk, but not all by far. One elk was lost to a coyote and one to a grizzly. To date there has been approximately 80 elk downed."

Once, Doris had a run-in with the game warden, and the warden lost.

"Dan and Eldon and Bobby Coverdell were bringing their elk out of Sheep Creek on snowshoes and backpacking every bit of it, so I decided I'd go meet them," Doris wrote in her journal on December 17, 1948. She hiked several miles up the track, then put on snowshoes to trek along Sheep Creek. She had snowshoed only about 1,000 feet when she spotted a big bull elk across the draw. Doris hollered to scare it away, but the elk didn't move. Then two

LUNCHEON AND DINNER MENU
SERVICE FROM 11:00 TO 6:00 PM
****

BEEF VEGETABLE SOUP

BOILED PORK SHANKS AND SOUR KROUT...........................1.15

BAKED SUGAR CURED HAM.......................................1.15

ROAST LOIN OF PORK**APPLE SAUCE.............................1.15

FRIED CALVES LIVER AND BACON 1.15

GRIED HAMBURGER **RAW ONION.................................1.15

T BONE STEAK..2.00

CLUB STEAK..1.50

STEWED JUNE PEAS   MASHED POTATOES

RICE CUSTARD PUDDING

COFFEE   TEA   MILK

****

HOME MADE PIES 20¢

APPLE   COCOANUT CUSTARD   CHERRY

MENU FORM NO 3

The Izaak Walton Inn and Hotel formed the center of the Essex community. Doris worked in the Inn restaurant to supplement income received from the Huffine Camp. To reach the Inn, Doris walked up a steep trail along a ridge behind their camp, and then across Essex Creek.

A host of wildlife came under the Huffines' care. When the couple found orphaned or injured animals, they brought them into their shop to rehabilitate them. The Middle Fork area was a major wintering grounds for elk, and the couple tried to nurse weakened elk. The Park Service ranger at Walton provided a mountain goat he found near the "Goat Lick" east of the camp. The Huffines raised one orphaned black bear for years.

men on the trail started shooting. The elk fell at the first shot, but soon got up. The man shot again, the elk went down, but stood up again. Doris, with her affinity for animals, reported that she was "desperate to watch such agony," so she started back down the trail in her snowshoes on the run. "Fell down about half a dozen times but finally got close enough that I figured he could hear me so I hollered, 'What in Sam Hill ails you down there, can't you shoot?' and he hollered back, 'I guess not', so I hollered 'my gosh, then get somebody that can.'"

The man had shot about 20 times and had run out of ammunition. Doris said she reached the man and found that he was Louie Haverlandt, the area game warden. His partner had crossed Sheep Creek and began struggling up the other side when Louie caught up with him and grabbed his gun. Then Louie fired three more shots at the elk at close range, finally killing it.

"Pretty good me bawling out the game warden," Doris concluded in her journal. "It sure did get me to see that thing suffer — couldn't hardly think of anything else for several days."

As she explained in her private writings, "natives" had a code of ethics regarding elk hunting. The code seemed to allow residents of Essex to shoot elk just about any time, anywhere, as long as they needed the meat. Most Montanans outside of the immediate Middle Fork canyon area, like residents of Kalispell, must obey game laws.

Doris typed in fine script on 3-by-5-inch paper how Dan, along with neighbors Eldon and Bobby Coverdell, actually "bagged" the elk they were packing out of Sheep Creek the day Doris scolded the game warden.

"Hunted since the season opened October 1st and finally got an elk on December 15th but a different way to get it than ever before," she wrote. "Two fellows, Homme and Leslie, from eastern Montana were staying here in a cabin hunting that day. They went up Sheep Creek on snowshoes and after dark here came Leslie staggering in and said, 'Where is Dan? and how many licenses do you folks have?' I asked Leslie what had happened and why he needed licenses, so he told me that he had gotten into a herd of elk and in the deep snow had shot five he thought. He said he would shoot and they would disappear and there would be another one so he would shoot again and when he went over there he was unable to dress them out as he had forgotten his knife when he left that morning.

"Any way you looked at the deal it was a mess," Doris continued. "At first we didn't know what to do, but thought something had to be done so those elk wouldn't lay up there and spoil. Well, we had to have another license so decided to go get our friend Eldon Coverdell and his license."

The men rounded up snowshoes, plenty of mittens, packboards, flashlights and extra batteries, and an old kerosene lantern. By 8 p.m., long after dark, they were ready to go. By the light of the lantern, the men snowshoed up the trail to the railroad tracks, along the tracks for two miles, then on up the Sheep Creek trail for 3 1/2 miles. When the party finally reached the kill site they found not five dead elk, but seven.

"Dan and Eldon were just floored at such a slaughter," Doris wrote, "and thought of just walking back and reporting Leslie to the game warden, but to save the meat it had to be dressed out that night. And as soon as they laid hands on it they were guilty too, so then there wasn't much to do but help and get their share no matter how they felt. There was one elk still alive with her back broken and that poor thing had to be killed too. By the time it was over they were all dead tired and almost sick with the smell and the cold."

Doris waited for them at the camp, kept soup ready, and made a cake. At 2 a.m., she fell asleep on the cot. Finally at 5 a.m. the men "came staggering in," Doris wrote, "and I do mean staggering as they were so sick they were almost crying. But there was no way to give up once they had started with that meat, nowhere to hide it without leaving tracks and that would never do.

"They were covered with blood," Doris continued, "and it was frozen all on their clothes and overshoes. When it thawed it flowed all over the kitchen

Doris (back row, third from right), taught as a substitute at the tiny Essex school, which served about a dozen students. Four teachers came and went at the school during the seven years the Huffines lived in Essex. Doris is about 46 in this photo but looks younger.

and I bet I mopped at least five times before it stopped dripping off. I've seen many messes but that was one of the worst."

The men worried that someone might find the elk so they rose early the next morning. In particular, Dan worried about losing his "Deputy Game Warden" status. "Until all the elk were tagged whoever did the shooting was sitting on a hot potato," wrote Doris.

The crew, accompanied by several men they'd hired, returned to the kill site the next day. "Dan, Eldon, and Bobby each got a quarter out for 5 days straight running," said Doris. "They were afraid of the weather going wrong on them and didn't dare take a chance on laying off a day so every day they went back and back until it just seemed like they couldn't go another day. Ho, how glad we were to see the last load in here."

Louie Haverlandt, the state game warden who Doris had scolded, could have used his ticket book on Doris and company had he followed her up the Sheep Creek drainage to the site of the seven-elk slaughter. By the time he was done, he'd have written tickets to a good portion of the residents of Essex, including Dan Huffine, the area's "Honorary Deputy Game Warden." Doris didn't seem to feel any guilt, though, because they were "natives."

Ironically, in her news column a few weeks later Doris lamented the illegal taking of elk in general, and criticized violators from Kalispell who had been caught. She even mentioned the names of the "non-natives" from Kalispell, to shame them sufficiently:

"Another party of game violators was apprehended Monday by the ranger and the game wardens," she wrote on December 31. "This time it was G.E. Hendrickson and John Fleming, Kalispell, who loaded an undressed elk into their car on the highway in the park just beyond the Walton ranger station. Three other elk carcasses were laying in the same spot. We cannot understand why people won't realize that crime doesn't pay, even if they have no respect for our game reserves. Need, we could understand, but the violators this season are far from needy. The fines can be as high as $500 and the guns and even the cars can be confiscated."

Doris penned another journal entry that showed she and Dan stretched Fish and Game laws. "Hunting season opened with a bang today," she wrote. "Dan went 'looking' in the timber across from Essex turn-in and just got down in there about 300 yards when other hunters began shooting up by the road so he stood real still and here came 5 elk. When they got just right he shot and his cow he had spotted didn't go down so he shot again. When he went over to get her he fell over a calf the first bullet had killed behind a tree so there he had two elk and only one tag.

"Well he dressed them out in a hurry and came home for me and my tag which I had to go up to Essex and purchase," Doris continued. "We went down there and pulled those two elk to the car. It seemed a long ways I tell you, but Dan said it was only 200 yards. It took us 3 hours to get them loaded."

During hunting season, Doris's column became a miniature outdoor magazine. Everyone went to Doris with their best hunting stories, which she gleefully recorded. "Many bear stories are heard in our district at this time of the year," Doris wrote one October. "The following told by a Texas fellow packing for the Bear Creek ranch is the best one heard recently. A hunting party composed of several men had packed into the upper Big River or Middle Fork country and had secured their elk and two grizzlies. When they reported back at camp that evening one hunter had failed to get his elk hung up on account of a grizzly showing up. He had to take for camp as he only carried a 30-30, and that's no bear gun.

"So," Doris continued, "this Texas packer decided he would go back and get the hunter's meat for him, grizzly or not, and with a saddle horse and two pack horses tied together he proceeds up the trail. While searching the mountainside for the meat there suddenly looms up a massive grizzly some distance above him and coming for him like a Diesel engine. This was just too much for the horses — the saddle horse did a flip flop which left Tex afoot, but he did manage to grab the ring on a pack saddle as they went by although he could not get on. One leg was partly over, then he was dragging again, on again, knocked this way and that by trees as that horse went snorting and crashing down through the timber on that hillside. But in the end when the horse stopped, Tex was still with him much the worse for the trip and still wondering if it would have been any worse to face the bear."

Essex, particularly the Huffine property along the river, was located in a major wildlife wintering zone. Doris felt protective about wildlife in the area and she publicly scolded people who did things she considered inhumane.

"Sportsman?" she wrote in her column. "Since last spring we had a beautiful brown mother bear roaming around Essex entertaining tourists and local residents. When first seen she had 3 baby cubs but before long a sportsman(?) had taken one of the cubs — then all summer there were two and they did no real damage but climbed trees and roamed around to the enjoyment of everyone. In September another sportsman(?) killed the second innocent little cub and this week a real sportsman(?) shot the mother herself and left the untaught baby to die during the winter. We have decided that men who do such unlawful killing have no respect for law, wildlife or its value to our country, and we fully appreciate Judge Martin's heavy fines for such sportsmen when apprehended."

As it turns out, that last cub didn't die that winter. Dan found him clinging to a limb, caught the cub, wrapped him in a blanket, and brought him into the Huffines' shop for the winter. Doris put a collar on him and chained him to the shop wall.

According to Doris, the cub "stayed awake all winter; he was warm don't you see. And he sure grew. We fed him scraps from the Izaak Walton Hotel. In the spring and summer we took him outside and chained him to a tree."

The bear became a tourist attraction. Dan trained him to sit back on his haunches, grasp a bottle of orange pop, and guzzle it down. Then for a while, the bear had a companion around the Huffine place when a mountain goat took up quarters in the basement.

It seems that one day the park ranger stationed at Walton had found a nanny goat lying on the ground near the goat lick. The ranger asked Dan to help him move it.

"They couldn't figure why the goat couldn't get up," Doris remembered. "Dan and the ranger decided that since we had the bear in the shop we might as well have the goat too. They put chains around its horns to control her and brought it down to our shop."

Because, as Doris said, "the goat was so vicious," Dan arranged bales of hay to separate the two animals. Though she was fond of the bear, Doris never developed a friendship with the goat. The next spring the goat died, apparently of old age, leaving just the bear in residence for a while.

That summer Dan's sister, Irma, and her two daughters visited from Bozeman. As the two girls played behind the camp Doris watched the bear "crawl back behind a tree and as the kids got in the circle (of its chain) the bear rushed out at them and scared them silly. So Dan said, 'This is it. We've got to get rid of that bear; it almost got those two little girls.'"

That evening, Dan released the bear miles south of the camp.

But that didn't mean Dan and Doris were through with keeping wild animals. It was not long afterward that they found Willie, their pet beaver, on the east side of Marias Pass. Dan had heard that the river had flooded over the road near Lubec.

"We went over to see the flood," recalled Doris. "The water ran deep over the road; you couldn't drive through. We were sitting there watching the water and we noticed this little teeny animal, about six inches long, washed up on the pavement.

"Dan got out and went over to pick it up — it was like a little drowned rat. And he said, 'Oh, it's a little beaver!' We were scared of the little rascal because we heard all these stories of beaver chewing things with their wicked teeth. So we put him in a wooden box. We took him home, warmed him up and fed him bread and milk. He loved that. We wrapped him up and put him in a pail, so he couldn't chew up our table and cupboards during the

"Willie" the beaver — named after the willows he loved — ranked as the Huffines' all-time favorite pet.

night. But we found out he didn't have any teeth, the poor little guy. We got him the first of June, but he couldn't bite a thing until his teeth came in that October. We had to put every bit of food in his mouth, all that time.

"In October he got to where he could chew tiny twigs," Doris continued. "I'd hold the twigs and he'd bite, bite, bite, right up to my fingers but he'd never bite me, never. One time he bit Dan. He never liked Dan, I don't know why. When I was in town for supplies the beaver wouldn't eat. He wouldn't take food from Dan."

Willie, named for the willows he loved, beefed up under Doris's care, quickly reaching a weight of 50 pounds. Each day Doris prepared milk and bread for Willie, talking to him as if he were her child. Willie "got bread to eat whenever he wanted, otherwise he'd eat your cabinets or chew holes in the doors and floors," Doris recalled. "He headquartered in the basement and the bathroom; we put water in the bathtub for him and he seemed real satisfied there."

Willie ranged around the camp, eating grass and small plants. Surprisingly, he never waddled down to the river. A snowfall during Willie's first autumn startled him. Doris watched Willie, only a foot long, "use his little front feet like a bulldozer and go this way and that way, backwards, forwards, to uncover his grass. He was so sad to see his greenery covered."

The beaver whined through his nose when he wanted food and loved to be held, especially when frightened. "Once," remembered Doris, "when the snow was deep, Dan came down the path and the beaver ran quickly to me and wanted to be picked up. So Dan took a picture of me holding him. Dan said the look on Willie's face said, 'I made it. You didn't get me this time.' I lifted the beaver every day of his life, so I was used to it even when he weighed 50 pounds."

By the summer of 1951 the Huffines had built the camp into a profitable business (Dan is on the right, Doris at left). They loved the mountains, huckleberries, bull trout and clear waters of the Middle Fork country, but were tired of fighting the winter snows.

Doris wrote Christmas letters in 1949 to her nephews and nieces from "Willie," describing his life at the Riverside Camp. "When I was real young, I didn't even weigh a pound," she wrote. "I am past one year old now and I weigh more than you maybe; I weigh 49 pounds this Christmas.

"There are lots of things I like to eat but I think I like apples best of all," continued "Willie." "I don't think I could live without my bread and willows every day. I cut the willow limbs into little pieces then I can take the bark off so fast and chew it up with my back teeth. Did you know I have two sets of teeth and two sets of lips? I have four long front teeth for cutting and one set of lips in front and one set of lips behind to keep water out of my mouth while I'm chewing branches underwater.

"You should see my nest. It is padded with the straw I made out of willow limbs. It looks like a big hen's nest but it just fits me. When I want something to do I just chew all the limbs into fine slivers until they look just like straw.

"Oh you don't know what my tail is like, do you? It is paddle-shaped, thick in the middle and thin on the edges. It is always warm and when I sleep I curl it under me and sleep with my feet on it. My stomach is covered with short, soft fur, just like the softest feathers on a goose. I would let you feel my stomach because I like little boys and girls.

"On Friday the folks went to town and left me all alone," Willie continued. "I was so lonesome and I wish you had been here to play with me. I made a dam out of the things in the basement. I piled up all my sticks and the old broom, and a lot of boxes near the opening of my pen. Finally I heard them come home and I got out of my nest and right over by the door. They came down the stairs and when the door opened I rushed up the stairs, I wasn't going to stay down there any longer. Oh, I was so glad to know they'd come back to me and I just did all my tricks so they would stay with me.

"Now I must go to sleep as I sleep all day long and only play towards evening," Willie concluded. "I go to bed every night at 10:30 but sometimes I stay up later when my folks forget to put me to bed. Merry Christmas, from Willie."

A few weeks later, Doris wrote another Willie letter to her six-year-old nephew, Charles, the son of Doris's sister, Shirley. "I didn't notice there was a nice green, pine smelly tree in our front room until nearly New Years. I thought oh boy, will that taste good and it will help me make a dam by my nest in the basement. I sat up on my tail and made a big jump right for it. I was dragging it towards my nest when my folks grabbed me. I scolded them and sunk my teeth into the base of the tree and began chewing it down; the whole tree fell over. When the folks grabbed the tree to save the decorations I just snapped off a big branch and dragged it off to my den. But those pine trees make a lot better dam than they do eating. I don't like the way the pine juice gets in my teeth. I am awful tired this time of day so I will go back to sleep now. Willie."

In another letter, Willie described his bath. "I have a little round tub that sets in the long white bathtub and when I get out of the water I just sit in the tub and drip off. Sometimes I have willow branches in the tub so I eat them and then go back in the water again. Lots of nights I stay in the tub for two hours or more. When I get tired of being in the tub I climb up on the side and sit on the very edge on my hind feet with my front feet in the air, like a squirrel. I am usually all wet and I make an awful puddle on the floor if they don't take me down and wipe me off before I run around. I don't like to be wiped and I sure do fuss and try to get away."

Willie's last letter was again to Charles, written the next spring. "Yesterday they left the basement door open so I could have more light and I went up the steps clear to the top. I didn't know how I was going to get back down and I was just sitting there when here came your Aunt Doris. She didn't see me and I didn't make a bit of noise and she nearly stepped on me. That would have been awful if we had both fallen down the steps but we didn't. I went into the front room and there was a big fern that I hadn't seen before; guess a woman left it at our house for a while. No one was watching me so I went over and pulled some of it down. Just then they saw me so I ran fast as all get out into the bathroom.

"Now it is time for me to get my apples. I can smell apples if they are even in the same room with me. Once they left some in a sack up on a shelf down in the basement and I worked all night long trying to build a dam so I could crawl up and get them. I drug everything there was over and piled it all in a heap. I had planks, boards, the broom, pasteboard boxes, canned goods, and everything but I couldn't get high enough. We hope you have a nice Easter but you can eat all the eggs as I don't like eggs one bit. I am, Willie."

Willie thrived under the care of Doris and Dan. He considered the bathroom and the basement his own. He clung to Doris and seemed jealous if any other animal got near her. In the early spring, after the Huffines had had Willie for two years, a well-meaning neighbor disrupted Willie's world. Eldon Coverdell, a good friend of the Huffines, was driving from Kalispell to Essex one day and spotted a beaver crossing the road. Thinking the beaver would be a good pal for Willie, Eldon stopped his car and tried to catch him.

"Eldon jammed on the brakes and ran over the bank after that beaver," remembered Doris. "He grabbed the beaver and the beaver took a big hunk out of Eldon's leg. That blood running down his leg made Eldon mad, so he ran back up to the car and grabbed some blankets, and went after him again. He caught the wild beaver, brought him to our house and put him in the basement with Willie."

But Willie, like a spoiled child, threw a fit. "The other beaver just scared our beaver silly," remembered Doris. "Willie wasn't going to put up with that. So he crawled high up on his pen and just flopped hard on the cement floor. We think maybe he got hurt, maybe he broke something inside."

Shortly after Willie's run-in with the wild beaver two or three round bald spots formed on his hide and he refused the water in the bathtub. "So," Doris recalled, "we decided to let him go. We thought something must be lacking."

Doris cried as she carried Willie down to the Middle Fork, which flowed bank-full. Willie refused to enter the water, so Dan threw him in.

"The poor little guy," recalled Doris. "He got out and was just shaking because the oil had gone out of his fur so we brought him back to the house. A few days later he got worse and couldn't eat and his stomach bloated. We did everything we could but he died that night."

The Huffines felt as much affection for Willie as other parents felt for a child. "I was really attached to the beaver and so was Dan, even though the beaver didn't like Dan. We were just broken up ... to lose the beaver. Both of us cried and cried about that — worse than losing a dog."

Doris ranked Willie as the best pet she'd ever had, even though other Middle Fork residents considered a beaver an unorthodox companion. "Some folks might have thought it odd that we kept a beaver in our bathtub, but it seemed natural to us. I loved that beaver."

Eventually, Doris worked through her grief over losing Willie. As spring advanced into summer, she promoted in her columns the outdoor activities for which Essex was famous. "These are busy days," Doris wrote. "We are attempting to crowd the entire summer into one month. Many are trying to see who can catch the biggest bull trout. Others are trying to bring in the biggest mess of flats (westslope cutthroat trout), and an awful lot of us are trying to pick five gallons of huckleberries in one day.

"Your reporter is limping around on one leg this week and having a fit about it, too, as the huckleberries are getting ripe." she continued. "These mountain huckleberry patches are bad enough with two good legs so one and a half just isn't enough. Saturday while putting oil into a car I climbed up on the bumper and slipped off as it was raining. My shin sure did hurt and I thought, there I've skinned it again, but it was worse than that as I had hit a bolt and cut an awful hole. Had to take time off and go to town and get ten stitches taken. Folks are sure having fun about the high priced oil Huffines put out these days.

"Odd things do happen to a person's berries in the huckleberry patch, but the following took the cake this week in our country," Doris wrote in one column. "We had set our packboard with the box partly filled with berries down about six feet from where we were picking, when all of a sudden a snowshoe rabbit going full force hit it and knocked it over spilling the berries. Nothing to do but pick the things up, and we had just accomplished this and gone back to picking when here came the rabbit from the other direction going just as strong, and if he didn't run into that pack again and knock it over from the other way. This almost caused us to stop picking and hunt up a stick in readiness for the third time, but thank goodness he never returned."

During the summer, Essexites often shared their town with black bears. Run-ins with bears made great copy for Doris's column. "Our bear have us worried and we don't know what to do about it," she wrote one July. "The other evening Mr. and Mrs. A.E. Havens were sitting in their living room when they noticed a black bear ambling towards the clothes line where the wash was hanging. The bear stopped and seemed to be looking the clothes over so Havens said, 'Look at that bear — he is trying to pick himself out the warmest pajamas'. But it wasn't pants that the bear was looking for as it grabbed one of Mrs. Haven's dresses and took off for the timber.

"Mrs. Havens immediately brought the remainder of the clothes in the house," Doris continued, "but left a rug and an old sack on the line to dry during the night. The next morning they were gone, so we are thinking our bear are getting very highly civilized when they want to wear clothes and have rugs in their homes. Mr. Bealey, the forest service ranger, suggested that the bear think winter is almost here and are trying to build up their nest. No, either way it just isn't good, and we do hate to furnish clothes for the bears."

The promise of good fishing fanned the Huffines' tourist trade and, in her column, Doris hyped the success of local anglers and of anglers boarding at the Huffine Camp. "Fishing has improved so there's lots of fun in the Middle Fork country these days. Folks are bringing in bull trout every day. Six and eight pounders are the average but who wants them any larger! Lola Gillispe caught an eight pound one the other day and this is her first summer to fish our waters. The flats aren't biting yet but they are usually a bit behind the bulls. The old river is just getting down to the good fishing level the last day or so.

"Even the young 'uns here are catching big fish," she continued. "Sunday, little Snapper Smith, who will start school this fall, landed a big 7-1/2 pounder all by himself. When asked, his dad informed us that he did not help one bit except with advice but that he did hold on to Snapper's coat tail so he wouldn't be pulled into the water. It was sure a beautiful big fish for anyone to land."

Doris and Dan had become mainstays in the community, and got along with everyone, with one exception. Frank Parma operated a "beer parlor" and seemed to be one of the wealthiest people in Essex. Doris and others thought that he came by his money illegally. He had been arrested for assault several times and often threatened people with guns.

Frank lived upstream and used the same water line as Dan and Doris, served by Essex Creek and a small spring. After several years of no disputes over water, Parma suddenly shut off the water valve. Parma believed he could bully the Huffines as he had others, but he failed to anticipate Doris's grit.

"I was working at the hotel today and at supper time Dan came in and said our water was turned off," Doris wrote on March 7, 1949. "Frank Parma was in there eating so I simply walked up the counter, looked him in the eye, and asked him what he knew about our water. Frank said, 'I shut off the valve. I need the water,' so I asked him how long he was going to keep if off, and he said, 'Oh, I'll maybe give you water 2 or 3 hours tomorrow.' "

Doris and Dan drove to Kalispell to see the county attorney, Ambrose Measure, about the dispute. Measure told Doris and Dan that Frank couldn't deny them their water rights and that he'd go right to court and get an injunction forcing Parma to restore the water flow.

On March 21 Doris and Dan "went in to see why the water hadn't been turned on. Frank had been there and told Measure that he wasn't ever turning it on again. Dan went up to Measure's office to see Measure, and there sat Frank Parma with Lee Compton on one side and Bob Wright on the other (small Capone and his henchmen). When we finally got to see Measure he told us what Frank had said, and then he told us to go to court would cost such an awful lot, and be such a long case that he thought we had better try to get the water out of the river. Sure changed his tune after seeing Frank, so we went to see another lawyer and he is handling the case. He says it's a cinch and we are hoping."

On March 26, Doris received a letter of support from the previous owner of the Essex camp: "Dear Dan & Doris: I have your letter of the 24th and am only sorry that I do not know all the answers for if ever I detested anyone it was that Frank Parma. I had a run-in with him when he lived in the old Sullivan house next to us. He was trying to get a beer license at the time and by taking it up with the State Board of Equalization, I finally kept him from getting it and I sincerely hope you beat him this time. Your place has been getting water through the line from the Spring for the last twenty years so am of the opinion that no Judge or Jury will stand to let anyone cut it off now."

In the trial held on April 28, the judge ruled that Parma had to allow the Huffines use of the spring. But the battle continued anyway.

On November 16, in a letter to the folks in Iowa, Doris wrote, "Oh, the water deal, I must tell you the latest on that. A week ago yesterday the old coot came over to the car where Dan was up at the post office and told Dan that he should get a pump in the river by yesterday as he was turning the water off. Well, we thought sure he would do it this time so we washed everything on the place again and even took a bath. We got all the tubs and pails full of water but the water is still running today and this is two days after it was to be turned off.

"I tell you," Doris continued, "it is hard and wearing on us and our clothes to be washed so much to keep up with that old bird and his turning off our water. If he turns off our water the Great Northern will turn off his water so I think that is what is holding him back."

In June 1950 Doris was still writing the county to get a court injunction against Parma. In the letter Doris said that "there is plenty of water for everyone if Parma didn't want to play pig."

Finally, the Huffines installed a different pipeline from the Great Northern spring. In September of 1950 the county served an injunction which forced Parma to allow the Huffines right of way through his land for the pipeline, and the battle ended. Frank Parma had proved to be a formidable foe, but Doris's persistence won in the end.

Through the years, Doris and Dan maintained friendships with the four Park Service rangers who had tours of duty at the Walton Ranger Station, just across the river from Essex. One January, Doris wrote a column about her favorite ranger. "Whenever a new ranger moves into a district, some of the folks always wonder, is he a tough one. We fully decided this week that our new ranger, Dave Stimson, is a tough one.

"Thursday morning the road crew reported to Dave that a rocky mountain goat must be hurt as it was standing just under the bed of the bridge up at the Goat Lick. Dave went up to see about the deal. He couldn't see under the bridge from the top because the goat had crowded close up against the support so he walked up the side of the draw a short distance and had taken about six steps down the steep bank in the snow when he fell on some ice and shot down the incline. He grabbed for something to stop himself, but found nothing, and in less time than it takes to tell, he hit the snowy creek bed almost 100 feet below.

"Landing on his shoulder and head," Doris continued, "he was still able to pick himself up, walk up the creek a distance, and get out on his own," Doris continued. "Looking back up where he started he will never understand how he escaped being cut on the rocks. Dave says it was comical when he looked up at the goat: It seemed to say 'what are you doing down there?'"

Later that winter, Doris wrote an account of how Stimson's son had a run-in with a bull elk. "Gordon Stimson had the once-is-enough experience of being charged by a bull elk this Saturday. He had gone with his father, Ranger Dave Stimson, on a ski trip into the headwaters of Ole Creek and coming out they were following this group of elk. The elk had just crossed a creek and were trying to get up the bank on the opposite side when Gordon and his father came up close enough to get a good picture.

"Gordon dropped his poles," Doris continued, "and was getting out his camera when his ski suddenly slid down an incline taking him within about 20 feet of the creek. This maddened the old elk so he turned and took for Gordon, but something caused him to turn down the creek as he was about half way across, thus saving Gordon. Bet Gordon has lost all interest in close up pictures of his dad's elk."

When Stimson left Walton, Doris lamented that Essexites barely got to know a ranger before he moved on.

The same seemed to be true for teachers at the Essex school. In the seven years Doris lived in Essex, four teachers came and went. "Helen Coverdell has handed in her resignation from the school here," Doris wrote in June 1951. "We are sorry to lose her as she taught here four years, the longest any teacher has remained so far up towards the summit of the Rocky Mountains."

Another teacher left after the next school year. In September of 1952 the Essex school year started late, and as Doris related, "Our school starts on Wednesday with a man teacher. That is going to be something different for Essex."

Doris was known for having the first nickel she ever made. While she was at Essex, she probably didn't buy herself a single new item of clothing. A letter to her family in Iowa illustrates the frugality for which she was famous.

"I have been making over a coat for myself and you should see it," she wrote. "I think it looks real nice considering what I started with. I even had enough fur left from the collar to make a little hat. I still have to get a buttonhole made in the front up near the collar but it is where I had to do some piecing so I think I will take it to town and get it made with a machine.

"I felt like we just didn't have the $5 to spend this fall on a coat for me. I tell you we sure haven't much left this fall to get through the winter on since we have had that water deal to pay for and then the new car and the tin roofs on this house. Guess we overestimated what we were going to make this summer. My old coat is 8 years old and the goods are wearing through in the back where the belt hits it but I will turn it and get some more wear out of it so I can wear it while I work on the old grey one."

Finally, after seven years, Doris, 51, and Dan, 47, decided that they'd had enough of shoveling all the snow in the Essex snow belt, and they listed the Riverside Camp for sale. A friend provided a tip on some land and buildings east of Kalispell that would be suitable for establishing a gift shop and campground, and after looking over the property, they decided to buy it. The Huffines sold the Essex camp in the fall of 1952 to Ray Dean for $12,000; Dean paid nothing down and the Huffines carried the loan.

Dan and Doris turned the camp over to the Deans on October 2. Mr. Dean and his family were supposed to have shown up in the morning but didn't arrive until 5 p.m. The Huffines operated the camp for them that day, then turned over the list of and bill for the inventory. Dean didn't have the money to cover the inventory, so Dan covered him with a loan.

The Huffines felt relieved to have finalized the sale of the camp. They looked forward to putting their energies into the new property they'd purchased in the Flathead Valley. The couple had collected many antiques, Indian artifacts, and other items during their years in the park and afterwards, and they planned on establishing a campground, gift shop, and museum. It was a natural conclusion to their many years of working with dudes and tourists, and gave them a chance to at least hope for a little easier life.

By 1953 Dan (right) and Doris (center) had converted a large building into a museum and gift shop. They didn't charge admission but accepted donations. South of the museum they established a campground and picnic area.

15
The Huffine Montana Museum, 1952-1984

"Only your help keeps our doors open!
No Government aid rec'd here."

From the time of their marriage, Doris and Dan had been collecting artifacts and antiques from Montana and elsewhere, hoping to establish a museum. The land they'd bought in the Flathead Valley, bordering U.S. Highway 2, 40 miles southwest of Essex and 10 miles east of Kalispell, was well suited for such a business.

A 24-by-26-foot log house with a picture window stood on 10 acres and looked out across Highway 2 to the front of the Swan Mountain Range, less than a mile away. The couple planted an attractive flower garden, a large vegetable garden, and a raspberry patch.

North of the house stood a large building that Dan had moved onto the site and then converted into a museum and gift shop. Soon, Dan added siding to the house and built a connecting room between the house and the museum. The couple put hundreds of pieces of Montana memorabilia on display in the museum and opened for business.

Adjacent to their land, Otto Schulz had operated a small fly shop since 1945. Doris sometimes plugged Otto's flies in her Essex News column. Dan and Doris had known Otto for years; he had given them the tip when the 10 acres came up for sale.

During 1953, the couple took in about $2,400 at the museum and gift shop. They sold a variety of souvenirs, gifts, and locally made crafts of horn, wood and agate. Visitors did not pay admission to the museum, but an an-

The Mountain View Fly Shop, operated by the Huffines' friend Otto Schulz, was covered with deer antlers. The Tally Ho Wagon can be seen between the fly shop and museum.

tique vase was strategically placed below a hand-lettered sign that proclaimed, "Donations: Only your help keeps our doors open! No Government aid rec'd here. Thank You!"

People from all over the United States and other countries signed the museum visitor log. The museum featured extensive collections of Blackfeet and other Indian artifacts. Doris's hand-lettered posters told stories about many of the mounted animals, firearms of all descriptions, and other items. Antique music boxes, spinning wheels, a Montana horse-drawn hearse, and an original "Tally Ho" wagon from Glacier Park formed the museum's centerpieces. The covered, horse-drawn Tally Ho stage was used to haul passengers around Glacier Park in the Lake McDonald area from 1911 to 1917. The Huffines later donated the wagon to the park.

"Whenever somebody had something they didn't want, we kept it," remembered Doris, describing the way they acquired many of their antiques. She and Dan also traveled around Montana and elsewhere collecting Indian artifacts and purchasing antiques and collectibles at auctions.

The couple hoped to concentrate their energies on their third and last effort to establish and build up a tourist business. To attract steady traffic to their establishment, for instance, Dan and Doris established a campground in the timber east of their house, adding picnic tables and outhouses as amenities. Then, like an unwanted boomerang, the Riverside Camp returned to their ownership when the Deans defaulted on their loan.

"One evening," wrote Doris in 1954, "the Deans stopped in with their

188

four little kids to talk about the Essex place. They said they could pay some of the interest but none of the principal on the loan we were carrying for them. We were just floored.

"When we asked them why they couldn't pay, they said they just didn't have it," Doris continued. "Didn't know why and didn't know where it had gone."

Doris and Dan felt sympathy for the Deans and their children, but that all changed later that year. During the 1954 hunting season, an incident occurred that led Doris to write: "Trouble hits us again and the last three days have been hard to take."

As she told the rest of the story, "Last Friday afternoon Tetraults came out and wanted Dan to go along hunting the next day up by Essex where it was open for elk. At first Dan didn't want to go as it meant getting up awful early but he finally decided to go and then Erna and I thought we would go too, and visit Katy. We got up about 4:30 the next morning and got to Essex by about 6:00."

The men went hunting while the women visited. Later in the morning, according to Doris, "Dan rushed in with the guns and said they had shot two elk, and it seemed that Ray Dean (the fellow who is buying our place) had come to where they were dressing out the elk and had told them that he was sure that was closed territory. We really didn't know enough about game laws to know just what to do in such a case but we thought surely Dean would know that Dan wouldn't go right out there in broad daylight and kill elk and dress them out if they had known it was in the wrong place."

The party thought they wouldn't be prosecuted because, as Doris related, "the park wants those elk killed since they just starve in the winter so they try to ignore the violations if they aren't too extreme."

They reached West Glacier without being pursued so the men began feeling safe and talked about how good the steaks would taste. Doris still worried.

The Huffines' Tally Ho Wagon was used to haul tourists from West Glacier to Lake McDonald in the early 1900s. It was one of Doris's favorite museum attractions. It was later donated to Glacier National Park.

Dan and Doris also displayed an old Montana hearse in the museum. John Clarke's woodcarving, "Old Trap, Bear, and Hunter," can be seen in the upper right of the photo.

"Well, we got back to Tetraults," continued Doris, "and got it all hung up, then we came on down to our place. Dan was so sure he wouldn't be arrested that he got cocky and instead of taking the side road before we got home and washing off the blood, like I wanted to do, we just came right down the highway to our place. The top of the car was all bloody and here sat the game wardens so then there just wasn't any use denying the deal. They said, 'Well, Dan there just isn't anything to do but take you in.' I asked the game warden who told them about the deal and he said 'That fellow at the bridge, Dean.'

"It was just awful to think that a fellow who's under as much obligation to us as Dean is would do a thing like that," Doris continued. "No one likes a squeaker especially when they can't see where it gains them any deal. We could appeal the case but it never pays to hire a lawyer if you can help it so we just had to take what they gave us, which was a fine of $202.50. And no meat either. Dean can't break the code of the Middle Fork natives and slap a person in the face like that and then expect to have us let him live there any longer for nothing. That kind of deal really makes me lose sleep and now we have to foreclose on him."

Dan and Doris took the Deans to court, paying more than $400 in court costs and legal fees. The camp returned to their ownership; they wrote off a business loss and netted about $1,500. Now they had two tourist camps to operate.

"I sure hope you don't mean to go back up to Essex," Maxine Conrad, Doris's sister, wrote from Washington. "It's an inspiration about some of the things you can raise in your garden that you couldn't raise up there. It is sure awful to get the darned place back again, but if you can sell it fast enough and often enough maybe you can make something yet."

Maxine closed the letter with complaints about handling her rambunctious boys in the suburbs, "Gotta go...kids are playing in a trash fire and carrying burning brands into our garage." That off-hand comment gave the ever-creative Doris an idea. She asked Maxine to bring her boys along, live at the Essex camp and operate it the next summer. Maxine said yes, as she

Doris continued to teach at schools around the Flathead Valley. Here she's pictured with students of the Boorman School, west of Kalispell, in 1959. Students remembered her as firm but well-liked.

had so many times in the past.

So it was that the Huffines operated both the Huffine Montana Museum and Campground, and the Essex camp, with Maxine's help, during the summer of 1955. Maxine managed the cabins and store at Essex while Doris and Dan spent most of their time improving and operating their museum and campground in the Flathead Valley. Dan traveled back and forth to Essex 20 times to maintain the camp and the couple invested another $800 in improvements.

"We were real busy with my job at the lumber company, Doris in the Museum, and Doris's sister running the cabins at Essex," wrote Dan in the couple's 1955 Christmas letter. "We had to run up there quite a few times to fix things." Then on to other important matters, just to prove that hardship did not encourage the Huffines to lose their sense of perspective: "We didn't raise any chickens this year but still have 19 hens from last year. We did raise 17 ducks, and still have our talking magpie, one raccoon, three chipmunks and 12 rattlesnakes."

Along with Dan's letter in 1955, Doris sent out a story about a neighbor with the title, "Fisher's Well and Coverdell's Cow." It was another delightful tale of animal hijinks.

"Well I must tell you about the cow falling in the well," she began. "Coverdells have just one milk cow and they always have the worst luck with it. Across the road lives Mrs. Fisher and she is a problem — always in trouble and having a struggle of some kind.

"This summer Fishers had to have a well drilled to 385 feet so that well cost them a mint of money and it's the most important thing in their lives at present. The other evening Mrs. Coverdell and her father were at home and they heard the worst noise on the back porch and said it was so awful it sounded like a bobcat got hold of their young bull dog. Then the door burst open and in came Mrs. Fisher with tears running off her chin and she was moaning and throwing her hands. Finally they got it out of her that their (Coverdells') cow had fallen into the 8-foot-deep hole that held the electric pump for Fisher's well.

"It seems that the top over the well was only 1-inch thick boards and when the cow walked over it, the boards broke and down she went," Doris continued. "Mrs. Coverdell got over to Fishers and there stood the cow wedged down there as calm as could be."

Mrs. Coverdell called her husband and he arrived from work driving a wrecker. He tied some ropes around the cow and hoisted her out of the hole. The cow walked home as if nothing had happened. Mrs. Fisher lamented that "the cow's puddling would spoil their new well and that she just didn't know what they would ever do about all the cow flops the cow left down there."

"I guess she did leave quite a few," concluded Doris. "Dan thinks the Fishers should start raising mushrooms as they need a fertilized dark place, but he hasn't seen Mrs. Fisher yet to suggest it."

All in all, the Huffines enjoyed their new location in the Flathead Valley. The museum and gift shop proved to be a success. On the gift shop alone between 1954 and 1956 the Huffines took in about $2,500 to $3,000 a year. Of course, they spent about $1,800 a year to buy gift shop merchandise and more antiques. During 1955 and 1956, Dan made about $4,000 a year working for the Rocky Mountain Lumber Company in nearby Columbia Falls, and he still drove occasionally for the Glacier Park Transportation Company. Doris was the main proprietor at the museum and gift shop, and she kept the business's books. Also, in 1956, the couple leased the Essex camp to several people, leading to an additional source of income. The Huffines received an annual payment of $300 to $400 and a percentage of the proceeds from the cabins and service station.

That same year, the U.S. Army Corps of Engineers proposed to build a dam on the Middle Fork of the Flathead River, four miles upstream from the camp at Essex. Backwaters would flood the magnificent Spruce Park Gorge on the river within what later became the Great Bear Wilderness Area. But rather than fighting the dam proposal, Doris chose economics over environment and supported it as a way to spur development.

"I am writing you in regard to the proposed Spruce Park Dam on the Middle Fork of the Flathead River," she wrote to Montana's U.S. Sen. James E. Murray on September 30, 1956. "I am asking that you do all in your power to get it built. We think this is a very wise improvement to our country."

Doris went on to list four advantages of building the dam. She noted that there would be no destruction of farmland or private land, and that the dam would add to the electrical production of Hungry Horse Dam on the South Fork of the Flathead River, create a new fishing lake, and provide two years of employment.

"It is so out of the way it wouldn't interfere with anyone," she continued. "From our viewpoint there is so much for Spruce Park Dam and so little against it. It seems that anyone who believes in the advancement and improvement of our country would be all out for this dam."

Despite such sentiments, the dam proposal was defeated.

Over the next several years the couple drove back and forth from the Flathead Valley to maintain the Essex Camp. In February of 1958, they had a string of bad luck. First, while cooking a chicken to take to Essex for lunch Doris was badly burned across her face when the chicken exploded. Then, later that month, they drove to Essex to meet the couple who would be renting the camp for the year. They shoveled about three feet of snow from the roof and did various repairs, then climbed into their pickup and drove west on the narrow highway along the Middle Fork of the Flathead River, enjoying their view of the snowy peaks of Scalplock, Rampage, and St. Nicholas in Glacier Park across the river. Suddenly, a car appeared in the rear-view mirror.

Recalled Dan in his diary, "We saw a car coming from behind and was sure he would hit us square on but at the last minute the car swung sideways and hit the corner of our pickup box. Doris's head hit the windshield, the glove compartment door opened and everything spilled on the floor." The couple drove back to Essex and called a highway patrolman, who arrived three hours later. Damage to the Huffines' truck amounted to $156.

Even though they had moved to the Flathead Valley, Dan and Doris still enjoyed the mountains. In their 50s, they often hunted in the backcountry. Each year they bought deer and elk tags, and often at least bagged a deer.

"Left for Strawberry Lake, went to end of the road and 1 1/2 miles up the trail," Dan wrote on November 15, 1958. "Saw a doe walking 50 yards away and then a big 5-point buck looking for the doe. The buck kept working closer to within 50 yards when I shot. Sure had a struggle getting him up to the trail. Doris lifted and pushed on the hind legs."

During the next hunting season, the couple took part in a meat-packing marathon with their neighbors, the Jorgensens. The ordeal was reminiscent of their elk packing adventures when they lived in Essex. Wrote Doris:

"Jim, Barbara, and David Jorgensen stopped in and had shot an elk up the North Fork, David said; then later he said he shot three bulls and wanted Dan's help and advice getting them out. The next morning Dan and I followed behind David, Jim, and two other men to help get the elk out. We went UP and UP through three feet of snow until it seemed like we couldn't go anymore, but still we hadn't reached the elk. Finally after we had been winded time and time again and had to rest dozens of times, Jim said, 'Those mountains over there will look like runts when we get up to where the elk are,' and he was right."

When the group found the first elk Doris wrapped up the heart and then continued on up to where the men were quartering the other two elk. The men tied ropes on the elk quarters and dragged and skidded them along the mountainside. After several hitches of pulling them along and getting them all together again, they reached the edge of a steep ledge and pushed them over the side. The elk rolled to the bottom of the canyon where the party had left a sled.

"The rest of us slid and slipped down the mountain," Doris said, "through brush and over rocks down to the elk. It was dark by then and we were all wet. My feet were so wet the water was squishing between my toes and if I stopped I felt like I would freeze."

At that point the group loaded some of the quarters on the toboggan. With the aid of two flashlights, and eating frozen Hershey bars for energy, the crew finally reached the trailhead. They loaded the elk quarters and started for home to recuperate from the ordeal. As Doris recalled, it wasn't easy.

"The first thing I did when we got in the house was to take off my wet shoes and try to get a fire going in the cookstove. We had been in deep snow from 8 in the morning until 8 in the evening. Dan and I had some supper and then just sat on the oven door. In the night we both woke up and Dan threw up but all I did was feel funny for about an hour or so. We didn't sleep much the rest of the night and at 7 the next morning we pulled out to get the rest of the meat before somebody stole it on us."

The crew finally hauled the rest of the meat out by late afternoon. Dan felt sick and could only help Doris and Barbara pack the six- and seven-point racks and the hides.

The next day the men worked all day getting the meat skinned and hung up in the trees around the Huffines' campground. Doris "fixed dinner for the crew so now all we have to do is get our aches and sore spots cured and we're ready for another wild party. But we do hope David doesn't go so far the next time as we might just not be able to make the grade. Jim says he is 60 this year and by next year he will be 65 if he has to go on another jaunt like this one."

The combination of backcountry adventures and the social aspects of life closer to town fit Doris perfectly. She regularly attended several ladies clubs, the Sunrift and the Handy Helpers in particular. She and Dan were very active in the East Side Grange and several other granges as well. Doris was the notekeeper for the Handy Helpers.

"The meeting was held at the Howell Home," she wrote one January. "There was to have been a meeting earlier this month but a big storm hit our country. Seven members were present and eight visitors so a nice group was gathered. Everyone lit right in on the quilt and the ladies had the quilt finished before lunch. A lovely lunch of roast chicken and mashed potatoes with various potluck dishes was served."

In 1958, Doris began teaching at Boorman School, west of Kalispell. During winter, Dan often drove her and another teacher 15 miles to the school in the morning and picked them up in the afternoon. Doris and the 10 students in her eighth-grade class summarized their 1958/59 school year in a four-page report: "Some of the boys outside ran Eddy Schultz's car over behind the light pole and he had quite a time getting it out," one of the students wrote. "Then ... somebody pushed the top off the boy's outside rest room." Doris made a box of fudge on student birthdays, and led them on a field trip to Glacier Park in the spring.

At the end of 1959, Dan summarized the couple's net worth. He listed

This rattlesnake was among the many animals Dan and Doris kept at their place in the Flathead Valley.

$2,000 cash in the bank, $26,000 for the museum and Essex camp, $10,000 for their home and 10 acres, and other items for a total of $41,275. He didn't assign value to the antiques in the museum or to the couple's rapidly growing savings bond collection. Doris's teaching added significantly to the couple's income and she seemed to enjoy it.

"It is a nice school and the money sure did help get some things done around here," wrote Doris in the couple's 1959 Christmas letter. "Dan went to work for the county assessing in May and finished in July. Then he went to work for the government as a census taker and finished in December, so he has been busy. Between jobs he has built a double garage and joined our house to the store with a connecting room.

"Our business in the store this summer was way down and to top it off the rains started on August 17 and never let up until it snowed — this ruined our fall trade.

"Oh sure, we hunted and had some wild experiences," she continued. "I was tracking an elk in timber for the rest of them — playing dog you know — and ran right onto a newly killed moose. They are not legal so a game warden had to come and save the meat."

In December the Huffines acquired an important piece for the museum when an artist friend who had some items on display at the museum stopped in. "When we got home John Clarke, the Indian Sculptor, was here to pick up his lamp and bear he left this fall," Dan noted in his diary. "He said (wrote) do you want my 'Old Trap, Bear and Hunter' cheap? He gave the price, I wrote the check, then took him to the Kalispell Hotel to catch the bus to Glacier Park." Clarke, one of Montana's best-known artists, was known as "Cutapuis, The Man Who Talks Not." Dan and Doris had known him well during their years as neighbors in East Glacier, and they loved his wood carvings.

In 1960, after taking care of two places for almost eight years, the couple finally sold the Essex camp for the $12,000 asking price (they received $3,465 down). Rent paid by Otis and Besse Sharp over the last few years applied to the purchase price.

"We have been well all year," Doris wrote in the 1960 Christmas letter. "After school was out I went home on the train to Iowa for two weeks; hadn't seen my dad and folks for three years. Found both my dad and aunt just fine and looking better than ever. On the way back I stopped in Minneapolis to see my cousins; sure had a nice trip. Now they have offered me the lower room in a school six miles from home so I plan to go to work January 3 and finish the term.

"Business this summer wasn't good," she continued. "Same amount of people but not interested in buying souvenirs or camping, too many free campgrounds offered by the government. The Forest Service and Glacier Park are putting big money into their free campgrounds and the little fel-

Doris and Dan still owned about half-interest in the Essex Riverside Camp (bottom center) when the 1964 flood roared down the Middle Fork of the Flathead. The Walton Bridge went with the flood, the Riverside camp was wrecked, but the Walton Ranger Station (top, right) within Glacier National Park remained intact.

This was all that was left of the Huffines' frame house at the camp following the flood. Floodwaters washed away most of the flat land which held the camp.

low can't compete."

Dan added a note at the bottom of the letter: "This may throw you but between the flu and the chicken barn smell at the fair I lost all taste for smoking after 40 years. Doris said if she had thought chicken would stop me smoking she would sure have chickened my cigarettes years ago."

Competition from government campgrounds remained a big issue with Doris for years. In 1963 she wrote a long letter to the regional forester in Missoula. The letter was vintage Doris, scrappy and fighting for her rights and the rights of others.

"Regarding the public campgrounds to be built at Hungry Horse, we would like to put in a protest against such an interference of the federal government in private business. There is no chance for the private owner to operate against government competition under the present high county and state taxes, not to mention all the federal taxes.

"My attitude is that, you men, in spending federal money, should look at all aspects of the case and not just the ones that make the biggest show. It seems that small things, such as people, have a place in our government if it shall survive as set up by our forefathers. As an old fashioned American citizen, I do hate to see government agencies competing with each other and against private enterprise."

Dan wrote the couple's 1963 Christmas letter. "Doris finished up a school year at Lake Blaine," he wrote. "Then the summer was spent in the museum and the huckleberry patches — huckleberries! We never saw such berries in all our years. They were so thick that you just wondered where to start picking and could pick as many as two gallons per hour. We used all we could and then dried 13 gallons.

Doris continued her outdoor interests such as hunting, huckleberrying and hiking well into her 60s (here she takes a break on Logan Pass in Glacier Park). She also remained active in ladies' clubs, the Grange, and many volunteer organizations. (She's fourth from left in photo above.)

"Me? Oh I had the usual cycle of assessing for two months, poisoning gophers for the U.S. Fish and Wildlife Service for two months, and my stint at the fair, with some days in the museum and huckleberry patch thrown in.

"Anyway," Dan concluded. "We've had a good year, both well, plenty to eat, lots of good friends, and what more do you need?" Doris added a card with the following:

I'm sending this card to tell you
That taxes have taken away
The things that I really need
My workshop, my reindeer, my sleigh.
I am now making my rounds on a donkey
He's old and crippled and slow
So you'll know if you don't see me at Christmas
That I'm out on my ass in the snow.
Signed, Santa

The following spring began normally, but in June a natural disaster of immense proportions struck western Montana: "The Flood of '64." Heavy rains on a melting snowpack swelled Montana rivers and streams to record levels, and within a few days 28 people perished and millions of dollars of property damage resulted. The 500-year flood swept through the Flathead drainage, destroyed the Riverside Camp, and cut off the steady payments the Huffines had received from the camp's sale.

"Raining like Hell," a disgruntled Dan wrote on June 8. "The Flathead came up like wildfire, Columbia Falls flat getting flooded. Saw Blankenship Bridge go under Old Red Bridge."

Dan reported on June 9 and 10 that 2,500 cattle were lost down the river along with miles of railroad tracks and many houses. "Red squirrel seen riding down the river on the roof of a house," he wrote.

Over the next few days, the Kalispell *Daily Inter Lake* reported that damage estimates in northwest Montana reached $50 million, and that the raging Middle Fork of the Flathead River had virtually destroyed U. S. Highway 2 above West Glacier. An aerial photo of the Huffine's ravaged Riverside Camp at Essex appeared in the June 12 edition of the paper.

Doris wrote a letter to her folks in Iowa on June 15 describing the flood and the destruction of their old camp. "Well, it is raining again today and rain just makes us shiver after what the rain started last week on Monday. You just can't imagine how awful it really was and it came so quick and so unexpected that it took so many unprepared. I wish that I could make you see how that old river went wild, and what it did."

Doris continued, "First I guess I will tell you about our place at Essex although we have no real firsthand word from there as the roads are still out and will be for a long time yet. It has been declared an emergency so the Bureau of Public Roads is taking over and all the big companies are joining together under the name Operation Bull Dozer and sending in their equipment.

Doris took up painting in her late sixties and over the next two decades produced a steady flow of outstanding nature portraits.

"We heard the destruction up the Middle Fork is beyond words. The entire Nyack Flats is nothing but a big pile of trees, just acres and acres of washed in trees. It took all the cattle off those flats, about 200 head, and just one of them rode that boiling river down the 8 miles to Belton and got out alive. The rest went to Flathead Lake, I guess, as they are using barges to get all the floating dead cattle, horses, dogs, cats, and chickens out of the lake this week.

"The road fills and culverts all went, so now they have had to go back to the old road up on the mountain sides like all of you remember — that twisty, narrow road — but they are so lucky that they had it to go back to as it stood up just fine. You know this is sure showing up these new young engineers and their modern ideas. All the old bridges and roads stood and all the new roads and bridges went down the river."

Doris added that the flood waters washed out the road from the Riverside Camp to Essex and the bridge across the river to the ranger station.

"We saw an aerial picture of our old place in the paper the other day," Doris wrote, "and you just can't imagine how awful it looks. The river bank looks like it breaks off abruptly under the front of our house, the 20' wood shed that was attached to the back of our kitchen has been washed out in front and has lodged against the service station, the cabins are at least half washed away and maybe more.

"The water didn't just come in and flood them calmly," Doris continued. "It roared in and it took all the ground as all the big trees are gone clear back to the bench and all around the house. The one big tree that stood to the north of our house must have easily been 200 years old so that is proof that nothing like this has happened for that long. We still have a bit over half interest in the place so I guess we saw quite a few of our dollars roll down the river."

Doris concluded her letter with a terse reflection. "Dan says he never wants to see it again and I guess that would be best, but I do wonder if those folks up there will feel the same and just walk off. It is sure just awful for them."

Doris wrote a letter to the unlucky camp owners, Otis and Ella Sharp, a few days later, offering to help them clean up at the camp. Later in the summer, Doris filed a protest on behalf of the Sharps with the county regarding the tax assessment on the camp. Later in 1964, Mrs. Sharp wrote a letter to Montana's famous U.S. senator, Mike Mansfield, complaining about the lack of federal aid to flood victims.

"We lost our business, income, home and contents as well," wrote Mrs. Sharp. "So far we have not been able to get one bit of aid, and the Blackfeet Indians got both loans and housing, though many of them didn't even get their feet wet."

Mansfield's reply wasn't long in coming. The senator advised them to seek a small business loan. The Sharps tried, but to no avail, even with letters of support from the Huffines and other friends. The remaining cabins and wrecked buildings were bulldozed and removed, the land reverted

Doris's trademarks were her flower gardens, raspberry patches, and beautiful landscaping (seen here on a vintage postcard).

back to the Forest Service, and the Sharps and Huffines lost nearly everything they'd invested in the camp.

The incident reaffirmed Doris's negative view of government. Dan shared her views and his letters from the period reflect his growing distrust of politicians. "Well, give our money away," he wrote on November 3. "Johnson got back in for president with Humphrey as VP. Minnesota and Wisconsin people say he is a commie. Guess the voters were afraid of a conservative (Goldwater) for President, they like easy government money with no thought of who is going to pay."

Dan kept a ticket in his journal with the message, "This is a free ticket — it's not good for anything, it's just free. Compliments of the Great Society." Cards and stickers from Dan's memberships in the National Republican Congressional Committee, National Rifle Association, Liberty Lobby, and the Gun Owners of America reflected his conservative outlook.

As the country's political leanings became more liberal in the '60s, Doris became even more conservative in reaction to it. Her upbringing and life had emphasized what she considered patriotism. "Dear Mr. Mansfield," Doris wrote to her U.S. senator in 1967. "I just now heard (the black militant Stokely) Carmichael speak from Paris on the Walter Cronkite news program. It seems to me something should be done about any person who deliberately states to the world that he is going to do all he can to undermine the U.S. government. I feel that it is up to you fellows back there in Washington to do something about all such trash, black and white. I am a teacher in the public schools and it is more than disgusting to try to explain to the coming citizens why nothing is done to Carmichael and his kind."

Although she often wrote letters to politicians, much of Doris's correspondence in the 1960s after her father died concerned the handling of land she and her brothers and sisters inherited. At first the land was held in trust by all of them, but Doris sought to see it divided so that each person had title to an equal share of land. Her brother Frank disagreed. Doris believed that Frank wanted to see the land sold at auction so that he could buy all of it at a reduced price.

"Frank, do you really think that you are doing right and fair when you keep all of us from getting the share of the land that our Dad left to us?" wrote Doris. "Until it is in our names as individuals, I do not consider it ours.

"The only thing that you would agree to is this public sale and I think it is a disgrace to put Dad's land, that he worked so hard to acquire, up at public auction. If he would have wanted it sold he would have so specified in his will. Whatever have I ever done to you that you begrudge me a tiny little 80 acres of land, compared to what you own?"

Eventually, the five Ashley siblings agreed to a division of the land. Shirley sold her portion, Frank and Eldon kept theirs, and Doris and Maxine leased their land to Eldon for several thousand dollars a year. Sometimes Eldon could pay the lease, sometimes he couldn't; the quibbling went on for decades.

One year Eldon had his daughter send Doris a note about the rent. "Dad told me to tell you that he's sorry but he can't pay your rent right now and he'll pay you interest when he pays you," she wrote. "I haven't had any livestock for several years," Eldon wrote to Doris in 1973. "I got rid of them so I could take it a little easy and draw Social Security in the winter. The corn prices have been staying at about a dollar a bushel, sometimes less, and if you remember, Dad got more than that some of the time 30 or 40 years ago. I just wanted you to know that I'm not trying to beat you out of the rent money I owe you."

Doris was lenient with Eldon because he had eight children and he was maintaining Doris's land and its value. Eventually he paid her or worked off what he owed.

Another estate dispute came up after Doris's Aunt Eva died. The state of Iowa tried to get unpaid land taxes and inheritance taxes from Doris and her siblings. Doris argued successfully that Eva's worth in the form of bonds was mostly given away as gifts years before Eva died. "Discrimination!" Doris wrote. "It was my understanding that the President outlawed discrimination. Why should just we five relatives be held accountable to the state for Aunt Eva Ashley's property? Why didn't her other relatives and friends get threatening letters from the state through lawyers about the gifts they received over the years?"

Doris and Dan invested all the lease money from Doris's Iowa land and from their other inheritances directly into bonds and timed deposits, building their now considerable net worth. True to their characters, they continued to live as if they were penniless. By the 1970s, Dan and Doris were not just calling themselves old-timers, they were certified examples. "We are mighty glad to be able to tell you that we have been unusually well and no lasting aches or pains," Doris, 72, wrote in their 1973 Christmas letter. "We had lots of raspberries and never thought we would with no rain at all.

"Business? Oh it went along," she continued. "We had stoppers but there was a difference because of the gas shortage although it wasn't a problem around here. We don't need as many tourists as we used to, to keep busy. Our joints are creaking 40 years louder. Last winter I did all the things that I want to do but never get time in the summer: sewing, painting, crafts, and attending my clubs."

Doris appeared younger than her age. This was especially impressive because she represented herself as being four years younger than she actually was. Even on Doris's Montana hunting licenses her age appeared as if she'd been born in 1905 rather than 1901. Ever since her marriage to Dan, she had wanted people to believe she was the same age as Dan, not four years older.

"When I met her in '71 she was not skinny; she was a little bit plumpish," remembered good friend and neighbor Lilian Carlson. "Her hair was still naturally wavy and brown. She started coloring her hair gradually just after that."

Lilian joined Doris in community service projects as soon as they met. Doris was known for her prodigious volunteer efforts. Together, she and Lilian served lunch at the senior citizens center each week. Doris was an officer, lecturer, and all-around central figure at the East Side Grange, and helped at the volunteer fire department, where Dan also participated.

One of the first projects that Lilian and Doris worked on together was a fund raiser. "We sold chances all over the valley to a quilt we'd made at the Sunrift club," remembered Lilian. They apparently went door to door, which caused something of a problem for Doris, who uncharacteristically for a woman who toyed with grizzlies and coyotes, was afraid of dogs.

"When there was a big dog she'd let me go first and put my hand out to check out the dog," Lilian remembered.

Doris also had become well-known for her painting, a skill she began developing in her late 60s. Her paintings reflected her keen eye for nature and her long experience in the outdoors. Her images of wildlife were very realistic; she often complained that locally famous Western artist Ace Powell, a friend of the Huffines, couldn't paint a properly proportioned animal.

She painted many scenes of Glacier Park, moose, waterfalls, rivers, mountain goats and old rural buildings, Indians, and other subjects. Her paintings were highly prized by relatives, friends and others who were lucky enough to receive them. Dozens of Doris's paintings, mostly oils, adorned the walls of her living room, kitchen and back room. She also painted scenes on moose antlers, plates and other objects. Doris attributed her productivity to staying up to at least midnight and getting up no later than 6 a.m. each day.

The museum was becoming an attraction for antique buffs all over Montana and elsewhere. Among showpieces there was the Tally Ho passenger wagon, a horse-drawn surrey that had operated between Belton and Apgar during the early years of the park. The couple also put a lot of work into acquiring more pieces. "Montana Museum," their business card proclaimed. "Hundreds of antiques, historic Montana hearse, live rattlesnakes, gifts and souvenirs — Highway 2 near Glacier Park."

For security, Dan had installed an intercom system between the museum and the house. The couple turned up the volume and could hear the cow bell attached to the door ring when visitors came into the museum. Dan, especially, looked forward to visitors and enjoyed talking to them about the museum pieces and other subjects.

In the mid-1970s as Doris neared 75, she retired after teaching at eight different schools around the valley. Most considered her a strict disciplinarian, but as many people attested, she was very popular and creative with her students. Once, for instance, Doris implemented a unique program to discourage students from having apple fights.

"I believe Doris was teaching at one of the rural schools at the time," remembered her sister Maxine. "They had lots of fruit trees there, big crab apples I think. Well, the kids got to picking the apples and throwing them at each other. Some of the kids got hit pretty hard with apples and complained to Doris.

"Then Doris got an idea," continued Maxine. "She made those kids pick all the apples from the trees and every last apple from the ground and make jelly from them. After that those kids never threw apples because they'd be afraid Mrs. Huffine would force them to make jelly. Doris sold some of that jelly at her museum store."

"Lots of times when I went somewhere with Doris, we'd see someone and they'd say, 'Hello, Mrs. Huffine,'" remembered Lilian Carlson. "Doris would study the person's face and usually recognize him or her. Lots of times the former student would try to hug her; her students always seemed to remember her fondly, even though she was strict."

One student called Doris "an unorthodox and colorful teacher" who always kept his interest. Doris often toured her classes through the museum, and used the museum exhibits to illustrate Montana history. One man, 35 years after having Doris as a teacher, described her as one of the few teachers he remembered vividly. "She was a take-charge kind of woman," he said.

As they aged, Dan and Doris developed illnesses from time to time but generally they remained in good health. Doris had taken heart medicine almost daily since her 1940s sick spell. Dan noted that Doris had to take extra digitalis when she woke up at night and sometimes after dinner when she felt weak, but Doris took the problem in stride. Then in 1976, a sudden, unexplained illness overtook Dan.

"Legs hurt all night," he wrote on September 2. "Had to sleep on the cot." His entries for the rest of the year often referred to leg pain and swelling.

In the back of a diary, Doris chronicled Dan's illness. "Dan was sick from September to Christmas," she wrote. "No strength, sleeping all the time, couldn't eat, losing weight. His hands were so swollen he couldn't use them. At first he couldn't walk hardly at all as his legs hurt so bad.

"The doctor gave him some preanisolone, three pills a day," she continued. "Dan got better the first day and in a week was almost well. They say it will take a year or 14 months for the disease to take its course and it is sure the truth as Dan doesn't seem to get altogether well."

In 1978, Dan's condition improved but he couldn't shake the weakness. Doris attributed his improvement to the medicine and to garlic capsules that he took and that Doris rubbed on his back. "His legs aren't a bit good but we can't lay that to the disease," she wrote. Doris referred to Dan's condition as "rheumatica."

From then on, Dan spent his days and nights on a davenport under the picture window. He could barely move the legs which had carried him on hundreds of 20-mile-plus ranger patrols in a single day over mountains and through deep snow. In his journals he recorded the names of old friends who died each year, what they died from, and how long he had known them. "Lost 125 friends in the last two years," he wrote in 1979.

Dan's legs improved for a short time in 1979 and he was even able to help Doris in the raspberry patch. "Dan and I picked over 170 gallons of raspberries this year off our patch," she wrote in 1979. "We are so fed up with raspberries they are coming out all over. Dan even wished for a blizzard to shut them off."

"Dan got worse — couldn't eat at all," Doris wrote in January 1980. "Lost over 40 pounds and never did anything all summer and fall; could hardly walk. Doctors never found a thing to do."

"Dan was not much better in 1981," she wrote at the end of the next year. "He can't walk any better and doesn't do much work, sleeps more than he should, eats pretty good."

Then for 1982 and 1983, she wrote: "Dan has no strength. Never able to do any work — just sleeps or sits all the time, miserable from weakness and can barely walk with a cane. Doctors can find nothing wrong."

Good friend Lilian Carlson believed that Doris thought Dan was lazy and could have done more during his illness. She pointed out, though, that Doris probably thought anyone who didn't work 16 hours a day was lazy. "She made him get up and do things when I thought she shouldn't have pushed him so hard," remembered Lilian. "She just wanted him to get out and work."

"When Dan got sick she didn't stay home for him, she just kept on going," Lilian continued. "She left him alone quite a bit. I believe that she was giving Dan the same business he gave her when she was sick with heart trouble in the '40s. Dan used to go out a lot at night to play the banjo and he left her alone. So I guess when he got sick she gave him the same treatment he gave her; that was my impression, anyway. She never complained about taking care of him, though. She said, 'He has to get out and keep going.'"

Doris kept a ditty written by one of her friends that summed up her feelings about Dan's bed riding:

Come on Daniel, Get out of that bed
Put your shoes on your feet and your hat on your head
Rise up and get going, there's much to be done
By staying in bed, you're missing the fun.

In the couple's 1983 Christmas letter, Doris, 82, described Dan's condition and added, "It really takes a lot of figuring and planning to get the work done around here without any help from Dan." She mentioned the help her sister Maxine gave her that year around the place. "Maxine helped pick the raspberries and I sure did appreciate that as I just don't see how I would have ever done it alone. We picked more than 125 gallons and were so lucky to get customers for all of them." Doris added that she sold the raspberries and spent the money on wood for their stove.

Dan's health deteriorated steadily in 1984. In August Doris described a "bad spell" when Dan couldn't get off the floor after trying to make it to the bathroom. "Took me two hours to get him back up on the davenport," Doris wrote. "He's heavy and couldn't help a bit. Had to change him all over and the bed." Over the next several months Doris had to phone for help many times to get Dan on the davenport.

Dan's diary entries, always nearly complete before, were sporadic and almost illegible in 1984. In his last entry, written on November 27, Dan wrote that he couldn't move all day. "I just couldn't make it to the little room in time. Doris had to wash my legs."

On December 1, Doris called her nurse neighbor and close friend, Esther Overland, for help. Dan couldn't eat, couldn't go to the bathroom, and couldn't move. "I finally rolled him onto a chair near the cot, then we couldn't get him from the chair on to the cot," Doris wrote. "He went to sleep right away and slept all night."

The next morning Dan "woke up at the usual time and helped me get his daytime clothes on but his legs were badly swollen. He didn't want to eat so I told him to just lie back down. He went right to sleep but about 10 o'clock he began breathing hard and at noon he was still breathing hard so I called Esther... and she came down."

Esther called an ambulance immediately. "I saw that his breathing was very labored, and he was in and out of consciousness," Esther recalled. "We got him ready; he didn't protest when the ambulance came. I drove Doris in to the hospital."

The doctors told Doris that Dan's kidneys had failed and that he had pneumonia. Dan was placed in the intensive care unit about 5 p.m.

"I felt Dan was closer to death than the doctors thought," remembered Esther. "They advised Doris to go home and call in the morning. She hadn't had much rest the last three nights, so I took her home."

"I thought," wrote Doris, "that I'd go back in the morning with our car and stay with him as much as I could, but the doctor phoned about midnight that he had gone. I never had an inkling he was so near gone. I felt so bad I wasn't there to help."

Esther believed that Doris didn't resent the eight years of caring for Dan during his illness, even though it kept Doris from doing many things. "They got along really well," recalled Esther. "She was the boss; Dan was easygoing. But he was the man of her life and that's just the way it was. And he was a good man, a darn good man. He was forthright, very bright and a practical joker. I never saw them clash on anything."

Dan's obituary detailed his work in Glacier Park (with the usual errors in date and place that come from recounting a life in third person) and read, in part, "Mr. Huffine enjoyed preserving and collecting antiques for the museum. He served as an assessor in the Columbia Falls area for 20 years and served with the Bad Rock volunteer fire department for 22 years. He was a member of the East Side Grange for 20 years."

Doris's sister Maxine came to help Doris with the funeral arrangements. Doris ordered a stone inscribed with a scene of deer in the mountains for Dan's plot at the Fairview Cemetery, 1 1/2 miles west of the museum. More than 150 people attended Dan's funeral. A friend wrote a poem that Doris liked well enough to put on Dan's remembrance card:

I farmed the land
I tramped the wood,
These are the things I understood.
No great schemes, they passed me by
I knew the brook, the hills, the sky.

Over the next few weeks, many visitors stopped by Doris's home to offer their condolences to her. Doris turned face down the couple's best photo, taken more than 57 years before in Bozeman, remarking that she couldn't bear to look at it.

Doris's feelings about Dan's death were a mixture of sadness, loneliness, and relief that he didn't have to suffer any longer. And, at 83, she must have felt some relief from the burden she'd borne over the previous eight years.

"She knew he couldn't get any better," recalled Esther. "And his mind wandered a lot over the last few months. She hated seeing him linger on after his desire for living was gone."

Doris owned a series of dogs to keep her company after Dan died. In this October 1985 photo, Doris holds Hobe in front of her museum and home (left). Doris and her friends worked hours each day to keep up the grounds around her 10 acre site. Maxine visited Doris each summer to pick hundreds of gallons of raspberries and each fall to trim and stake the raspberry canes. The self-sufficient Doris lived alone at her beloved home until the last few weeks of her life in early 1990. (Photo by author)

16
Raspberry Jam, 1984-90

"After a lot of arguing, the health inspector finally told me I could sell the jam I had, but when it ran out, that was it. I waited until the woman was out of earshot and said, 'Do you think it will ever run out, Maxine?'"

After Dan died, Doris avoided the painful job of organizing all the museum pieces and other things she and Dan had accumulated during nearly 60 years together. "She wanted to just leave things as they were," remembered Esther Overland. "She didn't want to look forward to the time she couldn't take care of the place any longer."

Now well into her eighth decade, Doris's body stooped and she stood four inches shorter than she had as a young woman jogging the trails of Glacier Park. She wore the casual clothes of rural life, but her bearing commanded respect. Friends knew her for that combination of razor wit and common sense gained only through age and experience.

Doris still moved with the easy grace of someone used to moving quickly in rough surroundings. That summer, while huckleberrying, a companion bent to pick a few berries, looked up, and Doris had vanished. She had dashed around the bend of an old logging road, bound for a long-ago favorite picking spot that she wanted to reach first. In addition to huckleberry-picking trips, she occasionally visited her beloved Glacier Park and took short hikes.

Without Dan, Doris found she had to spend nearly all her time maintaining the museum, house, property and gardens. Through skillful organization and by delegating tasks to friends and relatives, Doris was able to maintain her raspberry patch, vegetable and flower gardens, museum, and gift shop. She ran her place with the skill of a seasoned construction foreman, and she kept to-do lists for each friend and relative who visited regularly. Her grounds became a veritable work camp. Everyone kept coming, though, because it was worth the work to visit with Doris afterwards.

Doris maintained her financial independence. She collected about $600 a month from a combination of Social Security and her teacher's pension. Her raspberry patch provided a major cash flow, and it was very important to her although she lamented that she "might as well burn the darn things because the money from the berries goes right into wood for the cookstove." In the fall, with the help of her sister Maxine, she carefully manicured the canes, and in summer she picked hundreds of gallons of what she and her customers from both sides of the Continental Divide considered the plumpest and tastiest raspberries in the valley.

Always looking to add a few more E-Bonds to her collection, Doris continued to concoct her popular raspberry and huckleberry jams (steadily increasing the price) to sell in the gift shop. Just two weeks after Dan died, she made a new batch of jam from berries frozen the year before. "A customer wanted 12 jars of huckleberry jam so I made it for her," she wrote. "I charged $2 per jar and she gave me a broom doll also."

On one late summer day, a photographer from the Kalispell *Daily Inter Lake* saw Doris working in her flower garden and stopped to take photos. Doris reluctantly agreed and a photo of Doris tending the garden appeared on the front page that evening with the caption: "Montana Moment." Doris stood below the museum and gift shop sign which advertised, "Museum: Jam — Gifts, Antiques, Old Montana Hearse, Dinosaur Bones." The seemingly harmless photo began a series of events that solidified Doris's low opinion of the county government.

"Some woman who worked for the county health department and with nothing better to do saw the photo in the paper," remembered a disgusted Doris. "She looked in the books and found out I didn't have a food preparer's license to make and sell jam."

The health inspector came out, looked over Doris's jam-making utensils and kitchen and told Doris that she was in violation for making and selling homemade jam without a license. The inspector ordered Doris to take down her sign and stop selling the jam. She also told Doris she couldn't get a license to make jam for sale without a kitchen separate from her personal one.

"Maxine, who was visiting, and I, couldn't believe this woman was going to shut down my jam operation," remembered Doris. "But she was insistent so I said, 'Well what about all this jam I have on hand in the gift shop. I'll go broke if I have to throw it all away.'

"After a lot of arguing, the health inspector finally told me I could sell the jam I had, but when it ran out, that was it. I waited until the woman was out of earshot, then said, "Do you think it will ever run out, Maxine?"

Doris painted over her "JAM" sign, but her established clientele and word-of-mouth advertising kept her jam business humming.

Like many people who have lost a spouse, Doris acquired a small dog for companionship. "Woody" became a comfort to Doris, but he was always in some sort of trouble. "Woody got hold of a box of D-Con and ate a lot," Doris wrote on July 15, 1985. "We had to take him to a vet and have his stomach pumped — $17.50. Esther drove and Woody loved that. He never even got sick, thank goodness.

"Woody got killed on the highway about 8:00 at night," Doris wrote on July 31. "Dana [Dan's great-niece] came out and helped. Maxine got him out of the barrow pit and we buried him out behind the shop under a bush." It had been a difficult two days for Doris; the day before, Doris had gotten word that her good friend Ted Kunde, who had worked like a grounds keeper for Doris while visiting the Huffine Museum and Glacier Park each summer from Seattle, died of a heart attack.

Over the next few days, Doris and Maxine looked around to find a puppy similar to Woody. "Finally found one for $25," Doris wrote. "Male, 11 weeks old, no shots — mostly poodle but supposed to be mixed with dachshund." "Hobe" became a good pet for Doris. But about a year later, just after he was neutered, Hobe got killed on the highway too.

"Maxine and I had got home from the fair, had supper — Hobe was here and ate and was fine," Doris wrote in her journal. "I went out to feed the chickens and he went along but didn't come back in and we never saw him alive again. The next morning we found him along a neighbor's driveway. We buried him out under the tree in back."

A few days later, Doris bought another puppy from the same mother as Hobe. "Named her Pepper," Doris wrote. "She's black as coal." Pepper was Doris's companion from then on.

Despite Doris's advancing age, volunteer efforts for the community remained a high priority for her. She and neighbor Lilian Carlson enjoyed going to the Kalispell Senior Citizens Center to serve meals each week for a program called Nutrition. "I don't think Doris missed one Friday in the 14 years we'd been going in there together; she went whether she was sick or well." remembered Lilian. "One time someone asked us what we did every Friday and I said, 'We carry trays for old people.' And that person said, 'Well, what do you think you are?'"

One Friday, disaster struck.

"When coming down Fifth Avenue from Nutrition we stopped at the stop sign on Second Street," Doris wrote in her diary just before Christmas in 1985. "We waited for all the cars to get out of blocks on each side, then started to move across. We just barely got the front end of the car out in the street when, Bang! A car from the west hit us, Kerwhang! Hooked our front bumper, tore it off and dented the fender, threw our car half around. Police came and I got a ticket for being on the through street. You can't win! Lilian went back to see why we didn't see the coming car and there was a truck parked on the side of the street that cut off our view."

The fine angered Doris. Lilian described her as a "nickel-nurser who just hated it when her money went to something without a good return from it. When we'd go out to eat at a restaurant she was always taking things home with her, then she'd put them in the refrigerator. I don't know if she ever ate any of it, but she'd keep it anyway."

Friends found it hard to overstate Doris's penny-pinching. Some of her clothes were older than she was. She served wine that she made from huckleberries picked fifty years earlier. And some of the mold-covered, home-canned food in her root cellar belonged in her museum. When she visited Doris, Maxine always took the precaution of sifting Doris's flour to remove bugs before she baked anything. Needless to say, diners in the know ate cautiously while visiting Doris.

"We've got huckleberries on hand now that we dried in the '30s," Doris would say. "Any dried fruit if it doesn't mold or if the bugs don't get into it too bad is good forever."

Doris used a unique method of making sandwiches for grange functions and picnics. She piled the sandwich filling around the edges of the bread when she put the sandwiches together, giving them a bulging appearance but leaving the center of the sandwich almost without filling. Doris used the technique because "you can make twice as many sandwiches from a can of tuna that way."

As she had during so many periods of her life, Doris relied on her sister Maxine for moral support and help with work. Maxine got a lot of enjoyment from Doris's wit and crusty personality, and she had taken Doris's barbs gracefully since childhood.

"Doris used to heckle and tease Maxine mercilessly," recalled Lilian. "I remember one time we were driving to town and Doris said to her, 'If I had such a big belly as yours I'd do something about it.' After Doris got out of the car I asked Maxine if Doris hurt her feelings and she said, 'I'm used to it. Doris has been trying to order me around since I was six months old.'"

Maxine kept coming back for more not because she wanted to feel needed but "out of a desire to be entertained and to laugh. Every once in a while Dan and I used to go out back and just chuckle about Doris's way."

Doris and Maxine visited their relatives in Iowa for a week in the summer of 1986; they got back to Montana on the Fourth of July. It was one of the few times Maxine was able to talk Doris into traveling anywhere.

"Doris would barely let us stop to go to the bathroom," remembered Maxine. "She was just in a big hurry to get there and then she was in a hurry to get back to Montana. She wouldn't eat at any restaurants and complained about the price of everything."

Doris believed that restaurant food, especially along the interstate highways, was overpriced and preferred to eat sandwiches and snacks while on the road.

Living alone so far from town was a challenge Doris met without complaint, but she got increasingly anxious about her safety. In the summer of 1987 she was alarmed by a hissing noise behind her house. "Sure got an awful scare tonight; a hissing noise was taking place all day as I went by the shop door. Sandra came about 7 o'clock and she heard it — sounds like a rattlesnake. Neighbor Alice Harrington came down but she didn't know what it could be. Tried to open shop door — noise took off like six rattlesnakes inside — we got out of there!"

The women gathered their courage, re-entered the shop, and poked around the rafters with a fishing pole. They finally discovered that the noise emitted from a trapped bat.

Doris wrote about another scare on May 22, 1988. "I let Pepper out around midnight and she got to barking something awful; after she didn't let up, I went out, unlocked the doors and let her in. Then I re-locked the screen door, looked up, and there was a man about 8 inches from me through the screen.

"I said, 'What in Sam Hill are you doing around here?' He said, 'I was going by and stopped to look at your flowers.'" Doris told the man to head down the road. He asked to use the phone and Doris refused.

"I came in, shut the door and called the Sheriff," she wrote. "The guy went out here south of the house towards the car and it looked like he took off some of his clothes. He went to the back of our place and I turned out all the lights."

A sheriff's deputy arrived and searched for the prowler, but couldn't find him. The deputy thought the prowler had left, but Doris told him she thought the man was still around somewhere. Nonetheless, she turned out the lights again and went to bed.

About 4:30 in the morning Doris heard a tapping on the front screen door. "Pepper went wild," she wrote. "I came out of the bedroom and through the glass in the door saw a guy out there yelling, 'Let me in, I know you're in there!' I loaded my gun, and called the Sheriff again and just let Pepper bark until he got here. They drove up with the lights flashing and called to the guy; he went out to talk to them and they finally took him away."

Even with the isolation, Doris cherished her independent life and was reluctant to make any decisions on what to do with her place and all the museum pieces as she neared the point where she couldn't take care of things any longer. She slowly sold off a few museum pieces and some of her paintings, but in general she just went along like she'd be able to handle the place forever.

Many antique buffs and other museum owners offered to buy the Huffine collection. Gil Mangels, of the Miracle of America Museum in Polson, 50 miles south of Kalispell, stopped in to see Doris about buying her museum collection. He was especially interested in the old Montana hearse, and his efforts eventually paid off when Doris finally agreed to sell the hearse.

"When we went to pick up the hearse," remembered Gil, "I was worried about getting a rock chip on the trip home so I had made some high plywood sideboards and headboards for the trailer. I remember Doris and Maxine were impressed with that.

"We had to move half the museum and gift shop to get the hearse out of the building. I moved several items off the hearse including two driving whips. I asked Doris which whip went with it. 'Neither,' she said. 'It didn't have one.'"

Gil told Doris that all horse-drawn vehicles would have had a whip and that he'd sure like one. Doris refused, and wouldn't even sell him one.

"I started fuming over the principle of the thing," Gil continued. "I paid quite a sum and felt like a silly little whip could have been included."

Gil seethed for a while in Doris's driveway and then considered calling off the deal. He re-entered Doris's house and his wife followed, trying to calm him down. "Doris was sitting at her little table writing something and gave it to my wife," Gil remembered. "It turned out to be a check for one-third of what we had paid her," made out as a donation to the museum. "I sure had to eat humble pie."

Doris's 1988 Christmas letter reflected her loneliness and deteriorating health. "It has been a very bad year for me," she wrote. "This is the first time I have been able to use my hands on the typewriter since early last spring. My right hand began hurting in March — the doctor said I had to have surgery on the carpal tunnels to clear it up. In May it went into the other hand so I could barely use it. Finally in July I decided that I would have to have the operation and when I went to the hospital, they found out that I didn't have any blood and they couldn't operate.

"Then I had to have blood transfusions, a lot of them," she continued. "Finally had the operation and it relieved the pain but since then I have had no strength and can barely take care of myself."

She began receiving transfusions each month and kept going. Doris made light of her problems in her usual manner: "It's an awful thing, those doctors. I pay 'em to draw my blood for tests, then I pay 'em to put it back in again."

"She had a lot less energy once she had to start taking the transfusions," remembered Lilian. "One fall evening in 1989, we stopped by Doris's house to pick her up for Grange. We honked and honked but Doris didn't come out. So Edna went in and Doris was just sitting in her chair. She'd forgotten all about Grange; can you imagine Doris forgetting Grange? So Edna and I helped her get dressed and we went on to Grange."

As Doris's health deteriorated, Lilian tried to talk her out of going to Nutrition, but that only angered Doris. "Some of my friends and family didn't think I should be going with her," Lilian recalled. "Sometimes she'd almost fall asleep while she was driving. One time coming down Columbia Falls Stage Road we started to go off into the ditch, and I shouted, 'Doris!' She had nodded off. I grabbed the steering wheel and she came around."

From time to time, Doris accompanied Lilian to a reflexologist, or foot doctor. "I think Maxine got us started with that," remembered Lilian. "Doris kind of thought it was a fake, but finally she started going there anyway. I'm not sure it helped her, but she went fairly often."

Doris began to believe in the foot treatments, kept reflexology literature around her house and went to the reflexologist off and on during her last years. "I went to (the reflexologist) Stapley last week for foot treatment and going again today," Doris wrote in her journal.

On the second week of December in 1989 Doris and Lilian went to Nutrition for the last time. Lilian said that Doris "was just too weak, although she hung in there and carried trays. When I got home I called them and told them to find someone else, that we weren't coming back again."

Despite her advancing age Doris never missed a weekly shift at the Kalispell Food Bank, however. Her judgment and skill with people made her a valuable addition to the staff.

"She insisted on going to the Food Bank long after she should have quit," remembered Lilian. "She had to be there, even if all she could do was lay down on the sofa in the back room. They really didn't want her to come when she was that weak; they were worried about her."

"She reminded me of one of those little kids who say, 'I can do it myself,'" remembered Esther Overland, who worked in the Food Bank office with Doris for a dozen years. "She kept going even though she shouldn't have. Of course everyone cherished having her there. She could tell by looking at a person whether or not they were telling the truth. Personalities she could sort out like you couldn't believe; she was a great judge of people."

Eventually, Doris was diagnosed as having multiple myeloma, a condition which resulted in leukemia-like symptoms. She received chemotherapy for months, lost her hair, and acquired a reddish-brown wig. She dreaded going to the hospital for the monthly transfusions, but the treatment was the only thing that gave her enough strength to walk and take care of herself. Sometimes the transfusions seemed to do more harm than good.

"I had transfusions all day at the hospital," She wrote on June 7, 1989. "I drove myself — had two units.

"All day I was sick all over," she wrote the next day. "Couldn't eat a thing. Someone said it must have been a reaction to the blood." The next day she felt better and went to Nutrition and to the Grange in the evening. A month later she noted that she didn't have to have a transfusion when she went in and that it was the first time in a year she'd gone over four weeks without one.

During the summer of 1989 Maxine visited several times and once brought their sister Shirley, who had been visiting from Iowa. Doris worked as hard as she was able around her garden and raspberry patch; she harvested and sold 125 gallons of raspberries. In October, Maxine visited again and helped Doris trim and tie up the raspberries, a tradition the two of them had kept for decades. Doris's last journal entry on November 22 read, "Three more units of blood." Doris was very week, her legs were sore, and dark blotches had appeared all over her body.

With the help of Maxine and Maxine's son, Dennis, Doris began to plan for the distribution of her estate. She had decided to give most of the museum collection to the Miracle of America Museum in Polson. But she still couldn't bear to start moving anything from the property, and she insisted on staying at her place rather than getting an apartment, long after it became clear that she shouldn't be staying there alone. Friends and relatives visited her more often to help with the chores, and she hung on.

Maxine returned in mid-December. Doris was breathing with the aid of oxygen, and she couldn't find a place in her house where she could sleep comfortably. With a wood-burning cook stove as her only major heat source, she and Maxine feared that she might catch pneumonia. Finally on Christmas Eve, Maxine took her beloved sister to the hospital in Kalispell.

Doris sat on a bed in the emergency room while doctors administered another blood transfusion. Later that night, she was transferred to a private room.

Doris in a hospital bed looked as out of place as a mountain lion in a fabric shop. She hated it. But after two weeks of care she felt better. Doctors even felt cautiously optimistic that she had beaten the myeloma into remission. On January 4, Doris moved to the nearby Brendan House nursing home. She expected to return to her home east of Kalispell after she had built up her strength.

Of course, Doris didn't like being stuck in the nursing home any more than she liked the hospital; she hoped to go home as soon as possible. Many friends and relatives visited. After several days, Maxine returned to Washington with plans to return to Montana when Doris felt strong enough to go home. Doris resigned herself to her stay in the home and made friends with some of the workers there. Over the next week, she thrived in the nursing home, though she often slept when visitors called.

Then on the evening of January 19 she suddenly fell very ill as her kidneys began to fail. Earlier, she had specifically requested not to be hooked up to a dialysis machine in the event of kidney failure. "I'm not going to have those tubes sticking out of me," she had said to Maxine. Doctors called Doris's longtime friend Sandra (Lassiter) Rosetti, and Sandra came to be with Doris during the night. At 7 a.m. the next morning, just 12 days short of her 89th birthday, Doris died after saying to Sandra, "Stop talking now."

"I think she died from a combination of leukemia and malnutrition," remembered Esther Overland. "She just didn't eat right after Dan died. Often when you lose somebody you lose your desire to eat."

On Doris's death certificate, doctors listed kidney failure resulting from multiple myeloma as the cause of death. But Doris reigned victorious to the end; officials listed her age as 84.

GRANGERS REALLY
GET THERE !

Doris, self-portrait. Doris was a mainstay at the Eastside Grange, and the family held the reception there after her memorial service at Fairview Chapel. Doris's mind remained sharp and active until the last minute of her life.

17
Doris's Way

"It seemed that Doris's main goal in life was to have everything done the way she wanted it done."

Maxine recognized that Doris had a large extended "family" in the Flathead, so she gave Doris's friends a lot of say in the funeral arrangements. Services were held at the Fairview Chapel, where services for Dan had been held five years earlier.

"Doris thought the world of that little church," remembered Maxine. In 1957, Doris had written a brief article about the chapel and cemetery, urging people to support it and calling it "the resting place of our pioneers."

At the funeral, many people said a lot of nice things about Doris. Most referred to her wit, independence, ties to Glacier Park, outdoor life, and, of course, her raspberries. Doris was buried alongside Dan, with a full view of the Swan Mountain Front and some of Glacier Park's peaks. Later that day at the East Side Grange, friends and family gathered at a potluck to remember her. No one seemed sad; most people talked about stories Doris had told or reminisced about an experience or run-in they'd had with her. Hundreds of people attended each event.

"Doris was so connected with the Grange and it was a chance for everyone to visit about her and say goodbye," remembered Lilian Carlson.

Lilian remembered Doris fondly as a scrapper, a woman with whom it was sometimes hard to get along. "It seemed that Doris's main goal in life was to have everything done the way she wanted it done," Lilian said. "Once in a while my German would rile up, I'd rebel and say, 'OK Doris this time we're going to do it my way.' Sometimes I'd just ignore her and do it my way anyway. She didn't like to be hugged very much. Once I told her I was going

In her mid-80s, Doris could pick huckleberries and skip up a mountain road as quickly as a teenager. Here Doris is pictured with her sister and lifelong companion, Maxine (far left). Dana Fraley, Doris and Dan's great-niece and the author's wife, is between the sisters. (author's photo)

to kiss her on the cheek and she said, 'If you do Lilian, I'll slug you.' Like I used to tell her, she often made me mad but I loved her anyway."

"What I liked about Doris the most was she was highly intelligent," remembered Esther Overland. "She was a very brilliant lady. It was nothing for her to study until 2 or 3 in the morning on some subject she was interested in. She was always ready for a challenge."

Based on her nursing experience, Esther believed that anyone else would have died years before with the illness Doris had. Esther maintained that "death and Doris just didn't get along."

Maxine and her son, Dennis, who Doris appointed executor of her estate, struggled to plan how to handle Doris's home, land, belongings and especially the museum collection. Doris had made it clear to Maxine that, after the family selected some of the pieces for their keepsakes, she wanted the collection to go to Gil Mangels' Miracle of America Museum.

As Gil wrote in his museum's newsletter, that time came sooner than he expected. "If she'd given us some advance notice," wrote Gil, "we'd have readied the hearse for her last ride. Doris is probably chuckling from above over that. Her wit, wisdom and spunk were her trademarks."

Doris didn't specify in her will that her collection be given to the Miracle of America Museum. Antique dealers and auctioneers wanted to break up the collection for resale but Maxine protected the estate, and made arrangements with Gil. "Now," he wrote with delight, "our museum is the collection's legal owner. The 2000+ artifacts filled many gaps in our collections with minimal duplication.

"After the hearse," he continued, "my favorite is the large John Clarke carving depicting a mother bear caught in a trap, yet still trying to protect a couple of cubs from the man who is advancing with his rifle. This is carved from a single piece of wood and is one of the largest early pieces Clarke carved. The display around it shows a real bear trap, a bear skull, ammo belt, hunter's cap and model 95 Winchester carbine like the man in the carving is holding. Scarlet fever took Clarke's hearing and speech at age two, but he developed his other talents until he was considered the best portrayer of western wildlife in the world."

Gil set up a special display of Doris's and Dan's collection of Indian artifacts, including Blackfeet items like a horse hair lariat, dolls, a parflech medicine case, moccasins, and coup stick.

Like many men Doris met during her life, Gil was touched by Doris's grit and independence. Reflecting back on his dealings with Doris when he bought the hearse, he said, "We now have the whips she and I argued over; one is on the hearse. But I'd sure trade it for a visit from Doris."

Although Doris denied herself most things during her life, in her will she was very generous in the distribution of the wealth she and Dan had accumulated over six decades. Her savings bond collection had grown in value to six figures, and was distributed to many relatives and friends. Her Montana home and land she left to Maxine, and she willed her Iowa land to relatives in Iowa. The collection of canned food, some of it a half-century old, still resides in her root cellar out near the chicken coop. Curiously, no one has rushed in to claim it.

When relatives and friends opened one of Doris's ancient cabinets after her death, they found a box holding nearly one thousand ribbons, most of them blue, from Doris's entries in the Northwest Montana Fair over a 40-year period. Her needle arts, flowers, jam, and baked goods won so often that fair officials finally refused to accept her entries, noting that Doris's work as a judge over the years and her highly developed skills gave her an unfair advantage over other contestants. They were right. Doris, competitive to the end, wouldn't have had it any other way.

Maxine, who enjoyed traveling all over the world, was frustrated by Doris's refusal to accompany her. "I asked her to go everywhere I went," remembered Maxine. "She just wouldn't go, even if I offered to get her plane tickets."

According to Maxine, Doris simply couldn't leave her dogs, cats, chickens and raspberries, and was worried about the house and museum not being under her watchful eye 24 hours a day. "The thought of getting someone to house-sit her place scared her to death. Every minute she would think that they would be breaking up the dishes, or that the chickens wouldn't be fed properly."

Doris probably sent this photo to Dan for him to carry with him on his ranger patrols in the winter of 1926.

In her 80s, Doris seemed as vital and attractive as she did in her 20s. She never lost her keen mind, love for the outdoors, and zest for life (author's photo).

"A while back, before Doris died, I went to a seer, someone who looks into the past," remembered Maxine. "She said, 'You have lots of spirits around you, people who have gone before you. You have one who especially enjoys being with you; her name is Nellie.' I couldn't remember any Nellie. She said, 'You ought to get reacquainted with her, because she adores you. Her trademark is a white apron; she's forever changing that apron to keep it pure white.'"

Later, Maxine told Doris what the seer had told her and Doris said, "Maxine, you can't have forgotten Nellie. She was our hired girl all the time you were learning to read back in Iowa. You spent more time with her learning to read than you spent with anyone else. And Nellie did change her apron if there was the slightest spot on it."

Doris told Maxine she believed in spirits as the seer described, and that the Blackfeet had told her that when people died their shadows entered a shadow world and waited to be joined by their loved ones. Her spiritual belief closely followed that of the Blackfeet's shadow or spirit world; she didn't believe in a heaven.

In one of Maxine's dreams, a woman came to her, carrying a baby in her arms. The woman leaned over to comfort her. Maxine described the dream to Doris, and Doris urged her to give every detail of the woman's clothing. "Doris was firmly convinced," related Maxine, "that it was Mother and our baby brother, Bertie George. Doris definitely believed Mama waited for her somewhere and that I would end up there too."

Throughout her life, Doris needed Maxine to feel whole. From childhood, Maxine stood by Doris and labored for her. The two sisters had shared every aspect of their lives.

"Now," Maxine concluded, "I believe I have one more spirit around me. Doris is finally getting to travel. I went on a trip to Lake Chelan and on down to California and I kept feeling her with me. I'll bet I stopped to look around for that other person in our party 15 times."

Because of their love for the Park and its history, Dan and Doris in 1977 donated the historic Tally Ho Wagon to Glacier; the surrey was used to haul passengers to Lake McDonald from 1911-1917. (Courtesy of Hungry Horse News. Here's how the restored wagon looked in 1997 (Photo courtesy of Glacier National Park).

Epilogue

Doris's presence has lingered behind her in the Flathead in many ways. Certainly, she and Dan were important personalities in the shaping of the character of northwest Montana. The Huffines' lives were linked to Glacier Park from the time they both came west, she from Iowa and he from eastern Montana, and this book should help to establish their importance to the region. But there is a more substantive reminder of their love for Glacier Park that also continues to bear witness today. Almost 20 years ago, they donated the historic Tally Ho passenger wagon that had been among the most treasured of their museum exhibits to the Glacier Natural History Association. Park officials noted that it will eventually form an important centerpiece for a new visitor center when it is built on the west side of the park.

At first, the couple planned on selling the surrey to the park. In a 1976 memo, then Glacier Park Superintendent Philip Iverson wrote about the possible acquisition of the wagon and noted that the Huffines wanted $4,500 for it. But by August 1977, Iverson was on hand to help accept the donation of the wagon by Dan and Doris; it had been appraised at $15,000. The Huffines made a wonderful gift of the luxury wagon that had operated between Belton and Apgar during the first years of the park.

"The Tally Ho is an important part of the transportation story of Glacier," says Deirdre Shaw, Glacier Park's curator of museum and archives. "It tells us about the experiences of the earliest park visitors, and it's a beautiful piece, a significant artifact in its own right."

Shaw showed me the contract with a California museum and research center for restoration of the Tally Ho. In 1984, Glacier invested $20,000 to return the wagon to its original condition. The park displayed the wagon, which is pulled by three horse teams, in a 1985 parade. Then in 1997, the Tally Ho was included in a National Park Service history display in California. Now, the surrey is back in Glacier and awaits a suitable place for display in its home area of West Glacier.

The Tally Ho donation reflected the love Doris and Dan held for Glacier and its history. They often talked about the donation and they were very proud of it. Doris laminated the Hungry Horse News article about the restoration of the wagon and tacked it up on her wall; it was one of the last things removed from her little house after her death.

I think of Doris often because I spend a lot of time in the backcountry of the Middle Fork of the Flathead, and in my mind Doris and the Middle Fork are inseparable. As I look back on it, one of my favorite outings with Doris had to be our coal gathering trip on Stanton Creek, not far from the lodge that the couple once owned. Doris, Maxine, my wife, and I piled into Doris's sedan and drove across the Flathead Valley and up the canyon of the Middle Fork to the old bridge crossing on Stanton Creek. It was 1982 and Doris was in a hurry because she didn't want to leave Dan alone at home for very long. I was skeptical that Doris could actually lead us to burnable coal but she seemed sure the vein would still be there and that she could find it, even after 50 years.

Doris ignored my doubts and led the way through the timber and alder brush. We walked past a few bends in the narrow creek canyon and, sure enough, we came across an outcrop of clean coal that extended right into the fast-flowing stream. Maxine didn't seem surprised that we were able to find it. We gathered two gunny sacks full of the soft coal, dragged it back down the edge of the stream, and loaded the sacks into the trunk of Doris's car.

When we returned to the museum, Doris asked us to stay for dinner. As we sat down to eat, Doris held out a glass and said, "Here, John, try some of this, well, this drink." With my guard down, I gulped some of the liquid and too late felt the sharp bite of fermented juice of some kind; it hurt all the way down my throat. When I protested, Doris chuckled and admitted she had brought it home from a grange potluck a few weeks before, and that it wasn't too popular even then. "I guess it is too old," she said. I think that Doris was paying me back because I openly doubted she could find the coal vein. All in all, the trip and the drink were pure, vintage Doris.

Doris, Dan, Maxine, and their stories established in me a sense of place for the Flathead country and Glacier Park. I had hiked, skied and worked all through the area's backcountry, but I didn't really have a solid feel for it until Doris brought it back to an earlier time. For me, she put it all in perspective.

When I visited Doris in the Brendan House during the last weeks of her life I found her to be as sharp as ever. She seemed confident that she'd soon be returning to her comfortable little house. Throughout this last ordeal her appetite remained strong. When she was in the hospital before checking into the nursing home, Dana and I brought her a pumpkin pie; she ate a piece while the nurses administered a blood transfusion. After about a week in the nursing home, Doris began to crave certain foods. I smuggled in french fries and a chocolate milk shake. "I really can't eat anymore," she said as she gobbled the fries.

Doris's appetite for life stayed equally strong. One night sometime before her last trip to the hospital, she and I sat around her little front room which looks out to the Swan Mountains. Doris told me that she treasured her life, her little home, museum artifacts, friends, reading, and painting. Here was a woman, just short of 89, at the height of her mental powers. Despite her hardships, she cherished life and did not want to leave it.

Doris's love of local history never waned. Earlier, she had encouraged me to search out the story of one of the Middle Fork oldtimers, her friend Josephine Doody. A few days before Doris died, she sat up in her nursing home bed and completed a review of a story I'd researched and written about Josephine. "It might have happened that way," Doris said to me. That was the last time I talked to Doris. Her mind remained keen to the end; her words showed she understood the uncertainties of history.

Each summer I stop by the Fairview Chapel to visit the graves of Doris and Dan. They lie together, with a breathtaking view of the sharp ridges of the Swan Mountain Range. Sometimes I bring beargrass or paintbrush from the highcountry. At least once each summer, I bring raspberries from bushes in my garden which I started years ago from Doris's magnificent transplants. Raspberries were Doris's trademark. I think she would prefer them to flowers.

Sources

Chapter 1: Triple Divide

(1) Doris's quotes are from her journal of 1927/28, interviews with her that I recorded in 1984 and 1985, notes from other interviews with her from 1979-1990, and recollections and notes of other conversations with her.

(2) Information from the ranger station diary is from a photocopy of the original which is housed at GNP archives.

(3) Blackfeet names and stories: Schultz, James Willard. 1926. Signposts of Adventure. Houghton Mifflin Co., New York, NY; Schultz, James Willard. 1962. Blackfeet and Buffalo. University of Oklahoma Press, Norman; Schultz, James Willard. 1916. Blackfeet Tales of Glacier National Park. Riverside Press, Cambridge, MA.

(4) Interview with Otto Bessey Jr., Kalispell, MT, May 1997.

Chapter 2: Snake in the Cornpatch; and Chapter 3: Until Death

(1) Interviews, phone conversations and correspondence, October 1994 to April 1995, with: Shirley (Ashley) Reinking, sister of Doris; Maxine (Ashley) Conrad, sister of Doris; Norma Reinking, Shirley's daughter-in-law and friend of Doris; Sadie (Brune) Murphy, childhood friend of Doris; Bernice (Weaver) Manker, sister-in-law of Doris from Doris's marriage with Howard Weaver; Doris (Speke) Weaver, wife of Dale Weaver; and Frank Ashley, Doris's brother.

(2) Death certificate, Austa (Drake) Ashley.

(3) Information and excerpts from the Woodbury County History Book, supplied by Glenna Ferrone of the Woodbury County Genealogical Society; other vital records of Doris Ashley and Howard Weaver located by Ms. Ferrone.

(4) Taped interview with Maxine (Ashley) Conrad, October, 1991.

(5) Taped interviews with Doris Huffine and Maxine (Ashley) Conrad, 1984-5.

(6) Typed genealogical summary of the Huffine family, by Irma (Huffine) Fritts; phone conversations with and letter from Irma (Huffine) Fritts, November/December, 1994.

(7) Letters from Austa and Doris Ashley to Eva Ashley, 1905, 1906, 1910.

(8) Typed summary (two pages) of Eva Ashley's memories about early life in Iowa; typed and summarized by Doris Huffine.

Chapter 4: Native Son

(1) Taped interviews with Doris Huffine and Maxine (Ashley) Conrad, 1984-5.

(2) Typed genealogical summary of the Huffine family, by Irma (Huffine) Fritts; phone conversations with and letter from Irma (Huffine) Fritts, November/December, 1994.

(3) Papers, school records and correspondence of Dan Huffine.

(4) Dan Huffine's journal, 1924.

Chapter 5: Glacier

(1) Information on Glacier's people and places are from: Buchholtz, C. W. 1976. Man in Glacier. Glacier Natural History Association, West Glacier, MT.; Great Northern Railway Co. 1925. The Call of the Mountains: Vacations in Glacier National Park. Travel Guide; Hanna, W. L. Montana's Many Splendored Glacierland. Superior Publishing Co., Seattle, WA.; Hanna, W. L. 1988. Stars Over Montana: Men Who Made Glacier National Park. Glacier Natural History Association, West Glacier, MT.; Robinson, D. H., and M. C. Bowers. Through the Years in Glacier National Park: An Administrative History. Glacier Natural History Association and the National Park Service. West Glacier, MT. Schultz, James Willard. 1962. Blackfeet and Buffalo. University of Oklahoma Press, Norman.

(2) Information on Stevens' comments about his discovery of Marias Pass came from: Montana Historical Society. Glorious Glacier:The Exciting Early History of Glacier National Park. Montana Heritage Series Number Nine. Helena, MT.

(3) Some information on early Apgar and McDonald Lake events came from: Harrington, Leona, and the pupils of Apgar School. 1951. History of Apgar. Mimeographed.

(4) Information on Doris and Dan are from their journals and papers, interviews that I conducted with them, and notes Doris made in the margins of a copy of "Through the Years in Glacier Park."

(5) Quotes about the legislation to establish Glacier are from: Kalispell Inter Lake. February 11, 1910. "Glacier National Park Bill Passed." Flathead Co. Library, Kalispell, MT.; Kalispell Inter Lake. May 14, 1910. "Glacier Park Bill Ready for Signing." Flathead Co. Library, Kalispell, MT.; Kalispell Inter Lake. May 20, 1910. Comet's Tail to be in Place Tonight." Flathead Co. Library, Kalispell, MT.

Chapter 6: Maids and Jammers, Chapter 7: Lone Ranger, and Chapter 8: An Interesting Match

(1) Doris's quotes are from interviews with her that I recorded in 1984 and 1985, notes from other interviews with her from 1979-1990, and recollections of other conversations with her.

(2) Dan's quotes are from his journals of 1925-27, from a taped interview with him by GNP in 1982, and from my recollections of conversations with him from 1979-1984.

(3) Quotes from Doris's and Dan's co-workers are taken from the pages of their 1925-26 Glacier Park yearbooks.

(4) Quotes by Mary Roberts Rinehart: Rinehart, Mary Roberts. 1918. Tenting To-Night. Houghton Mifflin Co., New York, NY.; and Rinehart, Mary Roberts. 1916. Through Glacier Park. Houghton Mifflin Co., New York, NY.

(5) Information on Glacier Park Hotel and concessions: MacCarter, Joy,

Editor. 1984. History of Glacier County, Montana. Glacier County Historical Society, Cut Bank, MT. 299 pp.; Ober, Michael J. 1973. Enmity and Alliance: Park Service — Concessioner Relations in Glacier National Park. M.A. Thesis, University of Montana, Missoula; and from, Buchholtz, C.W. 1976. Man in Glacier. Glacier Natural History Association, West Glacier, MT.

(6) Information on Hileman comes from "Master Photographer — Mountain Goat Hileman," Montana Magazine, May/June 1993.

(7) Blackfeet information, names and stories: Schultz, James Willard. 1926. Signposts of Adventure. Houghton Mifflin Co., New York, NY; Schultz, James Willard. Reprinted, 1973. My Life as an Indian. Corner House Publishers, Williamston, Massachusetts; Schultz, James Willard. 1962. Blackfeet and Buffalo. University of Oklahoma Press, Norman; Schultz, James Willard. 1916. Blackfeet Tales of Glacier National Park. Riverside Press, Cambridge MA; and from, Buchholtz, C.W. 1976. Man in Glacier. Glacier Natural History Association, West Glacier, MT.

(8) Personal information from interview with Otto Bessey Jr., Kalispell, MT, May 1997.

Chapter 9: Winter at Cut Bank Ranger Station

(1) Doris's quotes are from her journal of 1927/28, interviews with her that I recorded in 1984 and 1985, notes from other interviews with her from 1979-1990, and recollections and notes of other conversations with her.

(2) Dan's quotes are from his journal of 1927/28, from a taped interview with him by GNP in 1982, and from my recollections of conversations with him from 1979-1984.

(3) The entries from the ranger station diary are from a photocopy of the original which is housed at GNP archives.

(4) I also referred to NPS memos and letters, and temperature records kept by Dan from the period.

(5) Blackfeet names and stories: Schultz, James Willard. 1926. Signposts of Adventure. Houghton Mifflin Co., New York, NY; and from, Schultz, James Willard. Reprinted, 1973. My Life as an Indian. Corner House Publishers, Williamston, MA; Schultz, James Willard. 1962. Blackfeet and Buffalo. University of Oklahoma Press, Norman; Schultz, James Willard. 1916. Blackfeet Tales of Glacier National Park. Riverside Press, Cambridge MA; Schultz, James Willard, edited by W. L. Hanna. 1988. Recently Discovered Tales of Life Among the Indians. Mountain Press, Missoula, MT.

Chapter 10: Indian in the Outhouse

(1) Primary Sources: Various taped interviews with Doris and Dan Huffine from 1982-1985; Many conversations and notes made from conversations with Dan and Doris from 1979-1990; Notebooks and miscellaneous papers of Dan and Doris dating from the period of 1928-1932; Dan's and Doris's journals from 1928-1932.

(2) Other information about the park and East Glacier from the following published sources:

Buchholz, C. W. 1976. Man in Glacier. Glacier Natural History Association, Inc. West Glacier, MT 59936. 88 pp.

Hanna, Warren L. 1988. Stars Over Montana: Men who made Glacier National Park History. Glacier Natural History Association, West Glacier, MT 59936. 204 pp.

MacCarter, Joy, Editor. 1984. History of Glacier County, Montana. Glacier County Historical Society, Cut Bank, MT. 299 pp.

Robinson, Donald H., and Maynard C. Bowers, 1960. Through the Years in Glacier National Park. Glacier Natural History Association, Inc., Glacier National Park, West Glacier, MT. Thomas Printers, Kalispell, MT. 127 pp.

Kalispell Daily Inter Lake, Kalispell MT. : June 7, 1928; June 9, 1928; November 1, 1928; November 5, 1928; November 7, 1928; March 1, 1929; June 18, 1929; December 3, 1930; December 24, 1930; December 30, 1930; December 8, 1931; February 5, 1932; March 16, 1932; March 31, 1932;

Chapter 11: Bull Cook

(1) Quotes from Doris are from interviews I recorded mostly in 1984 and 1985, various notes I'd taken in conversations with her from 1979 to 1990, and from recollections of things she often said over the same time period.

(2) Quotes from Dan are from an interview recorded by a representative of Glacier Park in 1982, his diary for 1929, notes I'd taken in conversations with him from 1979 to 1984(when he passed away) and from recollections of things he often said during that same time period.

(3) A.V. Emery's material is from his engineering reports, on file at the GNP library.

(4) Frank Kittredge's material is from his 1942 report on the Going-to-the-Sun Highway, written when he was Chief Engineer for the National Park Service. I photocopied the report at the GNP archives.

(5) Road distances, and some other specifics are from the book "Going to the Sun" by Rose Houk, 1984, MT's Many-Splendored Glacierland, by W.L. Hanna, 1976, and National Park Service brochures.

(6) Quote regarding the transmountain highway by Mary Roberts Rinehart is from: Rinehart, Mary Roberts. 1918. Tenting To-Night. Houghton Mifflin Co., New York, NY.

(7) Blackfeet names and stories: Schultz, James Willard. 1926. Signposts of Adventure. Houghton Mifflin Co., New York, NY; Schultz, James Willard. 1962. Blackfeet and Buffalo. University of Oklahoma Press, Norman; and from Schultz, James Willard. 1916. Blackfeet Tales of Glacier National Park. Riverside Press, Cambridge MA.

Chapter 12: Hidden Lake

(1) Quotes from Doris are from taped interviews, notes from interviews, miscellaneous conversations, her diaries from 1932-1940, and various other loose leaf writings by Doris from the period.

(2) Dan's quotes are from his diaries from the period, conversations I had with him, and from Doris's recollections of things he said.

(3) Maxine's quotes are from taped interviews.

Chapter 13: Bus Depot Operator

(1) Taped interviews with Doris Huffine, 1984-85.

(2) Taped interview with Dan Huffine, 1982, by Glacier National Park.

(3) Letters and V-Mail from Eldon Ashley, Norman Gray, and other GIs to Doris Huffine, 1941-1944.

(4) 1940 Census figures for Kalispell.

(5) Kalispell Daily Inter Lake, various issues, 1940-1945.

(6) Telephone conversation with Sandra Rosetti, long-time friend of Doris, Kalispell, MT, December 1994.

(7) Dan Huffine's Journals, 1940-45.

Chapter 14: Beaver in the Bathtub

(1) Quotes from Doris are from taped interviews, notes from interviews, miscellaneous conversations, her diaries from 1945-52, and various other loose leaf writings by Doris from the period.

(2) Material from Doris's "Essex News" columns appeared originally in the Hungry Horse News.

(3) Dan's quotes are from his diaries, conversations I had with him, and from Doris's recollections of things he said.

Chapter 15: The Huffine Montana Museum

(1) Taped interviews with Doris Huffine and Maxine (Ashley) Conrad, 1984-5; various other interviews and conversations with Doris through 1989 and with Maxine through January 1995.

(2) Taped interview with Dan Huffine by Glacier National Park, 1982.

(3) Dan and Doris Huffine's journals, 1952-84.

(4) Doris Huffine's papers, miscellaneous writings, and letters, 1952 - 1984.

(5) Letter from Bessie Sharp to Montana Senator Mike Mansfield, 1964.

(6) Various conversations and interviews with Doris's long-time friends Lilian Carlson and Esther Overland, December 1994.

(7) Dan Huffine's obituary, Kalispell Daily Inter Lake, December 4, 1984.

(8) Dan Huffine's memorial card, December 6, 1984.

(9) Death certificate, Dan Huffine, Flathead County, December 3, 1984.

(10) Various letters from Eldon Ashley and Frank Ashley to Doris Huffine, 1960s-1970s.

(11) Kalispell Daily Inter Lake, June 8-12, 1964.

Chapter 16: Raspberry Jam

(1) Taped interviews with Doris Huffine and Maxine (Ashley) Conrad, 1984-5; various other interviews and conversations with Doris through 1989 and with Maxine through 1995.

(2) Taped interview with Dan Huffine by Glacier National Park, 1982.

(3) Doris Huffine's journals, 1984-89.

(4) Doris Huffine's papers, miscellaneous writings, and letters, 1984-89.

(5) Various conversations and interviews with Doris's long-time friends Lilian Carlson and Esther Overland, December 1994.

(6) Interview with Sandra Rosetti, Kalispell, MT, January, 1995.

(7) Correspondence from Gil Mangels, Miracle of America Museum, Polson MT, November 15, 1994.

(8) Conversation with record-keepers at the Brendan House Nursing Home, Kalispell, MT, December 1994.

Chapter 17: Doris's Way

(1) Various conversations and interviews with Doris's long-time friends Lilian Carlson and Esther Overland, December 1994.

(2) Notes by Doris Huffine on the Fairview Chapel east of Kalispell, MT, 1957.

(3) Various conversations with Maxine (Ashley) Conrad, 1994-95.

(4) Taped interview with Maxine (Ashley) Conrad, October 1991.

(5) Correspondence from Gil Mangels, Miracle of America Museum, Polson MT, November 15, 1994.

(6) Miracle of America Museum Newsletter, June 1992.

INDEX

About the author

John Fraley came to Montana as a teenager and received fish and wildlife management degrees from both Montana Universities. He has worked for Montana's wildlife agency for 20 years, mostly in northwest Montana's Flathead country. John writes regularly for *Montana Outdoors*, and he has written articles on the Flathead's history and other topics for *True West*, *Montana The Magazine of Western History*, *Western Wildlands*, *Wild Outdoor World*, and other magazines. In 1980 he married Dana Dean, Dan and Doris Huffine's great niece. John, Dana, and their three children live north of Kalispell, 30 miles south of Glacier National Park. John and his family have a special love for the Park's backcountry and for the Middle Fork of the Flathead River.